JUSTIN WILSON'S
Homegrown Louisiana Cookin'

OTHER BOOKS BY JUSTIN WILSON

Justin Wilson's Outdoor Cookin' with Inside Help

The Justin Wilson Gourmet and Gourmand Cookbook

The Justin Wilson Number Two Cookbook: Cookin' Cajun

The Justin Wilson Cookbook

Cajun Fables

More Cajun Humor

Cajun Humor

The Wilson family. *Front row, left to right*: John Glen and William Edward (Ned); *middle row*: Olivette, Harry D. Wilson with Justin on his lap, and Menette; *back row*: Olivet Wilson.

Justin Wilson's

HOMEGROWN
Louisiana
COOKIN'

WITH

Jeannine Meeds Wilson

MACMILLAN PUBLISHING COMPANY · NEW YORK

COLLIER MACMILLAN PUBLISHERS · LONDON

Macmillan Publishing Company
866 Third Avenue, New York, N.Y. 10022
Collier Macmillan Canada, Inc.

Library of Congress Cataloging-in-Publication Data
Wilson, Justin.
    [Homegrown Louisiana cookin']
    Justin Wilson's homegrown Louisiana cookin'/with Jeannine Meeds
Wilson.
        p. cm.
    Includes bibliographical references.
    ISBN 0–02–630125–3
    1. Cookery, American—Louisiana style.   I. Wilson, Jeannine
Meeds.   II. Title.   III. Title: Justin Wilson's homegrown Louisiana
cooking.   IV. Title: Homegrown Louisiana cookin'.
TX715.2.L68W55   1990
641.59763—dc20   90-32891   CIP

Macmillan books are available at special discounts
for bulk purchases for sales promotions, premiums, fund-raising,
or educational use. For details, contact:

Special Sales Director
Macmillan Publishing Company
866 Third Avenue
New York, N.Y. 10022

10 9 8 7 6 5 4 3 2
Designed by Beth Tondreau Design/Jane Treuhaft
Printed in the United States of America

**THIS BOOK IS DEDICATED TO
MY MOTHER AND FATHER.**

Mama, Olivet Toadvin Wilson, lived her 97 years with great "vigorosity." She enriched the lives of those near her with the gift of happiness. She reared six children, wrote sparkling music, and created marvelous food for her family. I miss her and take comfort in my memories of her every day.

PapaBoy, Harry Dixon Wilson, was elected to serve his state for thirty-two years, from 1916 until his death in 1948, as Commissioner of Agriculture and Immigration. Under his inspiring and witty leadership, Louisiana welcomed peoples from many other nations to the safety of our soil, where they could pursue their dreams.

SPECIAL THANKS

We would like to thank Sharla Babin, our secretary, for her endless hours of work, invaluable suggestions, and persistence in the preparation of this manuscript.

The best sister in the world is Olivette Wilson Garrison. She helps every day, just by being there.

The personnel of the Louisiana Department of Agriculture and the State Archives of Louisiana have been willing and ready to help.

Louisiana State University School of Agriculture continues to develop ways to make the food producer and fisherman more productive. Chancellor Rouse Caffey can find the answer to any question we might have.

Bob Rice, a great photographer and friend, lent his years of experience to us for this project.

Maurice Dantin, our good friend, helped with tasting and advice on this project from start to finish.

Contents

Contents

x

Introduction

"During the early period of colonization all the aggressive nations of the Old World were quick to realize that whoever controlled the mouth of the Mississippi River would hold a firm grip on commerce to and from a vast and fertile area; whoever guarded the portals of the greatest inland waterway in the world, would control the artery that carried life's blood to the heart of a great country. This was ample reason for the feverish desire of diplomats and kings of the Spanish, French, and English peoples to possess that area through which the great river pushed its lazy waters into the Gulf of Mexico.

"And today Louisiana is the luxuriant and ornamental front-yard through which long trails lead to the Mississippi valley. It is here that the lavish hand of Nature let trickle through her long fingers an abundance of resources—oil, gas, sulphur, timber, fertile soil. And not being content with her generous gift of raw materials, she, in benignant affection, and guided by those words, 'Man does not live by bread alone' designed here a marvelous setting which would temper man's desire for riches with a complacent attitude toward material things. In this semi-tropical climate trees, flowers, and shrubs run riot in luscious growth and blossom in profusion, to the great delight of permanent residents and to the enchantment of tourists."*

* Harry D. Wilson, *Luxuriant Louisiana.* Baton Rouge, LA: Department of Agriculture and Immigration, 1947, p. 1.

· ❧ ·

In a state endowed with oil and minerals, fertile farmland, waters teeming with seafood, abundant wildlife, vast cypress swamps and pine forests, and the mighty Mississippi, Louisiana's greatest natural resource is still its people; people with imagination to turn what they found on the land and in the water into great-tasting food. "Great cooking," says Justin Wilson, "is nothing more than imagination and common sense in the proper proportions."

Madame Langlois, the housekeeper for Governor Jean Baptiste Le-Moyne, was the first great cook in Louisiana. It seems the few women who inhabited the settlement of New Orleans in 1722 were upset over the lack of familiar cooking ingredients so far away from France. The new colony experienced chronic supply problems with frequent short-ages of wheat, flour, garden vegetables, and herbs. The women marched on the governor's mansion clanging pots and spoons. Le-Moyne wasn't able to do much about the supply problem, so he asked Madame Langlois to show the settlers how to cook with the foods that were so plentiful in their new home.

Since then cooks in Louisiana have been taking native ingredients and combining them with imagination and common sense to create dishes without equal in the world. To understand why Louisiana's cuisine is so interesting one must realize that Louisiana is made up of many diverse and complementary groups of people. Each group has contributed to our culinary culture. Today new groups keep on arriv-ing to change the terrain. Like the continual flooding of a river over its banks, each wave brings a layer of sediment which joins with the earlier deposits to make a rich and fertile soil. Louisiana's culinary soil is fruitful and produces a fine and varied crop.

Madame Langlois learned her skills from the Indians, the first in-habitants of Louisiana. Indians arrived in Louisiana as nomads, but the abundance of food enabled them to stay. Shellfish supplemented by gathering and hunting turned these wanderers into village dwellers. Louisiana's subtropical climate and long growing season ensured a year-round food supply. Fruit and berries such as mayhaw, straw-berry, and blackberry were easily gathered along with ground arti-chokes, mushrooms, rice, maize, wild onions, and other root vegetables. They also gathered nuts and other grains. The Indians were masters at using all the resources available to them. They hunted bear, deer, turkey, squirrel, rabbit, and water animals which included alligator, catfish, and crawfish. The Indians used fish traps, then preserved their catch by sun drying or smoking. They had the rudiments of agriculture, using a digging stick to plant and cultivate their few crops. The Indians gave us filé powder for flavoring and made hominy. They taught the early settlers many valuable tricks about survival in the wilderness and about the plants and animals unknown to the Europeans who were slowly moving into the area.

Europeans, mainly of French, German, and Spanish extraction, gradually settled parts of Louisiana and gave names to two types of cooking still widely practiced. The chief characteristics of Cajun and Creole cooking are the use of herbs and seasonings with native ingredients. To differentiate between the two, a Creole menu closely follows the classical French order. Creole cooking originated and was perfected in the city of New Orleans with its ready access to markets and services. In contrast, Cajun cooking originated from the Acadians who settled along the bayous and on the prairies of southern Louisiana, and who were often isolated. Both cuisines are a mixture of other cultures—German, Spanish, Indian, and African. The entrées of either could include any seafood, a jambalaya, a casserole, a gumbo or rice, with any of a host of fish, beef, pork, fowl, or game dishes. Creole cooking tends to use more sauces and be more complicated, with a greater variety of ingredients. Cajun cooking, because it sprang from the countryside, tends to use wild ingredients or those that could easily be gathered or grown by a family. It also has many one-dish meals and is less detailed and structured than Creole cooking.

Among the people of New Orleans were a group of exiled aristocrats who were accustomed to fine foods and wines in France. The French Revolution brought displaced royal chefs to New Orleans, where they found many appreciative customers. They brought a finesse to their cooking through the rich sauces that have made many of their recipes treasures. They were also accustomed to having house servants and trained many blacks to cook for them, bringing the heritage of another whole continent into the mix.

From the French came their own set of spices and herbs. French settlers planted gardens that were patterned after ones they had grown in France, composed of a maze of vegetables and favorite herbs, revolving around a stand of fruit trees. They stored their food in a storeroom filled with vinegar barrels, preserves, and vegetable bins. Many foods were preserved by salting or pickling. These storerooms were built on the north side of the house to capture cool air, or if the house was near a stream, the storeroom was built so the running water could cool the space.

Cajuns were the exiled Acadians of Nova Scotia who after years of misery finally found a haven in Louisiana. The Creoles who had been living in the New World had a habit of shortening pronunciations, so before long Acadian was shortened to "Cadien." The Americans further corrupted the word to its present form, "Cajun."

After 1760, when the Cajuns began arriving in the wilderness along the Mississippi River, they often intermarried with the German families who had settled the same area in the early 1700s. In these instances of intermarriage, the Cajun wife was the mainstay of the home. She felt it was her job to see that her children carried on the Cajun heritage.

The children usually learned to speak the language of their mother. Many German names were Gallicized and cooking styles have blended together. In different regions of Cajun Louisiana one will find variations even in the familiar dishes. This variety indicates the influence in one area of some group not found in another area.

Spanish settlers and those from Latin America influenced Louisiana with their Spanish cuisine, showing the effects of the Aztec and Inca Indians conquered by Spain. Partial to cayenne peppers, pimentos, tropical spices, herbs, and garlic, the Spanish assisted in giving Creole and Cajun food the spiciness for which it is famous.

Thus, cooking in Louisiana began to develop from different nationalities into a combination of cookery from Europe and Spanish America, joined with the traditions of the local Negroes and Indians to form its own distinct yet ever-changing flavors.

Other groups have come into the state. Along the Mississippi River, south of New Orleans, there are many Slavic peoples who are known as accomplished fishermen. In the city of New Orleans and in the parishes of southeastern Louisiana, there are large Italian and Sicilian populations. These groups are some of the best growers and suppliers of produce and continue to practice their own traditions. Chinese, Greeks, Hungarians, and Irish came as well, and the last big group to invade the state were the Americans. Many Americans came overland from neighboring southern states. In fact, northern Louisiana has more in common with rural Georgia than it has in common with southern Louisiana.

Every group of immigrants has helped shape the culinary landscape of Louisiana. The reason that Louisiana has such distinctive food is that it is a melting pot of people and cultures. But it's more like a gumbo pot. First you make a roux—that's the land of Louisiana, from the rolling hills in the north, flowing down the alluvial valleys toward the coastal marshes in the south. Stir in the chopped seasonings—those are the people from all over the world that add their own distinct flavor to the mixture. Add the water, from the Gulf, the bayous, the lakes, and the Mississippi River. Then turn down the heat in our mild climate, and simmer over history. The longer this cooks the better it gets. Season to taste with Spanish and French colonial rule. Stir occasionally with the Revolution and the War Between the States. Put the lid on with Reconstruction and simmer some more. Serve over a bowl of rice, much like the urbanization of the population, and sprinkle with filé. All these ingredients with the proper amounts of imagination and common sense can't help but give you a great gumbo. And life in Louisiana is like a gumbo: you don't know what the next spoonful will be, but it will be interesting.

JEANNINE MEEDS WILSON

I'm glad you've come to my home, Louisiana.
My mama used to say, "When the Lord make Louisiana,
he must have been laughin'. . . . It's filled with so many
wonderful things" . . . the treasures of the sea, our rich delta soil,
and people with imagination to transform these riches
into our great natural resource—
Louisiana cookin'.
I love Louisiana. Welcome home!
Welcome to Home Grown!

JUSTIN WILSON'S
Homegrown Louisiana Cookin'

Appetizers

The only rules in the book of entertaining according to Justin Wilson are: Plenty to eat, plenty to drink, then let your guests enjoy themselves.

Louisianans use anything as an excuse for a party: Mardi Gras, the biggest, longest party, takes place throughout the southern part of the state from January 6 to Ash Wednesday; a football game, particularly when the Tigers play at L.S.U., has developed its own specialized partying technique called tailgating; and Christmastime gives rise to family-oriented parties with tables groaning under the weight of as many as fifty different dishes made by the hostess and others brought by the visitors who traditionally come to see the burning of the fires on the Mississippi River levee. Some of our governors have been great partiers. One governor served five hundred thousand hot dogs at his inauguation. Another held his inaugural party in the Superdome and invited the whole state.

Then there are the parties that begin for no reason. The beer after work that escalates into a full-blown crab or crawfish boil, the annual Justin Wilson *cochon de lait* roast that went from fifty invited couples to a three-day extravaganza with five hundred people or more. The words "small party" are a contradiction in terms at our house, and

Justin often cooks in large quantities because there are always people visiting. Any dish can be used as an appetizer; any appetizer can be used as a main dish. Frequently a host will serve dozens of tidbits so that the guests can try a little of everything. The idea is not to get full, it's to have a good time with the other people. In Louisiana entertaining or "chunkin' a party" is a full-time mission.

We use a great deal of seafood, because many people catch their own or are able to buy it fresh and cheap. Smoked meats are often made at home or at a local smokehouse. The garden provides peppers and other vegetables. Canapés are a tradition in New Orleans, where a great variety of spreads are served on the wonderful French bread.

So the next time you have friends over, remember, we're probably having friends over too, and we hope that you're having as good a time as we're bound to have.

Shrimp Dip

Shrimp dip is a very popular dish at parties.

8 ounces soft cream cheese	1 cup mayonnaise
¼ cup fresh lemon juice	Louisiana hot sauce or
1 pound shrimp, cooked,	ground cayenne pepper
peeled, and coarsely	to taste
chopped (see Note below)	1 tablespoon Worcestershire
2 cups finely chopped green	sauce
onions	Salt to taste

To soften the cream cheese, let it sit covered at room temperature several hours or microwave on low about one minute. In a medium-sized mixing bowl, mix the lemon juice and cream cheese together. Stir the shrimp and green onions into the cream cheese. Add the mayonnaise and stir in the hot sauce, Worcestershire, and salt. Turn the mixture into a serving dish and chill. This dish is a lot better if it is made a day or several hours ahead. Serve this dip with crackers, melba toast, or chips.

YIELD: *plentiful dipping for 10 to 15 guests*

NOTE: If using raw shrimp, bring 1 quart of water to a boil, to which 1 tablespoon salt and ¼ teaspoon ground cayenne pepper have been added. Add the shrimp, bring the water back to a boil, and let it boil for only 1 minute. Drain the shrimp immediately. Spread the shrimp out so that they cool quickly and then peel.

Shrimp Ceviche

Ceviche is often made with whitefish in Mexico. This version using shrimp is especially delicious.

1 pound small raw shrimp, peeled and deveined	2 large tomatoes, peeled and chopped into ½-inch pieces
½ cup fresh lemon juice	¼ cup olive oil
½ cup white vinegar	1 medium onion, chopped into ½-inch pieces
1 teaspoon salt	
2 teaspoons Louisiana hot sauce	10 sprigs fresh cilantro or parsley, coarsely chopped
1 green cayenne pepper, finely chopped	

In a medium-sized glass bowl, stir together the lemon juice, vinegar, salt, and hot sauce. Add the shrimp and let them marinate, covered, in the refrigerator for 4 hours. Add the remaining ingredients, mix well, cover, and return to the refrigerator for another hour. Serve as a cocktail or on a bed of lettuce.

YIELD: *20 appetizer servings or 6 to 8 salad servings*

Marinated Shrimp

I garontee there won't be any of this left after the party!

1 pound peeled, cooked small or medium-sized shrimp (see Note below)

½ cup fresh lemon juice

Louisiana hot sauce or ground cayenne pepper to taste

½ cup olive oil

¾ cup white vinegar

¼ cup honey

1 cup pitted green olives with juice

2 medium-sized white or purple onions, thinly sliced

Salt to taste

In a large mixing bowl, combine the lemon juice, hot sauce, oil, vinegar, and honey, and stir until the honey is dissolved. Add the olives and mix well. Then add the onions, shrimp, and salt, stirring gently. Cover and refrigerate for at least 1 hour or even overnight.

Y I E L D : *appetizers for 10 to 12 people*

N O T E : If using raw shrimp, bring 1 quart of water to a boil, to which 1 tablespoon salt and ¼ teaspoon ground cayenne pepper have been added. Add the shrimp, bring the water back to a boil, and let it boil for only 1 minute. Drain the shrimp immediately. Spread the shrimp out so that they cool quickly and then peel.

Marinated Crab Claws

This dish is also called crab fingers.

1 pound shelled crab claws

⅓ cup fresh lime or lemon juice

1½ teaspoons salt

½ teaspoon onion powder

¼ cup red wine vinegar

½ cup olive oil
1 tablespoon Worcestershire
   sauce

Louisiana hot sauce or
   ground cayenne pepper
   to taste
¼ teaspoon garlic powder

Place crab claws in a glass or plastic dish. In a small bowl, mix the remaining ingredients together, then pour over the crab claws, cover with a lid or foil, and refrigerate overnight, stirring several times.

YIELD: *appetizers for 10 to 20 people*

Crab Mold

You can use shrimp or fish instead of crab.

2 pounds crabmeat, carefully
   picked clean of shells
¼ pound (1 stick) softened
   margarine or butter
½ cup mayonnaise
8 ounces softened cream
   cheese

½ cup finely chopped pimentos
¼ cup finely chopped celery
½ teaspoon fresh lemon juice
   Salt to taste
   Louisiana hot sauce or
   ground cayenne pepper
   to taste

In a medium-sized mixing bowl, blend together the crabmeat and margarine to form a paste. Add the remaining ingredients, mixing well. Cover and refrigerate overnight. In the morning, press the mixture into a small bowl or mold. Return to the refrigerator for 4 hours. Turn out the mold onto a bed of lettuce and serve with crackers or French bread.

YIELD: *about 3 cups or 1 small mold*

• ⌒ •

Oysters Justin

Salt to taste	**One 4-pound box rock salt**
½ **teaspoon ground cayenne pepper**	¼ **teaspoon fresh lemon juice for each oyster**
½ **teaspoon garlic powder**	⅛ **teaspoon olive oil for each oyster**
1 **teaspoon onion powder**	¼ **teaspoon finely chopped green onions for each oyster**
½ **teaspoon finely crushed dried parsley**	
3 **dozen oysters in the shell**	

Preheat oven to 400°F. The saltiness of oysters varies a great deal, depending on where they grew and the season of the year. Taste the oysters for salt and adjust the amount of salt used in this recipe for personal taste. Mix the salt with the cayenne pepper, garlic powder, onion powder, and parsley in a small mixing bowl.

In a shallow 9-by-12-inch baking pan, pour enough rock salt to cover the bottom, about ½ inch thick. The rock salt helps to distribute heat evenly and to keep the oysters hot while serving. If the outsides of the oyster shells are dirty, rinse and brush them in cool water. Open oysters (see page 119), letting the oyster rest on the bottom shell. Nest the oysters on the half shell in the rock salt, keeping them level so that the oyster liquor doesn't run off. You should be able to bake 8 at a time. Sprinkle the oysters with the mixed seasonings, the lemon juice, olive oil, and green onions. Place in the oven and bake for 10 to 15 minutes, just until the edges of the oysters begin to curl. Serve with crackers.

YIELD: *6 to 8 servings*

Oyster Fritters

1 **pint shucked fresh oysters (reserve 1 cup strained juice)**	2 **teaspoons baking powder**
2 **cups all-purpose flour**	¼ **teaspoon baking soda**
	¼ **teaspoon ground cayenne pepper**

¼ teaspoon salt or to taste
3 medium-sized eggs, beaten
¼ cup buttermilk

1 cup oyster juice, strained
About 1 quart oil for frying

Fill a deep fry pot half full with oil and preheat to 375°F. Chop the oysters into ½-inch pieces. In a medium-sized mixing bowl, sift together the flour, baking powder, baking soda, cayenne pepper, and salt. In another bowl, beat the eggs, then add the milk and oyster juice. Pour this mixture into the dry ingredients and mix well. Add the oysters to the flour mixture. This batter should hold together well and not be runny. (If it's too wet, sift in a little bit more flour.) Using a long-handled spoon, carefully drop the batter by teaspoons into the hot oil. Fry about 3 minutes or until the fritters turn over and turn golden brown on both sides. (They should turn over by themselves, but if they don't, just give them a little push.) Drain the fritters on paper towels and serve hot.

Y I E L D : *about 3 dozen, depending on size*

Sausage and Oyster Sandwiches

20 fresh medium-sized oysters, shucked and drained
1 pound smoked sausage, cut into forty ¼-inch slices
2 cups dry white wine

1 teaspoon Louisiana hot sauce or ¼ teaspoon ground cayenne pepper
½ teaspoon salt
1 tablespoon Worcestershire sauce
1 tablespoon honey

Using a toothpick as a skewer, place an oyster between 2 slices of smoked sausage to make 20 little "sandwiches." In a large, high-walled skillet, combine the wine, hot sauce, salt, Worcestershire, and honey, and cook over low heat. Place the skewers in the sauce and heat gently, never boiling, until the oyster edges curl, about 5 minutes. Serve warm from a chafing dish.

Y I E L D : *20 "sandwiches"*

Fish Nuggets

DRENCH:

- 1 medium-sized egg
- 1 cup milk
- 1 teaspoon salt
- ½ teaspoon ground cayenne pepper
- 2 pounds fish fillets, cut into 1-inch cubes
- 1 quart oil, for frying

DREDGE:

- ½ cup corn flour
- ½ cup all-purpose flour
- ½ teaspoon ground cayenne pepper, or to taste
- 2 teaspoons salt, or to taste
- ¼ teaspoon garlic powder
- ½ teaspoon onion powder

Preheat oil to 350°F. In a medium-sized mixing bowl, beat the egg, milk, salt, and pepper together. In another medium-sized mixing bowl, combine the flours, pepper, salt, and garlic and onion powders. Dip the nuggets in the drench mixture. Drain, then coat well in the dredge mixture. Carefully place a few nuggets at a time in the hot oil and fry in batches until fish are golden brown and the pieces float, about 1 to 2 minutes depending on the thickness of the fish. Remove from the oil and drain on paper towels. Serve immediately with tartar or cocktail sauce.

YIELD: *2 pounds of nuggets, enough to serve 10 to 12*

Ham 'n' Eggs

- 6 hard-boiled eggs, peeled
- ¼ cup minced ham
- 2 tablespoons mayonnaise
- 2 tablespoons prepared mustard
- 2 tablespoons drained and finely chopped salad olives
- ½ teaspoon Louisiana hot sauce
- Salt to taste
- Olives or fresh parsley sprigs for garnish

Carefully cut the eggs in half lengthwise and remove the yolks; set the whites aside. In a small mixing bowl, mash the yolks with a fork, then mix in the ham, mayonnaise, mustard, olives, and hot sauce. Taste for salt; depending on the saltiness of the olives, you might not need it. Carefully spoon the dressing back into the egg whites. Serve on a plate of lettuce and garnish with cut olives or parsley sprigs.

YIELD: *12 stuffed halves*

Baby Back Ribs with Mustard Sauce

10 pounds baby back pork ribs, separated	Ground cayenne pepper to taste
Salt to taste	Mustard Sauce (see page 58)

Preheat oven to 300°F. Sprinkle salt and pepper on the ribs, then place them in a large baking pan, and bake in the oven until tender, about 1 hour. Drizzle with the mustard sauce.

YIELD: *serves 10 to 20*

Rich Shells

¼ pound (1 stick) butter or margarine, softened	3 ounces softened cream cheese
1 cup all-purpose flour	

Preheat oven to 400°F. Cut the shortening into the flour. Add the softened cream cheese and mix together well. This dough should have the consistency of a pie crust and be easy to handle. Pinch off enough dough to make a 1-inch ball. Drop into the bottom of a muffin tin and flatten out and up the sides with your fingers, or simply flatten with a roller or your hands. These can now be filled with meats, fruits, cheeses, spreads, or anything you might invent. You can leave them uncovered, fold them over, or draw them together like a small pouch. Bake until the pastry is slightly brown, about 10 minutes. You can drizzle the top with butter, or egg, or icing, or a savory sauce. These can be baked ahead, then filled like tarts or mini pies and refrigerated.

YIELD: *20 to 40 shells, depending on size*

Burgundy Bread

1 loaf French bread, sliced in half lengthwise	1 cup dry red wine
½ cup olive oil	Dash Louisiana hot sauce
½ teaspoon (one small clove) minced garlic	½ cup grated Parmesan cheese

Preheat the broiler. In a small saucepan over medium-high, heat the olive oil, then sauté the garlic. Stir in the wine and hot sauce, then remove from the heat and whip vigorously until the mixture does not separate. Using a basting or pastry brush, generously coat the cut sides of the bread with the wine mixture. Place on a flat baking sheet and sprinkle with grated cheese. Broil, about 6 inches from the element, about 5 minutes, until golden brown. Slice and serve immediately.

YIELD: *10 to 20 pieces*

Mardi Gras Doubloons

The Mardi Gras colors are purple, green, and gold—that's where this name comes from.

2 large carrots, sliced ¼ inch
thick or one 16-ounce can
sliced carrots
1 medium-sized purple onion,
sliced in ¼-inch rings
1 long green Anaheim pepper,
sliced in thin rings
½ cup olive oil

½ cup honey
¾ cup red wine vinegar
½ cup tomato or vegetable
juice
Louisiana hot sauce or
ground cayenne pepper
to taste

Boil fresh carrots in 1 quart salted water about 15 minutes until tender; then drain and discard the liquid. In a small saucepan, over medium heat, combine the olive oil, honey, vinegar, tomato juice, and hot sauce, and let simmer for 5 minutes. Place the carrots, onions, and peppers in a medium-sized bowl and toss them lightly. Pour the cooked sauce over the vegetables and toss again. Cover and refrigerate for 3 to 4 hours.

YIELD: *appetizers for 10 to 12*

Pecan Blues

½ pound blue cheese
1 pound cream cheese,
softened
1 teaspoon Louisiana hot
sauce
Salt to taste

1 teaspoon Worcestershire
sauce
1 tablespoon fresh onion juice
(see Note below)
2 cups chopped pecans

Blend the cheeses with an electric mixer or in a food processor. Add the hot sauce, salt, Worcestershire, and onion juice, then blend again. Shape the cheese mixture into a ball and refrigerate, covered, overnight or for several hours. Pour the chopped pecans into a medium-sized mixing bowl. Roll the cheese ball over the pecans, with a fair amount of pressure, to imbed the pecans in the cheese. Make sure the entire surface of the cheese ball is covered with pecans. Chill until ready to serve. Can be served on fruit or crackers.

YIELD: *one 5-inch ball, enough for about 20 servings*

NOTE: To get the onion juice, puree a medium-sized onion in a blender or food processor. Place the puree in a strainer and, using a wooden spoon, force the juice out. Commercial onion juice is often very strong and bitter-tasting.

Roasted Pecans

¼ cup oil or melted shortening
2 cups pecan halves
Salt to taste

Ground cayenne pepper to taste

Preheat oven to 300°F. Mix the oil, pecans, salt, and pepper in a medium-sized mixing bowl. Turn into a shallow baking pan, and roast until done, about 15 to 20 minutes, stirring every 5 minutes. Serve warm or cold.

YIELD: *2 cups*

Squash Squares

¼ cup olive oil
1 cup finely chopped onion
1 teaspoon minced garlic
2½ cups shredded zucchini or other summer squash
6 medium-sized eggs, beaten
1½ cups plain bread crumbs
¼ teaspoon ground cayenne pepper

½ teaspoon salt
½ cup chopped fresh parsley or ¼ cup dried parsley
2 cups grated cheese, whatever type you like
½ cup grated Parmesan or Romano cheese
¼ cup sesame seeds

Preheat the oven to 325°F. In a large skillet, sauté the onions in olive oil over medium heat until they are tender. Add the garlic and squash and sauté another 3 minutes. In a large mixing bowl, combine the eggs, bread crumbs, pepper, salt, parsley, grated cheese, and cooked squash. Grease a 9-by-13-inch baking pan with olive oil and turn the squash mixture into it. Sprinkle the top with the Parmesan cheese and sesame seeds. Bake for 30 minutes. After cooling, cut into 1-inch squares. Serve warm or cold.

YIELD: *about 100 pieces*

Stuffed Okra

20 fresh young okra, sliced in half lengthwise and seeded
1 quart oil for deep frying

1 cup white crabmeat, carefully picked free of shells

STUFFING:
1 cup corn flour
1 cup plain bread crumbs
1 teaspoon onion powder
½ teaspoon garlic powder
½ teaspoon ground cayenne pepper
2 tablespoons chopped parsley
2 teaspoons salt
2 large eggs, beaten
½ cup dry white wine

DREDGE:
2 cups corn flour
1 teaspoon salt
Ground cayenne pepper to taste

DRENCH:
1 large egg, beaten
½ cup dry white wine
Salt to taste
Louisiana hot sauce to taste

In a large mixing bowl, make the stuffing by mixing the corn flour, bread crumbs, onion and garlic powders, pepper, parsley, and salt. In a smaller bowl, mix together the eggs and wine, then pour into the flour mixture. Add the crabmeat and mix well. Refrigerate for 2 hours or until stiff, then stuff the okra halves and pat down to make firm.

Mix the corn flour, salt, and pepper in flat pan to make a dredge.

Make the drench by combining the egg, wine, salt, and hot sauce in a small bowl. Preheat the oil to 375°F. Put one okra at a time in the drench, then roll individually in the dredge, making sure to coat all sides. Fry in batches for 10 minutes or until golden brown. Drain on paper towels and serve immediately.

YIELD: *40 pieces or about 10 servings*

Stuffed Hungarian Peppers

10 **Hungarian peppers, halved lengthwise, seeded and stemmed**

2 **cups of any filling or spread**

Fill the pepper halves with any of the spreads which follow or your favorite fillings and refrigerate. Serve cold.

YIELD: *8 to 10 servings*

Pimento Cheese Spread

½ **pound sharp cheddar cheese, grated**

3 **ounces cream cheese, softened**

1 **teaspoon Worcestershire sauce**

1 **teaspoon Louisiana hot sauce**

½ **teaspoon Dijon mustard**

1 **teaspoon drained and chopped pimentos**

In a small bowl, combine all the ingredients and mix well. Refrigerate until ready to stuff peppers, or use as a spread on toast or crackers.

YIELD: *2 cups*

Sardine Spread

One 4-ounce can sardines
    packed in oil, mashed
1 tablespoon minced onion
1 teaspoon lemon juice

¼ cup mayonnaise
1 teaspoon finely chopped
    fresh parsley

In a mixing bowl, combine all the ingredients and blend to spreading consistency. Refrigerate until ready to use.

YIELD: *1 cup*

All-Day Spread

2 hard-boiled eggs, peeled and
    mashed
1 cup grated cheddar cheese
¼ cup minced ham
2 tablespoons mayonnaise
2 tablespoons finely chopped
    dill pickle

1 teaspoon Louisiana hot
    sauce
1 teaspoon Dijon mustard
Salt to taste

In a medium-sized bowl, mix eggs and cheese together, then stir in the ham. Add mayonnaise and the rest of the ingredients, mixing well. Refrigerate until ready to use.

YIELD: *about 2 cups*

VARIATION: Instead of ham, try different ingredients like boiled shrimp or crabmeat, or anything else you might want to experiment with.

Peanut Butter, Bacon, and Onion Spread

4 strips bacon
2 cups peanut butter, crunchy
    or smooth

½ cup minced onion

Fry the bacon until crispy, drain on paper towels, then crumble. In a small mixing bowl, combine the peanut butter with the bacon and onion; blend well. Refrigerate until ready to use.

YIELD: *2½ cups*

Chicken Spread

1 cup ground cooked chicken meat	1 tablespoon cream cheese, softened
1 tablespoon sweet relish, drained	½ teaspoon Worcestershire sauce
1 tablespoon minced onion	⅛ teaspoon Louisiana hot sauce
1 tablespoon mayonnaise	

In a small mixing bowl, combine all the ingredients and blend well. Refrigerate until ready to use.

YIELD: *2 cups*

Salads and Dressings

The imagination of the preparer is the only limit to a salad. So at Justin's house there is no telling what will find itself on the dish to the left of the fork. Seafood is a main ingredient because oysters, shrimp, crawfish, and crab are readily available and cheap. Green salads are used mainly as a base or starting place from which to add any other ingredient. Leftover rice and pasta are used in combination with meats, seafood, and vegetables to make a full meal. Often during the heat of the summer a cold plate of chilled meats, cheeses, and vegetables or a cold seafood salad with greens is perfect for the evening meal. The garden contributes fresh herbs and a parade of different seasonal vegetables. In the spring one can roam the woods and swamps to find wild plants that add exotic flavors to salad. It is essential if you are gathering wild species to be absolutely certain of the identity of the plant and its preparation. One part of a plant can be harmless while another part of the same plant can make you sick.

Jim, the old black man who used to tend Justin's yard, knew a great deal about plants. Jim, God rest his soul, never had to be told what to do; he always found something to do. Years before Jim came to work, Justin established a bed of watercress in a small ditch that led from the swimming pool to the pond. As running water will do, it created its own climate. The cress flourished along the ditch and gave fresh additions to many salads. One afternoon when Justin returned from a trip Jim reported, "Mister Justin Wilson, I done clint out that ditch from the pool and it sure is puddy now." Jim had no idea what watercress was, but he did know how to clean a ditch so that the water would flow. Justin never could get the cress started again.

Justin has a special wooden bowl for salad making and a special garlic-mashing fork that he uses to make vinegar and oil dressings. He then adds greens and vegetables to this bowl, then tosses the whole salad in it. He has had the bowl fifty years. "One of the few things I didn't lose in my first divorce," quips Justin. It's been through countless moves, floods, and hurricanes. It is never washed with soap, only rinsed with warm water and dried.

Because Justin likes the flavor of olive oil he uses it in his dressings. Many types of oils may be used, however; avocado, sesame, rice bran, corn, and a number of others are suitable. Making fresh mayonnaise is easy to do in the blender, but a high-quality prepared mayonnaise is suitable, too.

Don't let anything limit the makeup of your salads, and choose interesting combinations of foods that complement each other in flavor and texture. Many cooked vegetable dishes chilled and dressed make good salads: beets, okra, mirliton, cauliflower, or peppers. Always carefully wash fresh greens if you don't grow them yourself. Dry and chill them so that they will be crispy and the dressing will cling to them.

Benné Seed Dressing

Benné *is the French word for sesame.*

¼ cup sugar	¼ teaspoon ground dry
1 clove garlic, minced	mustard
1 teaspoon salt	1½ cups olive oil or
½ cup red wine vinegar	vegetable oil
¼ cup chopped onion	½ cup toasted sesame seeds

In a blender, add each ingredient in the order listed, then blend on medium speed until the ingredients are very well mixed. This dressing will keep for several weeks in the refrigerator.

YIELD: *about 3 cups*

Justin's Vinaigrette Dressing

This is delicious served over a fresh green or vegetable salad.

1 large clove garlic	½ teaspoon chopped fresh
2 teaspoons salt	parsley or ¼ teaspoon
1 cup olive oil	dried parsley
2 tablespoons fresh lemon	¼ teaspoon finely chopped
juice	green onion tops
½ cup red wine vinegar	¼ teaspoon minced ripe olives
1 teaspoon Louisiana hot	¼ teaspoon minced capers
sauce	1 teaspoon finely grated
1 tablespoon Worcestershire	hard-boiled egg
sauce	¼ teaspoon minced dill pickle
	1 teaspoon finely chopped
	pimentos

In a large wooden salad bowl, using a strong four-tined eating fork, mash the garlic together with the salt until they form a gritty paste.

One at a time, add the remaining ingredients, in the order listed, stirring after each addition. You can make this dressing several hours before you are ready to serve the salad. I make my dressing right in the same bowl that I use to toss the salad greens. But it can also be poured into a jar with a lid and stored in the refrigerator for several weeks. Olive oil will solidify and get cloudy if chilled. Bring the dressing back to room temperature before remixing.

YIELD: *about 1½ cups*

Justin's French Dressing

1 large clove garlic
2 teaspoons salt
1 cup olive oil
2 tablespoons fresh lemon
  juice
½ cup red wine vinegar

1 teaspoon Louisiana hot
  sauce
1 tablespoon Worcestershire
  sauce
1 teaspoon prepared mustard

In a large wooden bowl, using a strong four-tined eating fork, mash the garlic together with the salt until they form a gritty paste. Add the remaining ingredients, one at a time, in the order listed, stirring after each addition. You can make this dressing several hours before you are ready to serve the salad. I make my dressing right in the same bowl that I use to toss the salad greens. But it can also be poured into a jar with a lid and stored in the refrigerator for several weeks. Olive oil will solidify and get cloudy if chilled. Bring the dressing back to room temperature before remixing. You can use this dressing as a base and add many other herbs or spices, cheeses, or seasonings to it.

YIELD: *1½ cups*

• 🍃 •

Creamy Blue Cheese Dressing

I usually make a fresh batch of dressing every time I need it.

2 tablespoons olive oil or vegetable oil	2 to 4 ounces blue cheese, in small pieces
¼ cup mayonnaise	Salt to taste
1 tablespoon fresh lime or lemon juice	Louisiana hot sauce or ground cayenne pepper to taste
1 tablespoon red wine vinegar	
¼ cup sour cream or plain yogurt	

In a small mixing bowl, beat together the oil and mayonnaise until completely blended. Add the lime juice and beat some more. Then add the vinegar and beat again. Add the sour cream, blue cheese, salt, and hot sauce, and stir well. Serve over your favorite salad. This will keep in the refrigerator for several weeks.

YIELD: *about 1 cup*

Ranch Dressing

This is a ranch dressing even the cows would come home for.

1 cup buttermilk	1 cup mayonnaise
¼ teaspoon garlic powder	Salt to taste
¼ teaspoon onion powder	Louisiana hot sauce or ground cayenne pepper to taste
½ teaspoon dried parsley	
1 teaspoon dried chives	

Pour the buttermilk into a small mixing bowl, then add the garlic and onion powders and mix well. Add the parsley and chives and blend well. Blend in the mayonnaise until smooth, then add salt and hot sauce. This will keep in the refrigerator for several weeks.

YIELD: *2 cups*

Crawfish Salad

Lobster or shrimp can be used instead of crawfish.

2 hard-boiled eggs, grated	1 cup finely chopped green
1 pound peeled, cooked, and	onions
chopped crawfish tails (see	½ cup mayonnaise
Note below)	Louisiana hot sauce to taste
½ cup finely chopped celery	Juice of 1 lemon
1 cup fresh peas	4 cups shredded lettuce

In a small mixing bowl, combine the eggs, crawfish, celery, peas, onions, mayonnaise, hot sauce, and lemon juice. Put 1 cup of lettuce on individual salad plates, then add two heaping serving spoons of the crawfish mixture.

YIELD: *4 servings*

NOTE: To cook the peeled crawfish tails: In a saucepan bring 1 quart of water, seasoned with 2 teaspoons of salt and ½ teaspoon of ground cayenne pepper, to a boil. Add the crawfish tails to the boiling water, then bring back to a boil. Remove from heat, drain, let cool.

Pasta and Ham Salad

4 cups cooked pasta of your	1 teaspoon minced garlic
choice, drained and cooled	½ teaspoon prepared mustard
2 cups julienned ham	1 tablespoon mayonnaise
1 cup chopped green onions	Juice of 1 lime
1 cup salad olives	Salt to taste
1 cup halved cherry tomatoes	Louisiana hot sauce to taste
2 hard-boiled eggs, grated	Lettuce leaves
1 hot pepper, thinly sliced	½ cup pecan pieces
½ cup olive oil	¼ cup grated Parmesan cheese
¼ cup red wine vinegar	

In a large mixing bowl, toss together the pasta, ham, onions, olives, tomatoes, eggs, and pepper. In a separate bowl, whisk together the oil, vinegar, garlic, mustard, mayonnaise, lime juice, salt, and hot sauce. Drizzle over the pasta mixture and toss lightly. Serve on individual plates on a bed of lettuce, sprinkled with the pecans and cheese.

YIELD : *6 entrée servings*

Cole Slaw

This is great for a party or company or just to snack on.

1 large head of cabbage, shredded	1 tablespoon olive oil
4 medium-sized bell peppers, thinly sliced	1 tablespoon wine vinegar
2 medium-sized onions, thinly sliced	1 tablespoon Worcestershire sauce
	Louisiana hot sauce or ground cayenne pepper to taste
DRESSING:	Salt to taste
1 cup mayonnaise	1 teaspoon minced garlic
¼ cup Dijon mustard	Juice of 1 lemon

In a large mixing bowl, lightly toss the cabbage, peppers, and onions. In a smaller bowl, whisk together the dressing ingredients thoroughly, pour over the cabbage, and toss well. This can be kept in the refrigerator, covered, for several days.

YIELD : *10 to 12 servings*

• ✒ •

San Antone Salad

San Antonio, Texas, is one of my most favorite cities in the U. S. and A. The Mexican influence is very strong there and people seem to enjoy life almost as much as they do in Louisiana.

1 cup Justin's French (see page 20) or Vinaigrette Dressing (see page 19)
1 head lettuce, shredded
1 mirliton (chayote), peeled, seeded, and chopped in ½-inch pieces
1 cup drained kidney beans
1 cup chopped onion
1 cup drained hominy
½ cup chopped ripe olives
½ cup chopped bell pepper

1 tablespoon fresh lime juice
Salt to taste
Louisiana hot sauce or ground cayenne pepper to taste
8 ounces shredded cooked chicken meat (about 2 breasts)
Guacamole (see page 25)
Sour cream (optional)
Chihuahua cheese (see Note below)

Place the shredded lettuce in a large salad bowl. Drizzle ½ cup of the dressing over it, then toss lightly. In a large mixing bowl, combine the mirliton, beans, onion, hominy, olives, and bell pepper. Sprinkle the lime juice over the bean mixture, add the salt and hot sauce, then toss lightly. Spoon the bean mixture over the lettuce. Lay the shredded chicken over the bean mixture and put a big dollop of guacamole on the chicken and then a smaller dollop of sour cream. Drizzle with the remaining dressing and top with crumbled cheese.

YIELD: *4 to 6 servings*

NOTE: Chihuahua cheese is a strong crumbly cheese.

Guacamole

1 large ripe avocado
1 tablespoon fresh lime or
  lemon juice
¼ cup minced onion
¼ cup peeled, seeded, and
  chopped fresh tomato
1 sprig fresh cilantro

(coriander) or parsley,
  chopped
1 small hot chili pepper,
  minced
1 teaspoon minced garlic
Salt to taste

Cut the avocado through the skin and pulp lengthwise, then rotate the fruit until you're back at the starting point; pull the halves apart. Flick your knife blade into the pit, twist slightly to dislodge it, then lift the blade and pit out. Scrape out the pulp with a spoon or slice or cube the fruit while still in the skin. In a small bowl, mash the pulp with a fork, then add the remaining ingredients and blend well. To extend the mixture, sour cream, mayonnaise, or yogurt may be added to taste, and whipped to blend in well. Serve as a dip with tortilla chips or over a bed of lettuce as a salad or as a component of other salads such as San Antone Salad.

YIELD: *2 cups*

Brown Rice Salad

2 cups cooked brown rice
1 large tomato, peeled, seeded,
  and chopped
½ cup finely chopped fresh
  parsley
1 cup finely chopped onion
1 tablespoon finely chopped
  fresh mint

½ teaspoon minced garlic
½ cup olive oil
½ cup fresh lemon juice
Salt to taste
Louisiana hot sauce or
  ground cayenne pepper
  to taste

Combine the rice, tomato, parsley, onion, and mint in a large bowl and toss lightly. In a small bowl, whisk together the garlic, olive oil, lemon juice, salt, and hot sauce, then pour over the rice mixture and toss. Serve on a leaf of lettuce with a chunk of feta cheese and marinated olives.

YIELD: *4 servings*

Surplus Salad

This is the salad I make all summer when the tomatoes and cucumbers are abundant.

Bell pepper, sliced
Tomatoes, sliced
Cucumbers, sliced
Onions, sliced
Hungarian pepper, sliced

And anything the garden is
    supplying in surplus
Salt to taste
Louisiana hot sauce to taste
Your favorite salad dressing

Mix all the vegetables together in a large salad bowl. Use whatever salad dressing you wish. Pour over the vegetables, toss lightly, and serve immediately.

YIELD: *depends on the quantity of ingredients used*

Blue Crab Salad

Be careful—the crabmeat for this salad must be very fresh or you'll have to eat it in one day. Don't let it spoil.

1 pound lump crabmeat, picked
    over for shells

1 medium-sized onion,
    shredded

1 bunch red radishes, thinly
sliced
½ cup olive or vegetable oil
½ cup white vinegar
½ cup cold water

¼ cup fresh lime juice
Salt to taste
Louisiana hot sauce or
ground cayenne pepper
to taste

In a small, flat-bottomed glass dish, place a layer of onion, then a layer of crab, then a layer of radish. Repeat this step. In a medium-sized mixing bowl, whisk together the oil, vinegar, water, lime juice, salt, and hot sauce, and pour over the last layer. Cover and let marinate in the refrigerator for at least 2 hours. Serve on bed of lettuce with crackers.

YIELD: *6 servings*

Shrimp and Pasta Salad

4 cups cooked, drained, and
cooled elbow macaroni
2 cups small shrimp, cooked,
peeled, and deveined
4 hard-boiled eggs, chopped
½ cup chopped onion
¼ cup chopped celery
½ cup chopped black olives
½ cup chopped dill pickle

1 cup mayonnaise
2 tablespoons olive oil
Louisiana hot sauce to taste
1 teaspoon fresh lemon juice
2 teaspoons Worcestershire
sauce
1 tablespoon prepared
mustard
½ cup catsup

In a large mixing bowl, combine the eggs, onion, celery, olives, and pickle, then add the shrimp and macaroni and toss lightly. In a small bowl, whisk together the remaining ingredients. Pour over the macaroni mixture and mix well. Cover and let marinate at least 2 hours in the refrigerator before serving.

YIELD: *6 to 10 servings*

Cucumber and Onion Salad

2 medium cucumbers, peeled
  if desired, and thinly
  sliced
1 medium-sized onion, thinly
  sliced into rings
1 cup sour cream
¼ cup cider vinegar

Salt to taste
1 sprig fresh parsley, chopped
¼ cup mayonnaise
Louisiana hot sauce or
  ground cayenne pepper
  to taste

In a large mixing bowl, combine the cucumbers and onions. In a small bowl, combine the remaining ingredients, and mix well. Pour this over the cucumbers and onions and toss. Cover the bowl and marinate in the refrigerator for at least 2 hours.

YIELD: *4 servings*

NOTE: Some store-bought cucumbers are waxed; these must be peeled before slicing. Young, tender field cucumbers do not have to be peeled, but they may be peeled in strips or scored with the tines of a fork for decoration.

Beet Salad

4 fresh beets or one 16-ounce
  can beets, sliced ¼ inch
  thick
1 medium-sized onion, sliced
  into thin rings
1 cup olive oil
¼ cup cider vinegar

Salt to taste
2 to 4 whole cloves
1½ teaspoons sugar
Louisiana hot sauce or
  ground cayenne pepper
  to taste
Leaf or iceberg lettuce

If using fresh beets, place them in a large saucepan, cover with water, and cook, covered, over medium heat until tender, about 30 minutes. Let cool, peel, then slice into ¼-inch thick slices.

Put the beets and onions in a medium-sized bowl. In a small bowl, whisk together the oil, vinegar, salt, cloves, sugar, and hot sauce. Pour over the beets, cover, and let marinate in the refrigerator several hours or overnight. Serve over leaf lettuce on individual plates.

YIELD: *4 servings*

Potato Salad

Potato salad is often served with gumbo in southern Louisiana.

8 cups ½-inch boiled or baked potato cubes

5 large hard-boiled eggs, chopped

1 cup chopped dill pickle or dill relish

½ cup chopped olives

1 cup chopped onion

½ cup chopped celery

2 cups mayonnaise

2 tablespoons prepared mustard

Salt to taste

Louisiana hot sauce or ground cayenne pepper to taste

Combine the potato cubes, eggs, pickles, olives, onions, and celery in a large mixing bowl and mix well. In a medium-sized mixing bowl, whisk together the mayonnaise, mustard, salt, and hot sauce. Pour over the potato and egg mixture and gently combine. Refrigerate until ready to use; in fact, it's a good idea to make this salad a day before you serve it.

YIELD: *6 to 10 servings*

Pork Salad

This is wonderful-tasting dish that can be eaten as a salad or served on a lettuce leaf as a side dish.

1 pound raw pork or leftover cooked pork, torn into pieces
1 teaspoon onion powder
½ teaspoon garlic powder
Salt to taste
Louisiana hot sauce or ground cayenne pepper to taste

½ cup mayonnaise
1 tablespoon olive oil
1 tablespoon wine vinegar
¼ cup chopped celery
½ cup chopped bell pepper
½ cup chopped onion

If you are using raw pork, place it in a 4-quart saucepan, cover with water, and stir in the onion powder, garlic powder, salt, and hot sauce. Cover and bring to a boil. Reduce heat and simmer until the pork is tender, about 1 hour. Remove the pork from the broth and let it cool. After the pork has cooled enough to handle, pull it apart into small pieces.

In a large mixing bowl, beat together the mayonnaise and olive oil until creamy and smooth. Beat in the vinegar until well blended and smooth, then stir in salt and hot sauce. Add the celery, bell pepper, and onion, and stir to mix well. Add the pork and mix again. Serve on a bed of lettuce, as a sandwich filling, or stuffed in a tomato.

YIELD: *4 servings*

Wilted Bacon Salad

4 slices bacon
6 to 8 cups torn greens, such as romaine, parsley, spinach, or any leaf lettuce
1 large onion, thinly sliced
½ cup vinegar

½ cup water
Salt to taste
Louisiana hot sauce or ground cayenne pepper to taste
Croutons (optional)

In a medium-sized skillet over medium heat, fry the bacon until crisp. Remove and crumble; reserve the bacon drippings. Combine the greens and onions in a large salad bowl and toss lightly, then top with the bacon. Slightly heat bacon drippings in the skillet (be very careful not to heat the drippings too much or the grease may splatter when the water is added), add the vinegar, water, salt, and hot sauce; stir and mix well until heated through. Pour over the greens, toss, sprinkle with croutons, and serve immediately.

Y I E L D : *6 to 8 servings*

Crab Slaw

1 **small head cabbage, shredded**	¼ **cup wine vinegar**
1 **cup thinly sliced bell pepper**	½ **teaspoon garlic powder**
2 **medium-sized onions, sliced thin into half rings**	4 **tablespoons mayonnaise**
1 **pound white crabmeat, picked over for shells**	**Salt to taste**
¼ **cup olive oil**	**Louisiana hot sauce or ground cayenne pepper to taste**

In a large salad bowl, combine the cabbage, bell pepper, onions, and crabmeat. Mix well and refrigerate. In a small bowl, whisk together the olive oil, vinegar, garlic powder, mayonnaise, salt, and hot sauce. Pour the dressing over the vegetables and mix until coated. Serve immediately or refrigerate until ready to serve.

Y I E L D : *8 to 10 servings*

Snap Bean Salad

4 **cups fresh-cooked snap beans or canned, drained snap beans**	1 **medium-sized onion, thinly sliced into half rings**
1 **teaspoon salt**	½ **cup Justin's French Dressing (see page 20)**

Wash and snap fresh young beans. Half fill a stockpot with water to which 1 teaspoon salt has been added, and bring the water to a boil over medium-high heat. Add the fresh snap beans, and bring back to a boil. Drain and cool the beans. In a large salad bowl, combine the beans and onions and toss lightly. Pour the dressing over the salad, toss, and refrigerate until ready to serve. Mix once more before serving.

YIELD: *4 to 6 servings*

Peach and Pepper Salad

5 fresh peaches, peeled and sliced	¼ cup red wine vinegar
2 medium-sized bell peppers, sliced	Salt to taste
2 Hungarian wax peppers, sliced	Ground cayenne pepper or Louisiana hot sauce to taste
2 medium-sized sweet onions, sliced	

In a large salad bowl, combine all of the ingredients and mix together. Refrigerate for 2 hours and serve cold.

YIELD: *6 to 8 servings*

Oyster Salad

1 quart water	Louisiana hot sauce or ground cayenne pepper to taste
½ teaspoon garlic powder	
1 teaspoon onion powder	
2 teaspoons Worcestershire sauce	

1 tablespoon wine vinegar

1 pint or 2 dozen fresh oysters,
shucked and liquor
reserved

DRESSING:

4 tablespoons mayonnaise

1 tablespoon creole mustard

2 tablespoons olive oil

1 tablespoon catsup

Salt to taste

Louisiana hot sauce or
ground cayenne pepper
to taste

1 tablespoon wine vinegar

1 head of lettuce, cleaned and
torn

To the water in a medium-sized saucepan add the garlic and onion powders, the Worcestershire, hot sauce, and vinegar. Bring the water to a boil. Add the oysters and their liquor. Immediately remove from the heat, stir, and leave in the pan until the edges of the oysters begin to curl. When they do, drain and put the oysters in the refrigerator, covered, to chill completely.

In a small mixing bowl, whisk the mayonnaise and mustard together well. Slowly add the oil while continuing to whisk. Add the catsup while continuing to beat; add the salt, hot sauce, and wine vinegar. Tear the lettuce into a large salad bowl and pour in salad dressing and toss. Add oysters and mix in carefully.

YIELD: *4 servings*

Fish Salad

I usually make this out of leftover baked fish.

1 pound boned cooked fish

1 cup chopped onion

1 cup finely chopped dill pickle
or drained dill relish

1 cup finely chopped bell
pepper

2 large hard-boiled eggs,
chopped fine

2 tablespoons olive oil

Salt to taste

Louisiana hot sauce or
ground cayenne pepper
to taste

1 tablespoon wine vinegar

3 tablespoons mayonnaise

Crumble the fish into a medium-sized bowl, making sure that all the bones have been removed. Mix in the onions, pickle, bell pepper, and eggs. In a small bowl combine the olive oil, salt, hot sauce, wine vinegar, and mayonnaise. Pour over fish and mix well. Refrigerate until ready to serve.

YIELD: *6 to 8 servings*

· ❧ ·

Gumbos and Soups

A gumbo is like life in Louisiana, rich, varied, surprising, and full of flavor. You don't know what the next bite is going to bring you, but it's bound to be good. Gumbo comes from the Bantu word for okra, a vegetable native to Africa, and a primary ingredient in many gumbos. Gumbos are found nowhere else as they are found in Louisiana. A gumbo starts, of course, with a roux. Then the regional variations, the success of the hunt, and preferences of the wielder of the spoon take over. Generally, though, a gumbo is a thick, dark, and complex mixture that has cooked at least 6 hours (it gets better the longer it cooks) and is served over cooked rice. It contains either cooked okra or is sprinkled with filé. Filé, made from sassafras leaves, was long used by the Choctaw Indians in their foods, and the early settlers soon grew accustomed to its unique flavor. Gumbo season is eagerly awaited. Indeed, the first cold snap of winter will find cooks all over southern Louisiana firing up their gumbo pots and stirring a dark roux. Combine the roux with stock, seasonings, and an almost endless list of ingredients which include onions, garlic, bell peppers, parsley, celery, fowl, fish, and smoked meat that will eventually give a name to the particular pot of gumbo.

Justin tells a story about an Exotic Gumbo:

I was rode down de road one day an' dair was a li'l boy chirren drag
a bird wit' a wingspread about six feets. Now I got a big cur-rious,
like us Cajun, an' I ax, "Son, w'at you got dair, hanh?"
  He say, "A hawk," an' I say, "A whut?"
  "A schicken hawk, dass w'at I got."
  "What in de hell you gonna do wit' dat hawk?"
  "Make gumbo soup."
  "Oh, does hawk meat make pretty good gumbo?"
  " 'Bout like owl."

Besides gumbo, fish soups are popular because both fresh and saltwater seafood is cheap and plentiful. These include bisques, chowders,
and court bouillon. Soups or gumbos are eaten at least once a day by
many, a custom brought from Europe. Justin especially likes vegetable
soup with a clear meat stock. He even sprinkles filé on his hearty
winter soups. Nothing is wasted. A stock is made from leftover meat
or scraps from carving. The turkey carcass always finds itself antici-
pated as next week's gumbo. Especially flavorful for a stock base is the
tasty fat from roasted meat or the juices left in the water pan from the
smoker cooker.

The Indians, the Africans, and the Europeans all made contributions
to our talent for soup making. But what has evolved is a distinctive
style of art as soup.

Chicken Stock

1 chicken or other fowl or its scraps and bones	Parsley with stems
1 cup dry white wine	Ground cayenne pepper to taste
Water	Salt to taste
1 large onion, coarsely chopped	

Place the chicken or fowl scraps in a large stockpot and pour in the wine and enough water to cover. Put the lid on and bring to a boil. Scim off any scum that may form. Lower the heat, add the vegetables, pepper, and salt. Keep the pot covered and simmer for 1 hour. Remove the chicken or scraps and let cool, then remove any meat left on the bones and reserve it for other uses. Return the bones and skin to the stockpot and simmer for at least 2 hours. Remove any scum and strain the stock into containers and cover. This will keep in the refrigerator for 3 to 4 weeks or can be frozen and kept even longer.

YIELD: *about 1 gallon of stock*

Fish Stock

Use this with any seafood preparation.

Fish trimmings and bones or
   shellfish and scraps
Water
1 cup dry white wine (optional)
2 large onions, coarsely
   chopped

5 stems parsley
1 small lemon, quartered
Dill (optional)
Louisiana hot sauce or
   ground cayenne pepper
   to taste

Put the fish and/or shellfish in large stockpot. Add cold water to cover and the wine; cover and bring to a boil. Skim off any scum that may form. Reduce the heat to low, add the onions, parsley, lemon, and dill, and simmer covered for 3 to 4 hours. Strain into containers, cover, and keep well chilled until ready to use. This will keep in the refrigerator for 3 to 4 weeks or can be frozen and kept even longer.

YIELD: *about 1 gallon*

• 🌀 •

Ham Stock

Use this with vegetables, pork, or legumes.

1 cup dry white wine
Ham trimmings and cracked bones
Water
2 medium-sized onions, coarsely chopped
1 cup coarsely chopped celery
5 or 6 carrots, coarsely chopped
1 tablespoon coarsely chopped garlic
1 whole cayenne pepper or ½ teaspoon ground cayenne pepper

In a large stockpot, place the wine, ham bones and trimmings, and enough water to cover. Cover and bring to a boil. Skim off any scum that may form. Reduce the heat to low, add vegetables and seasonings. Cover and simmer for 3 to 4 hours, removing the scum as it forms. Remove the large bones and strain into containers and cover. Remove any unwanted fat after the stock is chilled. This will keep in the refrigerator for 3 to 4 weeks or can be frozen and kept even longer.

YIELD: *about 1 gallon*

Meat Stock

Use this in red meats or vegetable preparations.

Leftover or fresh beef, veal, pork, lamb meat, trimmings, and cracked bones
Water
1 cup red wine (optional)
2 large onions, coarsely chopped
½ stalk of celery, coarsely chopped
5 stems of parsley
1 teaspoon crushed dried mint
1 whole cayenne pepper or 1 teaspoon ground cayenne pepper
1 tablespoon chopped garlic

Put the meat and bones in a large stockpot. Cover with water and add the wine. Cover and bring to a boil, skimming off any scum that may form. Add the vegetables and seasonings. Reduce the heat to low, and simmer for 3 to 4 hours. Remove the large bones and strain into containers and cover. If not using stock immediately, chill and remove any unwanted fat. Keep refrigerated until ready to use or freeze for longer storage.

YIELD: *about 1 gallon*

Vegetable Stock

You may use a wide variety of vegetables for this stock. Avoid very strong flavors or legumes, which will make the stock cloudy. This is best used with light or dark meats or vegetable preparations.

2 medium-sized onions, coarsely chopped	3 medium-sized tomatoes, coarsely chopped
½ stalk celery, coarsely chopped	1 tablespoon chopped garlic
Greens or parsley, several sprigs	Whole cayenne pepper or bell pepper
	Water

Put all the vegetables in a large stockpot and cover with cold water. Cover the stockpot and bring to a boil. Reduce the heat to low and simmer for 3 to 4 hours. Skim off any scum that may form. Strain into containers, cover, and keep in the refrigerator until ready to use. This will keep in the refrigerator for 3 to 4 weeks or can be frozen and kept even longer.

YIELD: *about 1 gallon*

VARIATION: For a darker stock, leave the onion peelings on and brown the vegetables in oil before adding the water.

Seafood Gumbo

1 cup oil	Salt to taste
2 cups all-purpose flour	Louisiana hot sauce or
4 cups chopped onion	ground cayenne pepper
1 cup chopped bell pepper	to taste
1 cup finely chopped fresh	1 pound crawfish tails, cleaned
parsley	and deveined
1 cup chopped green onions	1 pound shrimp, cleaned and
1 gallon Fish Stock (see	peeled
page 37) or water	1 pound fish, cubed
2 tablespoons minced garlic	6 crab bodies, broken in half
2 cups dry white wine	Other available seafood
2 tablespoons Worcestershire	
sauce	

Heat the oil in a large, heavy pot over medium heat, then stir in the flour and make a dark roux (see page 56); this should take about 45 minutes. To the roux add the onions, bell pepper, parsley, and green onions, stirring after each addition. Cook, stirring frequently, until the vegetables are tender, then slowly add 1 cup of the stock, stirring until it forms a thick paste. Stir in the garlic, wine, and the remaining stock, then add the Worcestershire, salt, and hot sauce, and stir. Bring to a boil, then add the crawfish, shrimp, fish, and crabs. Reduce the heat to low and simmer, covered, for at least 2 hours, stirring occasionally. Serve over cooked rice with filé. Leftovers can be frozen in smaller portions.

YIELD: *6 to 10 servings*

Crab Bisque

¼ cup oil or shortening	½ cup chopped celery
½ cup all-purpose flour	1 sprig of parsley, chopped
1 cup chopped onion	1 cup chopped mushrooms

4 cups Fish Stock (see page 37),
    or Chicken Stock (see page
    36), or water
2 cups warm milk
1 cup lump crabmeat, picked
    over for shells

Salt to taste
Louisiana hot sauce or
    ground cayenne pepper
    to taste
2 tablespoons sherry
6 thin lemon slices

Heat the oil in a medium-sized pot over medium heat, then add the flour, stir, and make a light roux (see page 56). Add the onions, celery, parsley, and mushrooms, and sauté until the onions are clear. Slowly whisk in the stock and bring to a boil. Reduce the heat to low, cover, and simmer for 1 hour or until the vegetables are very soft. Remove from heat and strain, forcing the vegetable pulp through a sieve with a mallet or the back of a spoon. Whisk in the warm milk, stir in the crab, salt, and hot sauce. Serve with a thin slice of lemon and a teaspoon of sherry.

YIELD: *6 servings*

Court Bouillon

1 cup oil or shortening
2 cups chopped onion
½ cup chopped bell pepper
¼ cup chopped celery
½ cup chopped fresh parsley
½ cup chopped green onions
2 teaspoons chopped garlic
1 gallon water or Fish Stock
    (see page 37)
2 cups dry white wine
½ cup grated carrots
2 tablespoons lemon juice

5 cups large firm-fleshed fish,
    cubed, or a large fish head
1 tablespoon Worcestershire
    sauce
1 cup peeled and chopped
    fresh or canned
    tomatoes
Louisiana hot sauce or
    ground cayenne pepper
    to taste
Salt to taste

Heat the oil over medium-high heat in a large, heavy pot, and sauté the onions, bell pepper, and celery until the onions are clear. Add the parsley, green onions, and garlic, and stir. Then add the water and wine. Simmer for 15 minutes, then add the carrots, lemon juice, fish, Worcestershire, tomatoes, hot sauce, and salt, and bring to a boil. Reduce the heat to low, cover, and simmer for 3 to 4 hours. Do not stir, simply pick up and rotate pot. If you stir it, the fish will break up.

YIELD: *8 to 10 servings*

Fish Chowder

4 slices bacon, chopped
1 cup chopped onion
¼ cup chopped celery (optional)
½ cup chopped fresh parsley
2 tablespoons all-purpose flour
6 cups Fish Stock (page 37)
2 small turnips, peeled and cut into 1-inch cubes
2 medium-sized potatoes, cut into 1-inch cubes
3 cups 1-inch fish cubes
3 cups milk
¼ teaspoon crushed dried mint
Salt to taste
Louisiana hot sauce or ground cayenne pepper to taste

In a large, heavy pot, fry the bacon to render bacon drippings. Then sauté the onions, celery, and parsley until the onions are clear. Stir in the flour, but do not brown. Whisk in the stock, then add the turnips and potatoes. Cover and bring to a boil. Reduce the heat to low, add the fish and the milk, mint, salt, and hot sauce; cover and cook very slowly for 1 hour, stirring occasionally.

YIELD: *6 to 8 servings*

Fish and Tomato Soup

2 cups peeled and chopped
   tomatoes
½ cup chopped onion
¼ cup chopped fresh parsley
   Salt to taste
   Louisiana hot sauce or
   ground cayenne pepper
   to taste

8 cups Fish Stock (see page
   37) or water
1 cup dry white wine
4 cups firm cubed fish (sea
   bass, shark, catfish, etc.)

Put everything, except the fish, in a heavy medium-sized pot and bring
to a boil. Turn to low and continue cooking until the onions are clear.
Add the fish, cover, and increase heat to bring back to a boil. Lower
the heat again and let simmer, still covered, for 30 minutes.

YIELD: *6 to 8 servings*

Oyster Artichoke Soup

This is a very popular before-meal soup in Louisiana.

¼ cup oil or shortening
½ cup chopped green onions
½ cup chopped parsley
1 cup soft artichoke puree
   from 1 boiled artichoke, or
   chop some of the canned
   pieces, then puree
3 cups Vegetable Stock made
   with artichokes (see page
   39), or oyster liquor, or
   Chicken Stock (see page
   36)

1 tablespoon minced garlic
24 oysters freshly shucked,
   saving the juices, or 2 cups
   oysters and their liquor
   Louisiana hot sauce or
   ground cayenne pepper
   to taste
   Salt to taste

Heat the oil in a medium-sized pot over medium heat, then sauté the onions and parsley until the onions are clear. Add the pureed artichokes and stock, mix well, then add the garlic, cover, reduce the heat to low, and simmer for 30 minutes. Add the oysters and their liquor and stir. Turn off the heat, season with hot sauce, and check for salt. Serve when the oyster edges begin to curl.

YIELD: *6 to 8 servings*

NOTE: Some canned artichokes have very hard exterior leaves. These should be removed, the soft bottom choke scraped off and reserved, and the leaves discarded.

Oyster and Broccoli Soup

8 cups Fish Stock (see page 37) or water
2 cups broccoli flowerets, separated
1 cup dry white wine
4 tablespoons oil or shortening
½ cup all-purpose flour
1 cup chopped onion
1 cup chopped fresh parsley

1 teaspoon minced garlic
⅛ teaspoon crushed dried mint
Louisiana hot sauce or ground cayenne pepper to taste
Salt to taste
1 pint fresh oysters, drained and juice reserved

Bring the stock to a boil in a medium-sized saucepan over medium-high heat. Add the broccoli and wine and bring back to a boil. Remove from the heat and set aside. In a larger saucepan over meduim heat, warm the oil and stir in the flour to make a light-brown roux (see page 56). Add the onions and parsley, and cook until the onions are clear. Stir in 1 cup of the broccoli liquor to make a paste; add the garlic and cook, stirring, until the garlic gets very tender. Stir in the rest of the broccoli liquor with the flowerets, and add the mint, hot sauce, and salt. Reduce the heat to low and simmer for 20 to 30 minutes. About

5 minutes before serving, carefully add the oysters and juice, and heat just until the edges of the oysters begin to curl.

YIELD: *6 to 8 servings*

Leftover Thanksgiving Gumbo

½ cup oil or shortening or
    bacon drippings

1 cup all-purpose flour

1 cup chopped onion

1 cup chopped green onions

½ cup chopped bell pepper

½ cup chopped fresh parsley

¼ cup chopped celery

1 gallon of stock, more or less,
    made from the leftover
    turkey (see page 36)

1 tablespoon chopped garlic

½ teaspoon crushed dried mint

3 cups okra, sliced ½ inch
    thick (optional)

1 pound smoked sausage or
    andouille sausage, cut into
    ¼-inch slices

Any leftover turkey meat

Louisiana hot sauce or
    ground cayenne pepper
    to taste

1 tablespoon Worcestershire
    sauce

Salt to taste

Heat the oil in a large, heavy pot over medium heat, then add the flour and make a dark roux (see page 56); this will take about 45 minutes. To the roux add the onions, green onions, bell pepper, parsley, and celery, stirring after each addition, and cook until the onions are clear. Add 1 cup of the stock and stir well to form a thick paste. Stir in the minced garlic, then the remaining stock. Stir in the mint, okra, sausage, and turkey. Season with hot sauce, Worcestershire, and salt; stir to mix well. Reduce the heat to low, cover, and simmer at least 3 hours, stirring occasionally. Serve over cooked rice sprinkled with filé if you didn't use the okra. We usually don't use filé when the gumbo has okra because it is also a thickening agent. This can be frozen in containers to be eaten another day.

YIELD: *6 to 10 servings*

Chili Bean Soup

1 pound coarsely ground beef
2 cups chopped onion
½ cup chopped fresh cilantro (coriander) or parsley
2 tablespoons minced garlic
6 cups Ham Stock (see page 38) or Meat Stock (see page 38)

2 cups cooked or canned small red beans
2 cups tomato sauce
Chili powder to taste
Dash ground cinnamon
Louisiana hot sauce or ground cayenne pepper to taste
Salt to taste

Brown the ground meat over medium-high heat in a large pot. Then sauté the onions, cilantro, and minced garlic with the meat until the onions are tender. Add the stock, beans, tomato sauce, chili powder, cinnamon, hot sauce, and salt; stir well. Bring to a boil, then reduce the heat to low; cover and simmer for at least 2 hours, stirring often. Serve hot with extra chili powder, chopped onion, and grated cheese if desired.

YIELD: *6 to 8 servings*

Mock Turtle Soup

½ cup oil
½ pound beef (inexpensive cut), chopped
½ pound pork (Boston butt or roast), chopped
½ pound chicken, chopped
¾ cup flour
1 cup chopped onion

½ cup finely chopped green onions
½ cup finely chopped fresh parsley
2 tablespoons finely chopped celery
10 cups Meat Stock (see page 38) or water

½ cup tomato sauce
Salt to taste
Louisiana hot sauce or
    ground cayenne pepper
    to taste

2 hard-boiled eggs, chopped
    fine
Sherry (optional)
Lemon slices (optional)

Heat the oil in a large, heavy pot over medium heat and brown all the meat. Remove the meat from the pot and set aside. In the same pot, stir in the flour to make a dark roux (see page 56). To the dark roux add the onions, green onions, parsley, and celery, stirring after each addition, and cook until the onions are clear. Add 1 cup of the stock and stir to form a thick paste, then stir in the tomato sauce. Stir in the remaining stock, then add the meats, salt, and hot sauce. Reduce the heat to low, cover, and simmer for at least 2 hours, stirring occasionally. Add the eggs and simmer another hour. Serve with a teaspoon of sherry and a slice of lemon.

YIELD: *10 to 12 servings*

Oxtail and Lentil Soup

This is a hearty wintertime soup.

½ cup oil or shortening
2 pounds oxtails
2 cups chopped onion
½ cup chopped parsley
¼ cup chopped bell pepper
1 cup raw brown rice
1 gallon Ham Stock (see page
    38) or Meat Stock (see
    page 38)
2 tablespoons Worcestershire
    sauce
1 tablespoon minced garlic

1 large turnip, peeled and cut
    into ½-inch chunks
2 cups grated carrots
1 pound dry lentils, washed
    and picked over
2 medium-sized ripe tomatoes,
    peeled and seeded
Salt to taste
Louisiana hot sauce or
    ground cayenne pepper
    to taste

In a large, heavy pot over medium-high heat, heat the oil, and brown the oxtails. Then remove them and set aside. In the same pot, sauté the onions, parsley, and bell pepper until the onions are clear. Stir in the rice, then add the stock, Worcestershire, garlic, turnip, carrots, and lentils; bring to a boil, then add the oxtails. Squeeze the tomatoes into the pot, add the salt and hot sauce, and stir. Reduce the heat to low, cover, and let simmer for at least 2 hours, stirring occasionally. The soup is ready to serve when the rice and lentils are tender.

YIELD: *10 servings*

Rabbit Andouille Gumbo

3 pounds rabbit, boiled and deboned (save stock)

½ cup oil or shortening

1 cup all-purpose flour

3 cups chopped onion

1 cup chopped green onions

½ cup chopped bell pepper

½ cup chopped fresh parsley

10 cups Meat Stock made with rabbit (see page 38) or water

1 tablespoon chopped garlic

1 cup dry white wine

1 pound andouille or smoked sausage, sliced ¼ inch thick

Salt to taste

Louisiana hot sauce or ground cayenne pepper to taste

In a heavy pot, heat the oil over medium heat, then stir in the flour to make a roux (see page 56). Stir occasionally and continue cooking over medium heat; once the roux starts to brown, you will need to stir it constantly, until it reaches a dark chocolate color. This should take about 45 minutes. Add the onions, green onions, bell pepper, and parsley, stirring after each addition. Continue cooking until the onions are clear, stirring occasionally. Add 1 cup of the stock to the roux and stir until it forms a thick paste. Add the remaining stock, garlic, and wine, stir well, then add the andouille and rabbit. Add the salt and hot sauce. Cover and cook over low heat at least 3 hours or until you can't wait any longer, stirring occasionally. Serve over cooked rice with filé. Leftovers can be frozen in smaller portions to be eaten at a later date.

YIELD: *8 to 10 servings*

VARIATION: Almost any wild game can be substituted for the rabbit. We often use wild ducks, quail, or venison.

Turkey Noodle Soup

2 tablespoons oil or shortening
½ cup chopped bell pepper
1 cup chopped green onions
10 cups Turkey or Chicken Stock (see page 36) or water
1 cup dry white wine
2 medium-sized tomatoes, peeled and quartered
½ cup dried parsley
2 to 3 cups chunked turkey meat
1 cup uncooked small egg noodles
Louisiana hot sauce or ground cayenne pepper, if needed
Salt, if needed

In a large pot, heat the oil over medium-high heat, then sauté the bell peppers and green onions until the onions are tender. Add the stock and bring to a boil. Add the wine, tomatoes, parsley, and turkey, and bring back to a boil. Reduce the heat to low, add the noodles, taste for salt, add hot sauce, and stir. Cover and let simmer for 1 hour, stirring occasionally.

YIELD: *4 to 8 servings*

• 🌶 •

Corn Soup

¼ cup oil or shortening
½ cup all-purpose flour
1 cup chopped onion
½ cup chopped fresh parsley
¼ cup chopped bell pepper
6 cups Ham Stock (see page 38), or Chicken Stock (see page 36), or water
1 tablespoon minced garlic
1 cup chopped ham

2 cups freshly cut corn or canned corn with juice
2 cups peeled, seeded, and chopped fresh or canned tomatoes
Salt to taste
Louisiana hot sauce or ground cayenne pepper to taste

In a medium-sized pot over medium heat, heat the oil, then add the flour, and make a caramel-colored roux (see page 56). This will take about 30 minutes. To the cooked roux add the onions, parsley, and bell pepper, stirring after each addition; stir and cook until the onions are clear. Add 1 cup of the stock and stir well to form a thick paste. Add the remainder of the stock and stir to mix well. Add the garlic, ham, corn, and tomatoes, then stir in the salt and hot sauce. Reduce the heat to low, cover, and simmer at least 1 hour, stirring occasionally.

YIELD: *6 to 8 servings*

Minestrone

This is Italian for clean-out-the-refrigerator soup.

1 cup olive oil
1 cup chopped onion
¼ cup chopped celery (optional)

1 cup ¼-inch-thick sliced carrots
½ cup chopped bell pepper
1 gallon Meat Stock (see page 38)

2 tablespoons minced garlic
4 cups chopped tomatoes
8 ounces salt pork, finely
  chopped
2 cups dry red wine
¼ cup chopped parsley
1 teaspoon dried oregano

2 cups cooked or canned red
  beans
Salt to taste
Louisiana hot sauce or
  ground cayenne pepper
  to taste
Parmesan cheese (optional)

In a large, heavy pot over medium-high heat, sauté the onions, celery, carrots, and bell pepper in the oil until the onions are clear. Stir in the stock, then add the garlic, tomatoes, salt pork, and wine. Add the parsley and oregano and bring to a boil. Reduce the heat to low and add the beans, salt, and hot sauce. Cover the pot and simmer for 2 hours, stirring occasionally. If desired, serve with grated Parmesan cheese sprinkled on the top.

YIELD: *8 to 10 servings*

Red Bean Gumbo

White beans can be substituted for red beans, and you might want to try some meat other than smoked sausage or fish.

¼ cup oil, shortening, or bacon
  drippings
½ cup all-purpose flour
1 cup chopped onion
½ cup chopped bell pepper
½ cup chopped green onions
½ cup chopped parsley
10 cups Ham Stock (see page
  38) or water
1 tablespoon Worcestershire
  sauce

2 tablespoons minced garlic
1 pound smoked sausage, cut
  into ¼-inch slices
½ cup dry white wine
4 cups cooked or canned red
  beans, pureed with the
  juice
Salt to taste
Louisiana hot sauce or
  ground cayenne pepper
  to taste

Heat the oil in a large, heavy pot over medium heat, then stir in the flour to make a dark roux (see page 56); this will take about 45 minutes. To the roux add the onions, bell pepper, green onions, and parsley, stirring after each addition, and cook until the onions are clear. Slowly add 1 cup of the stock, stirring well to form a thick paste, then add the remainder of the stock. Stir in the Worcestershire and garlic, then the sausage and wine. Stir in the pureed beans, salt, and hot sauce. Reduce the heat to low, cover, and simmer for at least 2 hours, stirring frequently. Serve in a bowl over cooked rice and filé.

YIELD: *8 to 10 servings*

Vegetable Gumbo

This is for vegetarians (which I ain't). But I have some good-lookin' female lady girl women friends who are. I expand my kitchen brain when I cook for them.

1 cup olive oil	1 medium-sized turnip, chopped
2 cups all-purpose flour	
1 cup chopped onion	½ bunch mustard greens, chopped
½ cup chopped bell pepper	
½ cup chopped fresh parsley	1 tablespoon minced garlic
2 cups cold water	2 cups dry white wine
1½ cups sliced okra	Salt to taste
8 cups Vegetable Stock (see page 38)	Louisiana hot sauce or ground cayenne pepper to taste
½ small cabbage head, chopped	

In a large, heavy pot over medium heat, make a dark roux (see page 56) with the oil and flour. Add the onions, bell pepper, and parsley, and cook until the onions are clear. Add the water and stir. Add the okra and cook another 5 minutes, stirring to keep it from sticking. Stir in the stock, cabbage, turnips, mustard greens, garlic, and wine. Reduce the heat to low, add the salt and hot sauce, cover, and simmer for at least 2 hours, stirring occasionally. Gumbo is usually served over a spoonful of rice that has been sprinkled with filé.

YIELD: *8 to 10 servings*

Cheese Soup

¼ cup oil or shortening
½ cup all-purpose flour
1 cup chopped onion
½ cup grated carrots
¼ cup chopped celery (optional)
¼ cup chopped bell pepper
¼ cup chopped parsley
4 cups Chicken Stock (see page 36) or Ham Stock (see page 38)

2 cups grated cheddar or sharp cheese
1 tablespoon Worcestershire sauce
2 cups warm milk
Salt to taste
Louisiana hot sauce or ground cayenne pepper to taste
Chopped pimento (optional)
Chopped green onion tops (optional)

Heat the oil in a medium-sized pot over medium heat. Stir in the flour to make a light-brown roux (see page 56). Add the onions, carrots, celery, bell pepper, and parsley, and sauté until the onions are clear. Whisk in the stock, bring to a boil, then reduce the heat to low. Simmer covered, for 1½ hours, or until the vegetables are very soft. Remove from the heat, and strain, forcing the vegetables through a sieve, with a mallet or the back of a spoon. Stir in the grated cheese and Worcestershire, then whisk in the heated milk. Add salt and hot sauce, and keep warm and covered until ready to serve. Garnish each bowl with a spoonful of chopped pimentos and green onions.

YIELD: *6 to 8 servings*

Pastel Soup

Serve hot or cold as a first course or dessert.

4 cups fruit puree
   (strawberries, melons,
   berries, persimmons,
   peaches, bananas, or
   whatever you like)
1 cup fruity wine, white or
   red, depending on the fruit
   used

¼ cup honey
2 tablespoons fresh lemon or
   lime juice
1 cup lowfat yogurt
6 fruit slices to garnish
6 sprigs of mint to garnish

In a blender or food processor, puree the fruit, a little at a time. You
may need to add a little wine to help blend the fruit; if you're using
canned fruit, use the juice. Once the fruit is pureed, add the remaining
wine. Blend for a moment, then add the honey. Blend in the lemon
juice and yogurt. Serve cold or heat very lightly in a microwave or
saucepan. Garnish with fruit pieces or a sprig of mint.

YIELD: *6 servings*

CHAPTER 4

Sauces and Gravies

The phrase, "First you make a roux," begins many Louisiana recipes. Unfortunately, the writers assume that everyone knows how to make a roux, so they rarely give instructions. The roux is the base for many dishes and sauces popular in Louisiana. Creole cooks have been using sauces for centuries. The French Revolution displaced many royal cooks who eventually found their way to this French-speaking part of the New World. The combination of their great technical skill with new ingredients and different cultural influences began a tradition of cooking that continues today. New Orleans is easily the best eating city in this country.

Sauces are very important to classical French cooking. In Cajun country, sauces are often the rich juices and gravies that form in the same pot in which vegetables or meat were cooked. Common gravies in northern Louisiana are "saw mill," "red eye," and the roux-based brown gravy. The tomato, native to this hemisphere, has become a main ingredient in Creole sauce and in sauce piquant.

Sauces are used to emphasize an ingredient—a crab sauce over soft-shelled crab; to enhance the flavor of a food—mint sauce on lamb; or to provide a contrasting flavor for better definition of both flavors— mustard sauce on a sugar-cured ham. Justin's mama taught him much about sauces and gravy making. His papa used to compliment her cooking in an offhand way by saying, "Olivet, you could make a pine burr taste good if you put that sauce on it."

Gravies and sauces are essential for the successful completion of two characteristically Southern acts, soppin' and dunkin'. Soppin' is passive in nature, and the action takes place in a horizontal manner. Dunkin' is active and primarily vertical. Facility in the execution of these maneuvers is nearly as important to the enjoyment of a gravy or sauce as a well-made roux.

How to Make a Roux

1 part oil (shortening), bacon drippings, olive oil, cooking oil, lard, or a combination of these	2 to 3 parts all-purpose flour

If I want a thick roux, I use 3 parts flour to 1 part oil. If I want a thin roux, I use 2 parts flour to 1 part oil.

Mix the flour and oil in a heavy pot. A black iron skillet or a Magnalite skillet works best. Cook on medium heat slowly as the roux changes from a cream color all the way to a dark chocolate color. After the roux is past a medium brown, you've got to stir the roux constantly to keep it from burning. If you do burn the roux, throw it out, wash the pot, and start over. I've got a special roux stirring spoon that I don't use for anything except to stir a roux. The way I make a roux, it takes from 45 minutes to more than one hour before it gets as dark as I like it. I use a dark roux for all my gumbos and sauce piquants. For some gravies and sauces it is not as important to make the roux so dark. Some milk-based soups call for a light-colored roux. Even so, I usually make my lightest roux about the color of the water in the Mississippi at Baton Rouge.

Now, I have cooked a roux in a microwave oven, and in a regular oven without any fat. It doesn't make any difference to me; you can cook a roux a lot of different ways. You can even buy a roux off the shelf in the store, but this way that I just told you has worked for me for more than fifty years, and it works for many other people around Louisiana. I think it tastes better, too.

After my roux is cooked as dark as I want it, I add my chopped vegetables, like onion, bell pepper, and celery. I stir after each addition and love to hear the chopped onions sizzle in the hot roux. It starts to smell pretty good when the vegetables are added. Bell pepper and celery are taste killers, so don't use too much. You can use as much onion as you like. After the vegetables have cooked awhile and the onions are clear, put in the chopped parsley and green onions. I put in a little cold water or stock and then add fresh minced garlic, and I stir all the time. After the garlic has cooked awhile, I stir in the liquids and all the other ingredients to make a gumbo, brown gravy hash, or stew.

White Roux

White roux is the foundation of white and cream sauces.

1 part margarine, butter, or
   shortening
2 to 3 parts all-purpose flour

Stock or other flavoring
liquid, such as fruit juice,
milk, cream

Place shortening in a medium-sized heavy saucepan, and heat over medium heat. Add the flour and stir to mix well; cook but do not allow to get too brown. Add the stock slowly, stirring constantly to incorporate. Allow to come to a boil, stirring until the mixture thickens. Season to taste.

Lemon Butter Sauce

This is great over broiled fish.

¼ pound (1 stick) margarine
  or butter
½ teaspoon onion powder
1½ teaspoons salt
  Ground cayenne pepper
  to taste

1½ teaspoons lemon juice
1 tablespoon chopped fresh
  parsley or 1½ teaspoons
  dried

Over low heat in a small saucepan, melt the margarine and stir in the remaining ingredients; don't let it boil. Let heat through, then serve immediately.

YIELD: *about ½ cup*

VARIATION: *Crabby Lemon Butter Sauce:* For each serving, stir in after the parsley 1 ounce of shredded crabmeat and heat through. This is wonderful ladled over broiled or fried soft-shelled crabs.

Mustard Sauce

1 cup creole or other mustard
½ cup honey

1 cup dry white wine

In a small saucepan, mix all the ingredients together. Cook over medium heat until it comes to a boil, then remove from the heat and serve over meat.

YIELD: *about 2½ cups*

Smoker Sauce

This sauce is to use on meats that have been smoked in a water smoker or to give a smoky flavor to any meat or vegetable. It can even be used as a stock for delicious, hearty soups. Reserve the juice from your smoker, then skim off the fat and discard, or use ½ cup of it instead of the oil.

½ cup oil or shortening	Salt to taste
1 cup all-purpose flour	Ground cayenne pepper
2 cups seasoned juice, from smoker pan, strained	to taste

In a heavy saucepan over medium heat, heat the oil, then stir in the flour and make a brown roux (see page 56). Add the smoker liquid and stir well. Salt and pepper to taste, then simmer for at least 1 hour.

YIELD: *about 3 cups*

Barbecue Sauce

Spoon this on your meat after it's cooked.

¼ cup oil or shortening	¼ cup honey
3 cups chopped onion	2 tablespoons lemon juice
1 cup chopped bell pepper	1 tablespoon salt
½ cup chopped fresh parsley	3 tablespoons Worcestershire sauce
2 cups dry white wine	½ teaspoon crushed dried mint
3 tablespoons vinegar	1 tablespoon liquid smoke
1 tablespoon minced garlic	
2 cups tomato sauce	
Louisiana hot sauce or ground cayenne pepper to taste	

Heat the oil in a large saucepan over medium heat, and sauté the onions, bell pepper, and parsley until the onions are clear. Add the wine, vinegar, garlic, tomato sauce, hot sauce, honey, and lemon juice; mix well, cover, turn the heat down to low, and simmer for 1 hour. Add the salt, Worcestershire, dried mint, and liquid smoke; stir well. Cover and simmer at least 2 more hours, stirring occasionally. This stores well in the refrigerator. This may be thinned with water if necessary.

YIELD: *about 6 cups*

Meat Sauce

This is great served over hot dogs, pasta, or toasted French bread, topped with cheese. I'm giving you the directions for a big batch so you can freeze the leftovers in small portions.

5 pounds lean ground beef
2 tablespoons olive oil
4 cups chopped onion
1 cup chopped bell pepper
1 cup chopped celery
2 cups chopped fresh parsley
2 tablespoons chopped garlic
6 cups tomato sauce or peeled, seeded, and chopped fresh tomatoes

1 cup dry red or white wine
Salt to taste
Louisiana hot sauce or ground cayenne pepper to taste
1 tablespoon Worcestershire sauce
½ teaspoon crushed dried mint

In a large pot over medium heat, heat the olive oil and sauté the meat until it looks like sawdust. Add the onions, bell pepper, celery, and parsley, stir, and cook until the onions are clear. Add the garlic, tomato sauce, and wine; stir to mix. Add the remaining ingredients and stir; continue cooking until the liquid starts to boil. Lower the heat to a simmer, cover, and continue cooking for 2 to 3 hours.

YIELD: *15 to 20 servings*

Tomato Sauce

2 tablespoons margarine or
   butter or shortening
4 tablespoons all-purpose flour
1 cup finely chopped onion
1 cup finely chopped fresh
   parsley
4 cups peeled, seeded, and
   pureed tomatoes
1 tablespoon minced garlic

2 cups dry red wine or Meat
   Stock (see page 38)
1 tablespoon Worcestershire
   sauce
Salt to taste
Louisiana hot sauce or
   ground cayenne pepper
   to taste

In a large, heavy saucepan over medium heat, melt the margarine and
stir in the flour to make a medium-brown roux (see page 56), about 20
minutes. Add the onions and parsley, and sauté until the onions are
clear. Add the tomato puree, garlic, and wine, and bring to a boil,
stirring constantly. Add the Worcestershire, salt, and hot sauce, reduce
the heat to low, and simmer, covered, for at least 1 hour.

YIELD: *about 5 cups*

Oyster Sauce

This is great over a nice tender steak, rice, or potatoes.

½ cup oil or shortening
¼ cup minced onion
1 teaspoon minced garlic
1 tablespoon Worcestershire
   sauce
1 tablespoon dark brown roux
   (see page 56)

½ cup dry red wine
1 cup small shucked oysters,
   drained, liquid reserved
Salt to taste
Louisiana hot sauce or
   ground cayenne pepper
   to taste

In a medium-sized heavy saucepan, heat the oil over medium-high
heat, then sauté the onions and garlic until the onions are clear. Add

the Worcestershire, roux, and red wine, and stir to mix. Bring to a boil, stirring constantly. Reduce the heat to a simmer, then add the oysters and season with the salt and hot sauce. Simmer just until the edges of the oysters start to curl. Serve immediately.

YIELD: *1 to 2 servings*

Mint Sauce

2 cups water or stock
2 tablespoons vinegar
2 tablespoons sugar
1 cup chopped fresh mint
Salt to taste
Louisiana hot sauce to taste

In a small saucepan over medium-high heat, bring the water to a boil. Add the vinegar, sugar, mint, salt, and hot sauce, and reduce the heat to low. Cover and simmer for 30 minutes, then remove from the heat. Serve hot or cold over lamb or other meats.

YIELD: *about 2 cups*

Piquant Sauce

I like this on eggs.

½ cup oil
1 cup chopped onion
1 cup peeled, seeded, and
　　chopped tomatoes
½ cup cider vinegar
¼ cup finely chopped hot
　　peppers, cayenne,
　　jalapeño, or others
½ cup seeded and finely
　　chopped red bell peppers
1 tablespoon minced garlic
Salt to taste

Sauté the onions in the heated oil over medium-high heat, until the onions are clear. Add the rest of the ingredients and bring the mixture to a boil. Lower the heat to a simmer, cover, and cook for at least 1 hour. Serve over many foods, warm or cold. This can be stored in a covered glass container in the refrigerator for several weeks.

YIELD: *about 3 cups*

Mayonnaise

I frequently make fresh mayonnaise and use it as a base for salad dressings and other cold sauces.

1 large egg, at room temperature	2 tablespoons lemon juice or vinegar
1 cup vegetable oil	Dash ground cayenne pepper (optional)
½ teaspoon salt	Dash dry mustard (optional)

This can be made in a blender, with an electric beater, or by hand with a whip. The most important thing to remember is don't get impatient. Put the egg in the blender and whip it for 1 minute. Then, through the hole in the lid, slowly start adding the oil while the blade continues to run. Be careful to add only a very little bit of oil at a time, and only add more once that amount has been fully incorporated. After all the oil has been added, the mixture will be quite thick; it will stay on a spoon and not drip. Continue blending, adding the salt, lemon juice, and seasonings to taste. This can be stored for about 2 weeks in a covered glass container in the refrigerator.

YIELD: *almost 2 cups*

• 🐚 •

Blender Hollandaise

6 large egg yolks
½ pound (2 sticks) butter or
  margarine, melted
2 tablespoons lemon juice

Louisiana hot sauce or
  ground cayenne pepper
  to taste
Salt to taste

Place the egg yolks in a blender and pulse to mix. Slowly pour the warm melted butter into the egg yolks with the blender on low. Add the lemon juice, hot sauce, and a little salt if needed. A little warm water or warm stock may be added to make the sauce thinner.

YIELD: *about 2 cups*

Horseradish Sauce

This is great drizzled over boiled beef ribs or corned beef.

½ cup ground fresh
  horseradish or prepared
  horseradish
Salt to taste

1 hard-boiled egg, finely grated
1 cup mayonnaise
1 teaspoon Worcestershire
  sauce

Mix all the ingredients together in a small mixing bowl. This will keep in the refrigerator, covered, for several weeks.

YIELD: *about 2 cups*

Remoulade Sauce

This is very popular in Louisiana as a dressing for all types of cold seafood and salads. Howard Jacobs, a friend of mine, wrote a column for the daily New Orleans Times-Picayune *newspaper that he called*

"Remoulade." He used to write tidbits about this and that and then mix it all together, just like a remoulade sauce.

1 cup mayonnaise	2 tablespoons Worcestershire sauce
½ cup olive oil	Louisiana hot sauce or ground cayenne pepper to taste
½ cup Creole or Dijon mustard	
2 teaspoons prepared horseradish	Salt to taste
½ cup catsup	½ cup wine vinegar

In a large mixing bowl, slowly add the oil to the mayonnaise, whisking until the mixture becomes firm again. Add the mustard and whisk again until firm. Add the horseradish and continue to whisk, then add the catsup and whisk some more. Add the Worcestershire, whisking to incorporate, then add the hot sauce and salt and whisk again. Add the vinegar, whisking well, then refrigerate and use as needed. Keeps in the refrigerator several weeks.

YIELD: *about 4 cups*

Cocktail Sauce

This sauce can be served with hot or cold seafood.

1 cup catsup	1 teaspoon Worcestershire sauce
¼ cup prepared horseradish	Louisiana hot sauce or ground cayenne pepper to taste
1 teaspoon lemon juice	
1 tablespoon prepared mustard	Salt to taste

In a small bowl, combine all the ingredients and season to taste. Refrigerate, covered, and serve well chilled. This will keep refrigerated for several weeks.

YIELD: *1½ cups*

Cayenne Tartar Sauce

This is often used as a seafood sauce or as a base for a salad dressing.

4 cups mayonnaise	½ cup finely chopped onion
1 cup finely chopped dill pickle or drained dill relish	¼ cup finely chopped fresh or pickled cayenne pepper
½ cup finely chopped fresh parsley	1 tablespoon Worcestershire sauce
	Salt to taste

Combine all the ingredients in a bowl and mix well. Adjust seasonings to taste. Refrigerate and serve well chilled. This will keep for several weeks in the refrigerator.

YIELD: *5 cups*

VARIATION: For *Plain Tartar Sauce* leave out the hot peppers.

Stewed Fig Sauce

Serve as a complement to meats or breakfast or dessert dishes.

3 cups whole fresh figs	½ teaspoon vanilla extract
1 cup sugar	1 cup water

Place all the ingredients in a small, heavy saucepan. Over medium-high heat, bring to a boil, stirring frequently. Turn the heat to low, cover, and simmer, stirring occasionally, until the figs are tender.

YIELD: *about 4 cups*

Apples in Wine and Cinnamon Sauce

This is a good topping for ice cream, over fresh-baked biscuits, or over not-too-sweet cakes. Serve warm or cold.

¼ **pound (1 stick) margarine** **or butter**	1 **teaspoon ground cinnamon**
1 **cup dry white wine**	1 **cup sugar or to taste**
4 **cups sliced apples**	2 **tablespoons lemon juice**
	1½ **teaspoons vanilla extract**

Over medium heat in a heavy saucepan, melt the margarine, then add the wine and stir in the apples. Sprinkle the cinnamon and sugar over the apples and stir. Continue cooking for about 10 minutes, then stir in the lemon juice and vanilla. Lower the heat to a simmer and cover; continue cooking for 2 hours, stirring occasionally until the apples break up.

Y I E L D : *about 3 cups*

Strawberry Sauce

This is wondermous on smoked ham.

1 **pint fresh whole** **strawberries, washed,** **stemmed, and drained**	1 **teaspoon ground cinnamon**
½ **cup sugar**	½ **cup water**
	½ **cup strawberry wine or** **liqueur**

In a medium-sized saucepan, mix all the ingredients together and cook covered over low heat until thickened, at least 3 hours, stirring occasionally. If you wish, mash the berries with a spoon. This can be stored in the refrigerator for several weeks.

Y I E L D : *about 3 cups*

Pecan Praline Sauce

This is a great sauce for ice cream, bread pudding, and a variety of desserts.

¼ cup honey	2 cups pecan pieces
1½ cups water	½ teaspoon vanilla extract
2 cups firmly packed brown sugar	

Combine all the ingredients in a medium-sized saucepan. Cook, stirring frequently, over medium heat until thickened. Serve immediately.

YIELD: *about 4 cups*

Rice, Pasta, and Dressing

Since the early 1700s, when rice was introduced to the United States by French explorers, Louisianans have been growing it. In the 1880s mechanized farming methods moved south with a migration of Midwest farmers onto the Cajun prairie, and a whole region was transformed into a major rice-producing area. Currently the State of Louisiana holds second place in rice production in the United States. High annual rainfall and a subsurface layer of clay make Louisiana well suited to rice growing. The Wilson farm produced its own crop of "providence" rice when Justin was a boy.

In Southeast Asia and other parts of the world, labor-intensive rice culture produces a cooperative, highly regimented society. Conversely, rice growing in the United States is so machine dependent that rice is never touched by human hands. In this country rice seed is planted by gigantic tractors or sprayed from an airplane; herbicides are applied in the same manner, and harvesting is done by huge combines that cut the rice stalk and thresh it in one operation. Then it is dried, trucked to mills, stored in towering silos, milled by special machines which scour off the husk and bran, polished to the translucent pure white demanded by the consumer, graded by size, packaged, and finally transported to market. In spite of all this mechanization, we are reminded of that other rice farmer standing knee-deep in the paddy water when we hear that 70 percent of the rice produced in Louisiana is exported and sold on the world market.

Rice consumption in the United States has increased to about twenty pounds per person per year (this includes about three pounds per year that is used in brewing beer). Yearly per capita consumption in Louisiana is the highest in the nation, at about thirty pounds, but it pales when compared with Burma, where each person eats around four hundred pounds per year. Louisianans have long known that rice is an ideal food. It is low in calories, high in energy, and inexpensive. Because it is nonallergenic, it is used in many baby foods. It is nutritious, delicious, and combines well with any other food or flavor. Rice is used in jambalaya, boudin, and dressings, with gumbo, vegetables, sauce piquant, and even in beverages. In southern Louisiana rice is the starch staple and is used almost to the exclusion of other starches. Justin tells how popular rice is in southern Louisiana:

> Dere was a Cajun brought hisse'f in one dem restaurant-café in Lock Charles. An' he clam' up on de stool an' a good-lookin' girl waitess lady female brought herse'f an ax him, "What can I did fo' you, hanh?" An' dat damm fool say, "I'm hongry, I want a hamberger." She axed, "All de way?" an' he say, "No, cut de rice."

In the rice country around Crowley, every October a grand festival honoring and promoting rice is celebrated. The International Rice Festival was started in 1936 by a group of citizens intent on increasing the awareness and demand for rice. Justin Wilson and Bob Schlicher were co-chairmen of that first festival, more than fifty years ago, which has grown into a three-day jubilee with parades, contests, art displays, and, the best part, a cooking competition. New recipes and variations on old standards are prepared by children and adults alike. The names of the winners through the years would indicate that cooking skill is genetically transmitted. In categories from main dishes to breads to desserts, cooks from all around the area create wonderful dishes using rice as the main ingredient, since in the hands of a skilled, imaginative cook, rice can do anything.

Rice

You might try one of the new special nut-flavored rices.

Rice	**Salt to taste**
Water	**1 tablespoon oil or shortening**

Put the rice in a heavy pot. Add enough water to cover by 1 inch. Add the salt and oil. Cook over medium heat, uncovered, stirring occasionally, until you can't see the water; it will make a sputtering sound. Reduce the heat to low, cover, and simmer about 45 minutes. Don't raise the cover to check. When it's done each rice grain should stand apart, and not be gummy or mushy. I wouldn't call it fluffy, however. One cup of long grain rice can yield as much as three cups of cooked rice.

Seasoned Rice

2 cups raw rice	**½ teaspoon ground cayenne**
Water or stock	**pepper**
1 cup chopped fresh parsley	**1 teaspoon minced garlic or**
1 cup chopped green onions	**¼ teaspoon garlic powder**
2 teaspoons salt	

Place the rice in a medium-sized saucepan, with enough water to cover by 1 inch. Stir in all the seasonings, and bring the water to a boil over medium heat, stirring occasionally. Continue boiling until no water can be seen on top of the rice. Reduce the heat to low, cover, and let simmer until the rice is tender, about 45 minutes. Do not lift the lid until the rice is done.

YIELD: *4 to 5 cups*

Dirty Rice

Dirty rice can be used as a stuffing, a side dish, or as a main meal.

2 tablespoons bacon drippings	1 tablespoon minced garlic
½ pound lean ground beef	8 cups cooked rice
½ pound lean ground pork	1 cup dry white wine
1 cup chopped onion	1 teaspoon crushed dried mint
½ cup chopped celery	2 tablespoons Worcestershire
½ cup chopped fresh parsley	sauce
½ cup chopped green onions	Salt to taste
1 pound chicken giblets,	Louisiana hot sauce or
boiled and chopped	ground cayenne pepper
4 cups reserved giblet stock	to taste

In a large, deep saucepan over medium heat, sauté the ground beef and pork in the bacon drippings until crumbly. Add the onions, celery, parsley, and green onions, and cook until the onions are clear. Stir in the chopped giblets, stock, garlic, rice, wine, mint, and Worcestershire. Add the salt and hot sauce, then mix everything together well. Cook, stirring occasionally, for about 20 minutes. Reduce the heat to low, cover, and cook 1 hour. Leftover dirty rice can be eaten with eggs for breakfast.

YIELD: *10 servings, or enough to stuff one large hen, or 8 to 10 bell peppers*

• ❧ •

Chicken and Sausage Jambalaya

This is a traditional favorite at festivals, parties, and weddings.

1 small chicken (2 to 3 pounds) cut into 2-inch pieces, rinsed, and dried
½ cup oil
2 cups finely chopped onion
½ cup chopped bell pepper
1 cup chopped fresh parsley
1 cup finely chopped green onions

2 pounds smoked sausage, sliced ¼ inch thick
3 cups long grain rice
8 cups Chicken Stock (see page 36) or water
1 tablespoon chopped garlic
Salt to taste
Ground cayenne pepper to taste

In a heavy, high-walled chicken fryer over medium heat, brown the chicken in the oil, stirring the meat around so it won't stick. After the chicken has browned, remove it from the pot. Then add the onions, bell pepper, parsley, and green onions, and sauté until the onions are clear. Stir in the sausage, rice, stock, garlic, chicken, salt, and pepper. Continue cooking until nearly all the water has boiled out, then reduce the heat to low, cover, and let simmer until the rice is done, about 1 hour. Do not lift the lid for at least 1 hour.

YIELD: *about 10 servings*

Money Rice

8 cups cooked rice
½ pound grated cheese, your favorite kind
1 cup milk
1 medium-sized egg, well beaten
1 teaspoon minced garlic
1 medium-sized bell pepper

1 cup chopped fresh parsley
1 cup chopped green onion tops
Water or stock
Salt to taste
Louisiana hot sauce or ground cayenne pepper to taste

Preheat the oven to 350°F. In a large mixing bowl, combine the rice, cheese, and milk, and mix well. Add the eggs and mix again. In a blender or food processor, puree the garlic, bell pepper, parsley, and green onion tops with a little water or stock, just enough to moisten. Add this to the rice and mix well to get the green color throughout the dish. Stir in the salt and hot sauce. Pour into a 9-inch greased casserole dish, cover, and bake for 45 minutes. To get a crusty golden brown top, take lid the off for the last 10 minutes or put under the broiler briefly.

Y I E L D : *6 servings*

Rice and Crowder Pea Casserole

This is a dish made from leftovers.

6 cups cooked rice

2 cups cooked peas, drained well (see White Beans recipe page 179)

2 cups grated cheddar cheese

¼ teaspoon crushed dried mint

1 cup finely chopped fresh parsley or ¼ cup dried parsley

4 slices bacon fried and crumbled (reserve some drippings)

3 large eggs, beaten

1 cup dry white wine

Louisiana hot sauce or ground cayenne pepper to taste

Salt to taste

1 teaspoon onion powder

½ teaspoon garlic powder

Preheat the oven to 350°F. In a large mixing bowl, combine the rice, peas, cheese, mint, parsley, and bacon; set aside. In another bowl, beat together the eggs and wine, then add the hot sauce, salt, and onion and garlic powders, and beat well. Pour the egg mixture into the rice and mix thoroughly. Pour into a greased 9-inch casserole dish and bake for 45 minutes to 1 hour.

Y I E L D : *6 to 8 servings*

How to Cook Pasta

Pasta and noodles were brought early to the state by immigrant populations from Italy and Germany. Much pasta is still made fresh in the home. Louisianans have the great ability of taking ingredients from their homelands and combining them with native Louisiana ingredients to produce wonderful results. A favorite Italian restaurant in Baton Rouge serves a crawfish sauce over angel hair pasta.

Water, about 1 gallon for each pound of pasta	**¼ cup olive oil**
Salt to taste	**Pasta, whatever kind you want**

Fill a large pot ¾ full with water. Add the salt and olive oil. Bring the water to a rolling boil over high heat. Add the pasta while stirring, then stir occasionally after the water returns to a boil to prevent the pasta from sticking together. The pasta is done when it's "al dente," soft on the outside with a little firmness on the inside. You can test it by squeezing it between the thumb and finger. Sometimes I test for doneness by throwing a piece of spaghetti against the wall: if it stays, it's done. Drain and place on a platter. Pour a little more oil over it and toss to keep the pieces separated. Serve alone or with your favorite sauce. To reheat cold pasta, put it in a collander and run it under very hot tap water.

YIELD: *one pound of pasta yields about three pounds of cooked pasta*

VARIATION: Toss cooked pasta in a bowl with olive oil, Louisiana hot sauce, and some grated Romano cheese.

Macaroni and Cheese

This is one of my favorite dishes.

1 pound macaroni, cooked and
  drained
1 cup grated cheddar cheese
½ cup grated Romano or
  Parmesan cheese
½ cup chopped onion
½ cup chopped bell pepper
1 tablespoon olive oil

2 medium-sized eggs
1 cup dry white wine
1 tablespoon prepared
  mustard
Salt to taste
Louisiana hot sauce or
  ground cayenne pepper
  to taste

Preheat the oven to 350°F. Grease a 9-by-12-inch casserole dish. In a large bowl, combine the macaroni, cheddar cheese, and half the Romano and set aside. Over medium-high heat in a medium-sized saucepan, sauté the onions and bell pepper in the heated olive oil until the onions are clear. In a separate bowl, beat the eggs, then add the wine, mustard, salt, and hot sauce; mix well. Add the egg mixture and sautéed vegetables to the macaroni and mix well. Pour into the casserole dish, top with the rest of the Romano cheese, and bake for 45 minutes; the top should be crusty and slightly brown.

YIELD: *10 servings*

VARIATION: I chill the leftover macaroni and cheese, then slice it in pieces and eat it as a salad the next day.

DRESSING

Dressing can be made from anything grown or gathered in Louisiana. Frequently fish, fowl, or land animals, plus vegetables of many kinds, are used to make dressing. Because cornbread is so popular, leftover pieces are added to dressing. Nuts are often used to vary the texture.

Cornbread Dressing

3 cups crumbled 2-day-old
   cornbread
3 cups crumbled stale bread
   or toast
2 cups Chicken Stock (see
   page 36)
¼ cup vegetable oil
½ cup chopped fresh parsley

½ cup chopped celery
1 cup chopped onion
½ cup chopped green onions
½ teaspoon crushed dried mint
Salt to taste
Ground cayenne pepper
   to taste

Preheat the oven to 325°F. Mix the crumbled cornbread and bread together in a large mixing bowl, pour in the stock, and set aside. Over medium-high heat in a medium-sized skillet, heat the oil and sauté the parsley, celery, onions, and green onions until the onions are clear, then pour into the bowl with the bread. Add the mint, salt, and pepper, and mix well. Pour into a 9-by-9-inch greased casserole dish, or stuff a hen or turkey, and bake for 60 minutes or until the bird is done.

Y I E L D : *about 10 cups, enough to stuff a large hen with some extra*

V A R I A T I O N : Add 1 cup chopped oysters, 1 pound thinly sliced smoked sausage, or both, and mix well.

Oyster Dressing

½ cup chopped celery
1 cup chopped onion
½ cup chopped fresh parsley
2 tablespoons oil or shortening
1 cup cooked and chopped
   fowl gizzard and heart
2 cups giblet stock
2 cups cooked rice

3 cups crumbled dry bread, in
   ½-inch pieces
½ teaspoon crushed dried mint
1 pint chopped oysters with
   their juice
Salt to taste
Ground cayenne pepper
   to taste

Preheat the oven to 350°F. In a large saucepan, sauté the celery, onions, and parsley in the oil until the onions are clear. In a large mixing bowl, combine the giblets and stock with the cooked rice, bread, mint, and oysters with juice; mix well. Add the salt and pepper. Pour into a greased medium-sized casserole dish and bake for 45 minutes, or stuff a large bird and bake until the bird is done.

YIELD: *about 10 cups, enough to stuff a large hen*

Rice Dressing

2 tablespoons oil or shortening	Salt to taste
1 cup chopped onion	Louisiana hot sauce or
½ cup chopped bell pepper	ground cayenne pepper
½ cup chopped fresh parsley	to taste
1 tablespoon chopped garlic	1 tablespoon Worcestershire
1 pound lean ground beef	sauce
1 pound lean ground pork	6 cups cooked rice
3 cups stock	

Preheat the oven to 350°F. In a large skillet over medium-high heat, sauté the onions, bell pepper, and parsley in the oil until the onions are clear. Then add the garlic and sauté another 5 minutes. Stir in the meat, making sure it mixes well with the vegetables, and cook until the meat is browned. Pour in the stock, taste for salt, then add the hot sauce and Worcestershire, and mix well. Stir in the rice, mix well, then pour into a small greased casserole dish and bake for 45 minutes.

YIELD: *8 to 10 servings*

Pecan Dressing

2 cups pecans, pieces or halves	4 cups crumbled dry bread or toast

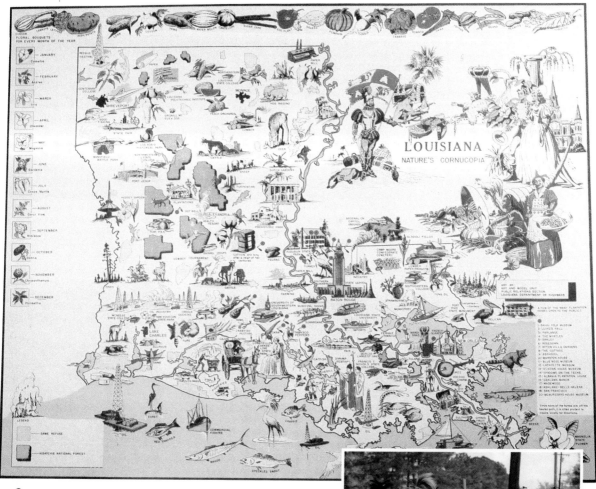

🦆 Louisiana's cornucopia of nature.

🦆 Two future beauty queens
eating fresh Louisiana strawberries. I ate them when I was
their age too.

🌶 Here's how it should look when you make a roux.

🌶 *Opposite:* This catfish is not
going to fit on the scale, no. But
I know he's gonna taste good
come suppertime.

Mayhaw jelly, pickled peppers and sweet peppers, pepper jelly, garlic in olive oil, and cherry jelly.

These homegrown collards were rinsed in the washing machine, then cooked with wine.

I'm not sure who's consecrating more on this jambalaya, my friend Maurice Dantin or me.

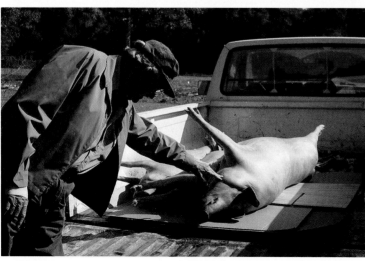

My frien' the P-I-G, Hog.

These are blooming may-haw trees. My dogs, Charlie and Phideaux, love to play in the swamp.

I just got to have fresh pepper to cook.

Leo calls this his Justin Wilson decor. We're wearing both a belt and suspenders —
not taking any chances.

Charlie Johnson is still my chief taster. He's getting to be a good cook, too. If you notice, he has the same name as my dog! Here we're deep frying a turkey.

½ cup oil or shortening
1 cup chopped onion
½ cup chopped celery
½ cup chopped fresh parsley
1 cup boiled and chopped
    gizzard and fowl heart

(leftover chicken or turkey
    can be used along with
    giblets)
2 cups reserved fowl stock
Ground cayenne pepper
    to taste
Salt to taste

Preheat the oven to 300°F. Combine the pecans and bread in a large mixing bowl and set aside. Heat the oil in a large saucepan over medium-high heat, and sauté the onions, celery, and parsley until the onions are clear. Add this to the bread and pecans and mix well. Add the giblets and pour in the stock to moisten well, season, and mix. Pour into a greased medium-sized casserole dish or use as a stuffing. Bake for 45 minutes if not used for stuffing.

YIELD: *about 7 cups, enough to stuff a small bird, or 6 servings*

Crumb and Cheese Dressing

This can be used to stuff artichokes, eggplant, shrimp, and other seafood.

1 cup grated mozzarella
    cheese
1 cup grated Parmesan cheese
3 cups bread crumbs
½ cup olive oil
2 tablespoons fresh lemon
    juice

Mashed anchovies or
    anchovy paste to taste
    (optional)
1 teaspoon dried basil
1 teaspoon garlic powder
1 tablespoon dried parsley
Salt to taste
Ground cayenne pepper
    to taste

In a medium-sized mixing bowl, combine all the ingredients and mix well. Use to stuff seafood or vegetables when they are baked or fried.

YIELD: *about 5 cups*

Seafood Dressing

This can be used as a stuffing or as a side dish.

¼ cup olive oil
1 cup chopped onion
1 cup chopped green onions
½ cup chopped bell pepper
1 cup chopped fresh parsley
1 tablespoon chopped garlic
3 cups crumbled cornbread
1 cup cubed fish
1 cup peeled, deveined, and
   cubed shrimp

1 cup crabmeat, picked over
   for shells
3 cups Fish Stock (see page
   37)
1 tablespoon Worcestershire
   sauce
1 teaspoon crushed dried mint
Salt to taste
Ground cayenne pepper
   to taste

Preheat the oven to 325°F. Using a large skillet over medium-high heat, heat the olive oil and sauté the onions, green onions, bell pepper, and parsley until the onions are clear. Add the garlic and cook another 5 minutes. In a large mixing bowl, combine the cornbread, seafood, and sautéed vegetables. Mix the stock and Worcestershire together, then pour into the cornbread mixture and mix well. Stir in the mint, salt, and pepper, then turn into a large greased casserole dish and bake for 1 hour or stuff in a whopper and bake until done.

YIELD: *about 8 cups or 6 servings*

Sweet Potato Dressing

1 cup giblets
1 cup dry bread in ½-inch
   pieces
3 cups peeled and grated
   sweet potato

½ cup chopped pecans or other
   nuts
½ cup finely chopped onion
1 cup giblet stock
2 large eggs, beaten

½ **teaspoon salt**

½ **teaspoon crushed dried mint**

½ **teaspoon ground cayenne pepper**

Place the giblets in a small saucepan and add enough water to cover by 1 inch. Season with salt, hot sauce, garlic powder, onion powder, and Worcestershire. Bring the water to a boil, then lower the heat to medium, cover, and cook until tender, about 30 minutes. Reserve 1 cup of the stock, drain and let giblets cool, then chop.

Preheat the oven to 350°F. In a large mixing bowl, combine the bread, sweet potatoes, pecans, onions, stock, and giblets, and mix well. Add the eggs, salt, mint, and pepper; mix again. Bake for 2 hours and serve with fresh pork.

YIELD: *about 6 cups or 4 servings*

Eggplant Dressing

Some varieties of eggplant don't need to be peeled. This is a good stuffing for many vegetables, fish, and fowl.

3 **cups peeled eggplant, cut into 1-inch cubes**

1 **tablespoon salt**
Water to cover eggplant

¼ **cup oil or shortening**

1 **cup chopped onion**

¼ **cup chopped celery**

¼ **cup chopped fresh parsley**

3 **cups cubed dry bread or toast**

½ **cup dry white wine**

2 **tablespoons Worcestershire sauce**

½ **teaspoon crushed dried mint**
Salt to taste
Ground cayenne pepper to taste

Preheat the oven to 375°F. In a large mixing bowl, cover the eggplant cubes with water and stir in the salt. Let them soak for at least 30 minutes. Rinse and pat dry. In a medium-sized saucepan over medium-high heat, sauté the onions, celery, and parsley in the oil until the onions are clear. Add the eggplant and heat until it begins to soften, about 10 minutes. Place the bread cubes in a large mixing bowl, and add the vegetables and eggplant, mixing well. Add the wine, Worcestershire, and mint, and mix well, then add the salt and pepper. Turn the mixture into a large, greased casserole dish and bake for 45 minutes, or use as a stuffing.

Y I E L D : *about 7 cups or 6 servings*

• ❦ •

CHAPTER 6

Poultry and Eggs

Eggs are a most versatile food. They are used in making everything from appetizers to desserts. They are suitable to be served at each meal and as snacks. They are also one of Justin's favorite foods. One day he and a friend prepared eggs thirty-seven different ways. That friend was in the egg business big time and had more than a million laying hens. They were doing product research and having a good time, too. When Justin's friend Travis was just starting in the chicken business, he encountered a problem:

He didn't have but a hunert schickens dat he was raisin' an' gettin' dem aggs, but he live r'at on a highway an' shoom, shoom, shoom, shoom, dem peoples go by an' kill dem schickens as fas' as he could get 'em up big enuf to lay aggs.

So he start callin' de State Police. "You got to did somet'ing 'bout dese drivers drivin' so fas' an' killin' my schickens." Well, de State Police was jus' doin' dere bes' to he'p, so dey came out an' put a big sign: Slow, Plant Entrance. Shoom, shoom, shoom, look like it speed 'em up.

An' ol' Travis call 'em every day, at leas'. "You got to did somet'ing. Dat 'plant entrance' sign did not did some good." Well, dey

say, "Hokay," an' dey come out an' dey sen' de Highway Depaht-
ment out an' dey put a sign: Slow, Children at Play, an' dat really
speed 'em up, shoom, shoom, shoom. Well, he call an' he call an'
he call. Finally he call up one day an' he say, "Look, Cap, do you
min', is it legal fo' me to put ma' own sign, hanh?" De captain jus'
wan' to get rid o' him so he say, "Go 'head on. Put you' sign up. Jus'
do anyt'ing, dat gon' slow dem peoples up."

Well, dat policemans didn't hear from ol' Travis for t'irty days.
An' one day de captain ax his sergeant, "Bill, you heard from Lobell?" "Oh, no, Captain. T'ank goodness." "Well, I ain't heard f'om
him' in t'irty days, so I guess I better call him up an' see w'at he did,"
de captain say. So he call him: "Mister Lobell, dis is Captain Walker
wit' de State Police."

"Well, hello dair, Cap. How you are? I jus' want to let you know,
Cap, dat I put a sign dat slow dem devils down. I ain't got a schicken
kill in t'irty days."

Captain Walker say, "You don't mean to tole me."

Travis say, "Dat's r'at. T'ank you, Cap, I got to go." An' he hung
up.

De captain say, "We better go scheck on dat sign. It may be
somet'ing we can use in a lot o' places." So he sen' Lieutenant
Melancon. He drove up to Travis's place in Springfiel' an' dair's a
great big sign, a whole piece of plywood: Slow, Nudist Colony.

Nowadays most of the eggs and poultry sold commercially are produced in immense, efficient plant complexes. The U.S. Department of
Agriculture inspects and grades products available in most grocery
stores. But when Justin was growing up he gathered yard eggs from
the family chickens. Yard eggs are still easily purchased throughout
Louisiana, and you can even hear a cock crow at dawn in New Orleans.

Justin cooks with double-yolk jumbo eggs. Several years ago he
recorded a promotional radio spot for the Louisiana Egg Commission.
Instead of using the traditional line, "The Incredible Edible Egg," Justin's version was, "The Unbelievable Eatable Egg." The spots were
popular, and Justin constantly comes up with new ways of using the
double-yolkers that the commission supplies to him.

What about cholesterol? "Well," he says, "PapaBoy lived to be eighty;

Mama was almost ninety-seven when she passed away, and we ate dozens of eggs each week, plus rich cream, hog lard, and many organ meats. My level is normal. I think the reason we weren't concerned about it is 'cause we couldn't spell it. I still can't."

Justin is concerned about cleanliness, though, so he always rinses a chicken well before cooking it. And from personal experience he has learned to break each egg in a separate cup before adding it to other ingredients.

Because poultry and eggs are so versatile, any recipe in this section can play host to many substitutions. Omelettes can be filled with virtually anything, and the list of quiche flavorings is endless. Different fruits and seasonings can be combined with poultry. Justin would be pleased if you did him one better and came up with thirty-eight different ways to fix eggs.

Baked Chicken with Rice Dressing

One 5- to 6-pound hen	2 cups Chicken Stock (see
Salt	page 36) or water
Ground cayenne pepper	4 to 5 cups Rice Dressing
	(see page 78)

Preheat the oven to 350°F. Rinse the hen well and pat it dry. Salt and pepper it inside and out, then stuff with the rice dressing. Place on a raised rack in a roasting pan and pour the stock into the bottom of the pan. Cover and bake for 1½ to 2 hours or until the hen is tender and no longer pink at the bones.

YIELD: *6 to 8 servings*

Chicken à la Creole

One 3-pound fryer, cut in pieces	2 cups Chicken Stock (see page 36) or water
2 tablespoons olive oil	
2 cups chopped onion	2 pounds fresh or canned tomatoes, chopped
1 cup chopped bell pepper	
1 cup chopped fresh parsley	2 tablespoons soy sauce
1 cup chopped green onions	Salt to taste
1 teaspoon crushed dried mint	½ teaspoon ground cayenne pepper or 1 teaspoon Louisiana hot sauce
1 tablespoon minced garlic	
1 cup dry white wine	

Rinse the chicken well. Simmer the chicken to make a stock (see page 36). After the chicken is boiled, remove from stock, let cool, and then debone and save meat. In a large, high-walled skillet, heat the olive oil over medium-high heat, and sauté the onions, bell pepper, parsley, and green onions until the onions are clear. Then add the mint, garlic, wine, and stock. Stir in the tomatoes and soy sauce; bring to a boil. Add the chicken, salt, and pepper, and bring back to a boil. Turn the heat down to low and simmer, covered, for at least 1 hour, stirring occasionally. Serve over cooked rice.

YIELD: *8 to 10 servings*

Smothered Chicken

This dish is so easy and so good.

One 2- to 3-pound chicken, cut into pieces	Louisiana hot sauce or ground cayenne pepper to taste
2 tablespoons soy sauce	
Salt to taste	2 tablespoons oil

2 cups chopped onion
½ cup chopped bell pepper
½ cup chopped fresh parsley

1 cup dry white wine
2 teaspoons chopped garlic

Rinse the chicken well, pat dry, then season the chicken with the soy sauce, salt, and hot sauce, and set aside. In a large, high-walled skillet, heat the oil, then sauté the onions, bell pepper, and parsley over medium-high heat until the onions are clear. Add the wine and stir; add garlic and stir, then add the chicken. Mix everything together, then lower the heat to medium, cover, and cook for at least 2 hours, stirring occasionally. The chicken should be so tender that it falls apart. Serve over cooked rice.

YIELD: *4 to 6 servings*

Mama's Fried Chicken

Mama used to fix this on Sundays for the family dinner.

DRENCH:

2 cups dry white wine
1 large egg, beaten
1 tablespoon Worcestershire sauce
1 teaspoon salt
Louisiana hot sauce or ground cayenne pepper to taste

About 1 cup oil, enough to fill the frying pan ¼ inch deep

DREDGE:

4 cups all-purpose flour
1 teaspoon garlic powder
1 teaspoon onion powder
½ teaspoon ground cayenne pepper
2½ teaspoons salt

One 3- to 4-pound chicken, cut into frying pieces

Mix all the drench ingredients together in a large mixing bowl. Then sift all the dredge ingredients together over a large, flat-bottomed pan. Pour the oil into a deep 12-inch frying pan and heat over medium-high.

Rinse chicken well and pat dry. Dip the pieces in the drench. Remove and roll individually in the dredge mixture, making sure to coat well. Place the chicken in the heated oil and fry until golden brown, about 15 minutes. Turn and fry the other side about 10 minutes. Make sure the chicken is thoroughly cooked. If you are frying more than one chicken, just add more oil as needed and let it heat through before adding more chicken.

YIELD: *6 to 8 servings*

Chicken and Dumplings

One **3- to 4-pound chicken**
3 cups chopped green onions
2 cups chopped fresh parsley
1 cup dry white wine
1 teaspoon ground cayenne
      pepper
2 tablespoons Worcestershire
      sauce
1 teaspoon garlic powder
1 teaspoon finely crushed
      dried mint
      Salt to taste
½ cup all-purpose flour

3 tablespoons oil
2 cups English peas
2 cups thinly sliced carrots
      Salt to taste

DUMPLINGS:

2 cups all-purpose flour
2¼ teaspoons baking powder
¼ teaspoon ground cayenne
      pepper
1 teaspoon salt
1⅓ cups milk or buttermilk

Rinse the chicken well and place it in a large stockpot with the onions, parsley, wine, and seasonings. Pour in enough water to cover; bring to a boil, reduce the heat to low, and simmer at least 1 hour. Remove the chicken from the pot, let cool, and cut the meat into chunks, and refrigerate. Leave the pot of stock on the heat at a slow simmer.

In a heavy 12-quart pot, make a small light roux from the flour and oil (see page 56). When the roux is medium brown, slowly add 2 cups of the reserved stock, stirring all the while. Slowly stir in another 2 cups of the stock, making sure that it has no lumps. Pour in the remaining stock and stir. Add the peas, carrots, and salt to taste. Let cook, stirring occasionally, until the carrots are tender, at least 30 minutes, while you make the dumpling batter.

In a large mixing bowl, combine the flour, baking powder, pepper, and salt (if you use buttermilk, also add 1 teaspoon of baking soda). Add the milk and stir until the flour is all wet; don't stir too much. Turn up the heat under the stock to medium so that it boils. Drop the batter by spoons into the boiling stock, cover, and cook for 20 minutes. Return the chicken to the pot to heat it through.

YIELD: *8 to 10 servings*

Fry-baked Chicken

3 to 4 pounds chicken pieces
2 cups all-purpose flour
1 teaspoon salt
½ teaspoon ground cayenne pepper
1 cup oil or shortening
2 cups finely chopped onion
2 cups finely chopped bell pepper
1 clove garlic, minced
2 pounds canned or fresh peeled tomatoes
1 cup dry white wine
½ teaspoon chopped fresh parsley
1½ teaspoons salt
Louisiana hot sauce or ground cayenne pepper to taste

Preheat the oven to 350°F. Rinse the chicken pieces well and pat dry; remove the skin. In a flat pan, mix together the flour, salt, and pepper; then roll the chicken pieces in the flour. Heat the oil over medium-high heat in a large skillet. Brown the meat in the hot oil, then remove and place in roasting pan. Over medium heat in the same skillet and oil in which the chicken was fried, add the onions, pepper, and garlic, and sauté about 20 minutes. Add the tomatoes, wine, and parsley, then stir in the salt and hot sauce. Simmer about 20 minutes, stirring frequently. Pour the sauce over the chicken, cover the roaster, and bake for at least 1 hour or until chicken is tender and no longer pink at the bone. Serve with rice.

YIELD: *8 to 10 servings*

Peachy Chicken

Fresh Louisiana peaches give their wonderful flavor to this dish.

DREDGE:

2 teaspoons salt
1 cup all-purpose flour
¼ teaspoon ground cayenne
   pepper
½ teaspoon garlic powder
½ teaspoon onion powder

One 3- to 4-pound chicken, cut
   into pieces
2 tablespoons olive oil
½ cooking apple, sliced
⅓ cup dry white wine
1 pound fresh or canned
   peaches, sliced
⅓ cup brandy

Combine the salt, flour, pepper, and garlic and onion powders in a flat-bottomed pan or large bowl. Rinse the chicken parts well, pat dry, then roll in the seasoned flour. Heat the olive oil in a large skillet over medium heat, and brown the chicken. Add the sliced apple, wine, and peaches, and cook covered for 20 minutes. Then turn the chicken over and pour in the brandy. Bring to a boil, then reduce to low, cover, and simmer another 20 minutes. Remove the chicken from the pan; pour the sauce over it when serving.

YIELD: *6 to 8 servings*

Savory Giblets

At our house we fight over the giblets, so sometimes I make this dish so everybody can get enough.

1 teaspoon garlic powder
1 teaspoon onion powder
   Salt to taste
   Louisiana hot sauce or
      ground cayenne pepper
      to taste
1 cup dry white wine

2 tablespoons Worcestershire
   sauce
2 cups water
2 pounds chicken giblets:
   hearts, gizzards, and/or
   livers (see Note)

Place all the ingredients in a medium-sized saucepan. Stir well to mix. Cover and bring to a boil over medium-high heat, then turn to low and simmer until the gizzards are tender, at least 30 minutes. Serve over cooked rice or potatoes.

YIELD: *6 to 8 servings*

NOTE: Some people don't care for the taste of liver. This same dish can be made with either hearts and gizzards or just with livers.

Duck with Pears and Wine

One 4- to 5-pound duck
Salt to taste
Ground cayenne pepper
to taste
½ cup finely chopped fresh
parsley

1 cup dry white wine
1 cup water
1 tablespoon honey
4 fresh pears, halved

Preheat the oven to 350°F. Rinse the duck well and pat dry. Using a shaker, sprinkle salt and pepper over the outside and inside of the duck, and place in a baking pan. Sprinkle the parsley over the duck. Mix the wine, water, and honey together, then pour around, not on top of, the duck. Place the pear halves around the duck and bake, covered, for 1 to 2 hours, basting every 30 minutes, until tender.

YIELD: *2 to 4 servings*

Deep-fried Turkey

I first made a turkey this way in the 1930s, when I lived in Crowley, Louisiana. Some friends—Mike Hession and Dominic Leger—and I had no luck in our hunting, so we killed a yard turkey and fried it in freshly rendered lard. I've been doing it ever since. It's the best way to cook turkey that I know of. This turkey doesn't get dry like most baked turkeys do.

One 12- to 15-pound turkey	Ground cayenne pepper
Salt	4 to 5 gallons peanut oil

Rinse the turkey well and pat dry inside and out. Using a shaker, sprinkle the bird inside and out with salt, then shake on cayenne pepper in the same manner, making sure to rub the seasonings into the meat. Wash your hands! Pour enough peanut oil into a large 40-quart pot to insure that the turkey will be covered when fully lowered into the pot. Make sure the pot is large enough that the oil won't overflow when the turkey is submerged. Also, I use a steamer rig to keep the bird off the very bottom of the pot, where the oil is much hotter. Heat the oil to 350° to 375°F. Then, holding on to the legs, very SLOWLY and CAREFULLY lower the bird all the way into the hot oil, being careful not to splash any oil. I wear cooking mitts to make this easier. Fry about 3 to 4 minutes to the pound. (Smaller birds cook more quickly; larger birds might have to cook 5 to 6 minutes per pound.) A 15-pound bird will be done in 50 to 60 minutes. Some long tongs or a large fork make handling the turkey much easier. Test for doneness at the bone at the thigh joint. Carefully remove the turkey from the oil, allowing it to drain, and stand it upright on its legs and pope's nose so that the excess oil will drain from the cavity onto paper towels. Carve as usual, and be sure to savor the crunchy skin.

Smoked Turkey

I sometimes put this on to smoke about 10 P.M. so it cooks all night while I'm asleep. Smoking is the easiest way to cook that I know.

One 15- to 20-pound turkey	1 cup dry white wine
Salt	1 onion
Ground cayenne pepper	½ bell pepper cut into 4 pieces

1 clove garlic
1 tablespoon liquid smoke
1 teaspoon crushed dried mint

6 tablespoons chopped fresh
  parsley
2 tablespoons Worcestershire
  sauce
Water to almost fill pan

Rinse the turkey well and pat dry. Prepare the smoker according to the manufacturer's instructions. While the briquettes are starting to burn, place aromatic wood chips to soak in some water. I use pecan wood because it's widely available in Louisiana and I like it, but you could use any fruit wood, nut wood, or mesquite if you like it. Sprinkle the carcass and cavity with salt and pepper, rubbing the seasonings into the meat with the palm of your hand. Wash your hands! Place the wine, onion, bell pepper, garlic, liquid smoke, mint, parsley, and Worcestershire in the water pan; lower it into the smoker. Put the rack in place, then carefully pour water to within ½ inch of the top of the pan. Place the turkey on the rack; if you have a two-story smoker, the turkey should go on the bottom rack so you can smoke a roast or ham on the top rack and let the juices drip onto the turkey. Put the wet wood chips on the briquettes so that they will begin to produce smoke. Put the smoker assembly together over the fire and let it do the rest of your work. I usually don't even have to check this once it's on. Allow to smoke according to manufacturer's instructions or overnight. Smoking generally lengthens storage time considerably.

Y I E L D : *serves the whole family, and the scraps make the best gumbo*

Scrambled Eggs with Avocado and Cheese

1 ripe avocado, peeled and
  mashed real well
1 teaspoon fresh lemon juice
1 cup grated cheddar cheese

Salt to taste
Louisiana hot sauce to taste
6 to 8 large eggs
2 tablespoons olive oil

Mash the avocado in a large mixing bowl, then add the lemon juice and cheese (reserving some of the cheese for topping), and beat well. Add salt and hot sauce to taste. In a large skillet over medium heat, heat the olive oil and cook the eggs, always stirring, until still soft and fluffy. Add the avocado mixture, stir, and remove from heat. Place on an ovenproof platter, sprinkle with the remaining cheese, and broil for about 1 minute.

YIELD: *3 to 4 servings*

Crab Quiche

Many vegetables or seafoods can be substituted for the crab.

One 9-inch unbaked pie shell
  2 tablespoons oil or shortening
  ¼ cup finely chopped green onions
  ¼ cup finely chopped fresh parsley
  1 cup lump crabmeat, carefully picked free of shells

1½ cups grated cheese, Monterey Jack or one with a delicate flavor
  ½ cup finely chopped mushrooms
  3 large eggs
  1 cup milk or cream
  ½ teaspoon salt
  ¼ teaspoon Louisiana hot sauce or ⅛ teaspoon ground cayenne pepper

Preheat the oven to 375°F. In a small skillet, sauté the onions and parsley in the oil over medium-high heat until tender. In a large mixing bowl, combine the crabmeat, cheese, and mushrooms, then spread it evenly in the pie shell. In a separate bowl, beat together the eggs, milk, salt, and hot sauce. Add the cooked vegetables to the eggs and mix well. Pour the egg mixture over the crabmeat. Bake for 40 to 50 minutes or until a knife inserted in the center comes out clean.

YIELD: *one 9-inch quiche; 6 to 8 servings*

Oyster Omelette

Any seafood and many vegetables and meats can be substituted for the oysters. One of my favorites is an omelette made from Crawfish Étouffée (see recipe on page 109).

3 large eggs	1 teaspoon oil
Salt to taste	6 fresh oysters, coarsely
Louisiana hot sauce or	chopped
ground cayenne pepper	
to taste	

In a bowl, beat the eggs together with the salt and hot sauce until frothy. Heat the oil in an omelette pan over medium-high heat and pour in the beaten eggs. As the eggs cook, rotate the pan and use a fork or spatula to draw the eggs into the center of the pan. Tilt the pan so that the unsolidified eggs run to replace those that have been drawn to the center. This may be done several times to bring the liquid eggs to the bottom of the pan. When the eggs are slightly set but still moist, add the chopped oysters to the center of the pan. Tilt the pan down at an angle, with the handle toward you. Using a fork or spatula, fold the top half over the filling and the bottom. Return to the heat to brown and slightly cook the oysters. Invert onto a plate to serve.

YIELD: *1 omelette*

Pepper Eggs

2 bell peppers, thinly sliced lengthwise	1 tablespoon minced onion
2 red pimentos, thinly sliced lengthwise	¼ teaspoon salt or to taste
Oil or shortening	Dash garlic powder
6 large eggs	Dash ground cayenne pepper or Louisiana hot sauce

Preheat the oven to 350°F. Grease an 8-inch casserole dish, and place a layer of bell peppers and then one of pimentos on the bottom of the dish. In a small bowl, beat the eggs together with the onion, salt, garlic powder, and pepper. Pour the beaten eggs over the peppers. Add another layer of bell pepper and pimentos. Bake for 30 minutes.

YIELD: *4 servings*

VARIATION: Boiled chicken chunks, seafood, cheese, and other vegetables can be added to give variety.

Pickled Eggs

I put beet juice in with the vinegar because I like the pretty pink color it gives to the egg. These are usually sold in bars in Louisiana.

1 **dozen hard-boiled eggs, peeled**	1 **part water**
	1 **teaspoon salt**
Hungarian peppers (optional)	1 **tablespoon minced garlic**
4 **parts white vinegar**	3 **tablespoons minced onion**

Place the eggs in a quart jar along with some whole Hungarian peppers, if you use them. In a 2-quart saucepan, mix together the remainder of the ingredients and heat until you can't hold your finger in it. Pour this mixture over the eggs, making sure to cover the eggs completely. Seal and let stand 1 to 2 weeks. Store in the refrigerator after opening.

YIELD: *12 pickled eggs*

Seafood

Visitors from around the world are amazed at the variety and volume of Louisiana seafood. They can't imagine being able to eat as many shrimp as they want, or fresh salty oysters costing only a quarter each. But when they are introduced to crawfish, given an eating lesson, then told they can join their hosts in feasting all afternoon from long tables heaped with mountains of the bright-red crustaceans, they know that they are in a place where eating is a major pastime—and seafood cooking and eating occupy a prominent place in that pastime.

Louisiana leads the nation in commercial production of fish and shellfish. Shrimp is the most valuable fishery product of Louisiana but, in total tonnage, menhaden, a fish processed for use in animal feeds and for its oil, leads all other species. Fishery resources are considered renewable and with wise management and prudent conservation practices all fish and shellfish production could continue to be a great source of revenue and enjoyment. In the last few decades, however, every consumer has had to become concerned about contamination of seafood. Not only in Louisiana's fertile marine nursery, but in the once-pristine coastal waters off Alaska, and in California's agricultural runoff, dangerous chemicals and bacteria are ruining the water and eventually the seafood that humans consume.

Recently a reporter asked Justin for his comments about an all-too-common occurrence. It seems that a company had been spewing a known carcinogen into the Calcasieu River for years and that fish caught in the area had high levels of several chemicals. The health department stated that it was perfectly safe to eat these fish so long as one first boiled them for twenty minutes, and threw the water away. The chemicals were deadly and unpronounceable. Justin said he preferred flavoring his fish with the more traditional seasonings of salt and cayenne pepper. Until game and commercial fishermen decide they will not tolerate any more contamination, irresponsible parties are going to continue dumping their deadly sewage into our food supply.

Aquaculture is a hope for the future. Already alligators, catfish, and crawfish are farmed in large-scale operations in several states. Research continues at Louisiana State University and other sites to devise effective ways to raise shrimp, crawfish, redfish, and oysters in controlled environments.

The most wonderful thing about seafood in Louisiana is that it is available to everyone at very low cost. A cane pole and an afternoon mean dinner is on the table. Many families catch enough crawfish in the spring to last them until crawfish are again in season. Crabs inhabit nearly every bayou in the coastal zone. We don't recommend a certain type of fish for each recipe because the luck of the cast always plays a role in determining the menu. Then there are what Justin calls "unknown delicacies," the trash fish that most people throw back in spite of their fine eating qualities. Ten years ago a connoisseur of seafood would have shunned a red drum, or redfish, as an inferior eating fish, but a different manner of preparation has created a fad that has seriously endangered the red drum population. Again, it is wise management and conservation practices that ensure visitors and residents alike will enjoy plentiful and healthy seafood in Louisiana for many years to come.

CRABS

The Atlantic Blue Crab ranges from Nova Scotia to Uruguay, but the sediment-laden Mississippi River provides their favored muddy bottom and makes the blue crab plentiful all along the Gulf Coast. Because blues adapt to differing water conditions, they will be found in salt, fresh, and brackish areas. Blue crabs eat plants, small fish, and other crabs. Although they are very good at defending themselves, they nonetheless are eaten by larger fish, turtles, and by man.

Like other crustaceans, crabs must shed their shells in order to grow. And a crab may molt as many as twenty-five times in a complete life cycle. Often crabs caught just before a molt will be kept in tanks so that they can be sold as a soft-shell. A crab's shell begins to harden immediately after a molt, so they are frozen just after molting.

It is easy to catch crabs. All that is needed is a string with a piece of meat tied to it. The bait is lowered to the bottom, where the crab latches on to it. The string is then pulled to the surface, and a net is used to catch the crab and put it in a bucket. Special crab nets and larger crab traps are also used to catch crabs in greater quantities. Crabs should be cooked alive, so keep them moist with moss or a burlap bag. As with other seafood, crabs must be kept chilled to avoid spoiling.

How to Crack Crabs

1. Remove the two large claws and set them aside to pick later. Hold the crab belly up. Pry under the shell with your fingers or with a knife along the "T" or triangular seam. Lift the center shape out.
2. Turn the crab over. Hold the crab firmly with one hand; with the other hand, pull the top shell off.
3. Remove the internal organs and eggs from the center.
4. Brush away the lungs, or "dead man"—the tubular organs that lie on both sides of the crab.
5. Break the body in half.
6. Pull off the small legs and swimmerets.

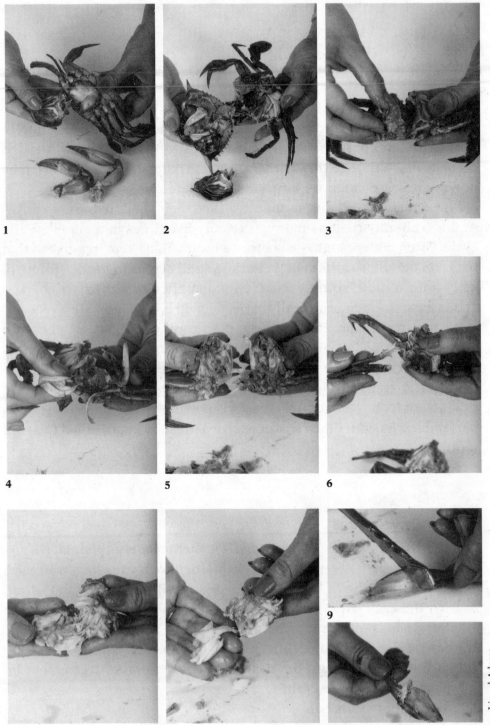

1

2

3

4

5

6

7

8

9

10

7. Carefully open the chambers that contain the white meat on each half of the body.

8. Remove the meat with your fingers or a knife. The meat from the largest chamber is called "lump" crabmeat.

9. Crack the two large claws. Place the claw flat with the moveable part up. Sharply tap the joint with a knife handle. The shell should crack at the point where it was hit. Gently pull the pinchers away from the rest of the claw. Carefully break off the bottom pincher.

10. You'll be left with a crab finger. Claw meat is generally a little darker and coarser than white meat. The flavor is slightly different, too, but it's all very good.

It takes about a dozen picked crabs to make a pound of meat.

Crab Albany

Around the town of Albany they grow the best collards, so when I thought about putting collards and crab together I thought about Albany.

2 cups cooked and drained collards or frozen greens	¼ cup finely chopped onion Salt to taste
1 cup lump crabmeat, picked clean of shells	Louisiana hot sauce or ground cayenne pepper to taste
1 cup tomato sauce	
1 cup grated mild cheese	½ cup plain bread crumbs

Preheat oven to 350°F. Place the greens in a layer on the bottom of a greased 9-by-9-inch casserole dish. Then, in a large bowl, mix together well the crabmeat, tomato sauce, cheese, and onion. Mix in salt and hot sauce, then pour over the greens. Sprinkle the top with the bread crumbs and bake for 30 to 40 minutes.

YIELD: *4 to 6 servings*

Crab Capricho

Capricho is just what I had when I put this dish together.

¼ cup olive oil or bacon
  drippings
1 cup raw rice
½ cup chopped onion
2 teaspoons minced garlic
2 cups stock or water
1 cup tomato sauce

1 cup finely chopped ham
Salt to taste
Louisiana hot sauce or
  ground cayenne pepper
  to taste
1 pound crabmeat, picked free
  of shells

Heat the oil in a large saucepan over medium heat, then add the rice, onions, and garlic. Stirring occasionally, cook until the rice becomes golden brown, about 15 minutes. Add the stock and tomato sauce, then stir in the ham, salt, and hot sauce. Add the crab and bring to a boil. Reduce the heat to low, cover, and simmer 30 to 40 minutes or until the rice is tender.

YIELD: *6 to 8 servings*

Crabmeat au Gratin

This is a traditional way to prepare crabmeat.

6 tablespoons margarine or
  butter
1 cup chopped onion
½ cup chopped green onions
¼ cup chopped fresh parsley
½ teaspoon chopped garlic
1 pound white crabmeat,
  picked clean of shells
Salt to taste

Louisiana hot sauce or
  ground cayenne pepper
  to taste
2 tablespoons all-purpose flour
1 cup water, stock, or milk
1 cup grated mild cheddar
  cheese
½ cup grated mozzarella
  cheese

Preheat the oven to 350°F. Melt 4 tablespoons of the margarine in a medium-sized saucepan over medium heat. Sauté the onions, green onions, and parsley, until the onions are clear. Stir in the garlic, crab-meat, salt, and hot sauce; reduce the heat to low and continue cooking. In a separate small saucepan, melt the remaining 2 tablespoons of margarine over medium heat. Add the flour and lightly brown it, stirring constantly. Slowly stir in the stock and continue cooking, stirring constantly, until the mixture begins to thicken. Add half of the cheddar cheese, stir until melted, then pour the mixture into the crab and carefully combine the two. Turn into a small greased casserole dish and top with the mozzarella and remaining cheddar cheese. Bake 20 to 30 minutes, until all the cheese is melted and browned around the edges.

YIELD: *4 to 6 servings*

Stuffed Crabs

If you've got two pounds of crabmeat, use it instead of the fish. Sometimes I have to put stretchers on crabmeat.

1 pound crabmeat, picked clean of shells	½ cup dry white wine
1 pound fish fillets	Louisiana hot sauce or ground cayenne pepper to taste
½ cup chopped fresh parsley	
½ cup minced onion	1 tablespoon Worcestershire sauce
2 tablespoons margarine	
1 tablespoon minced garlic	Salt to taste
2 large eggs, beaten	1½ cups plain bread crumbs

In a food grinder or processor, grind together the crab and fish until they are well mixed, then store it in the refrigerator until needed. Preheat the oven to 350°F. Melt the margarine in a large saucepan over medium heat, then sauté the parsley and onions until the onions are clear. Add the garlic and crab-fish mixture and stir. In a separate bowl, beat together the eggs, wine, hot sauce, Worcestershire, and salt. Remove the crab mixture from the heat and combine it with the egg mixture. Stir in the bread crumbs and let the mixture sit for about 15 minutes before stuffing it into well-scrubbed crab shells or ramekins. Bake for 20 to 30 minutes. These may also be deep fried in oil for about 5 minutes at 350°F.

YIELD: *about 10 stuffed crabs, enough to serve 5 people*

Broiled Soft-shelled Crabs

Around Lacombe and Mandeville, we used to see dozens of kids selling soft-shells on Sunday afternoons. They stood near the highway with the biggest, juiciest crabs nestled in a bed of Spanish moss. We often fixed these broiled and fried. I like to make sandwiches from broiled crabs.

> **2 soft-shelled crabs per person**
> **Crabby Lemon-Butter Sauce**
> **(see page 58)**

Pull off the "T" or triangular sections of the crab's belly. Clean the crabs by carefully lifting the carapace, or top shell, and removing the gills or "deadman." There are 6 elongated white gills on each side. Then pull off the eyes and the mouth area. Before they molt, crabs do not eat for several days so they are clean internally. Their shells are very fragile, so always handle them carefully.

Brush a small amount of the lemon-butter sauce on the surface of the broiler pan and lay the crabs belly up on it. Using a carving fork, you may puncture through the body of the crab. Broil about 5 inches from element. Carefully turn over and broil another 5 minutes. The meat should be opaque white and hot. Some people prefer the crab shell crispy, so they broil crabs longer and a little closer to the element. Drizzle the sauce over each crab and serve immediately.

• ❦ •

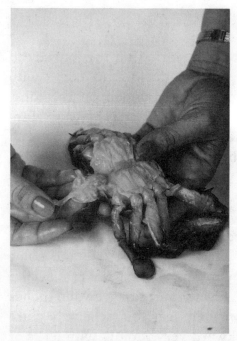

Pull off the "T," or triangular shaped, section of the crab belly.

Carefully lift the carapace, or top shell.

Lionel Adams

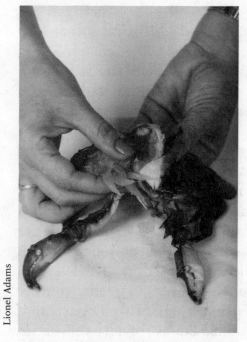

Remove the gills, or "deadman."

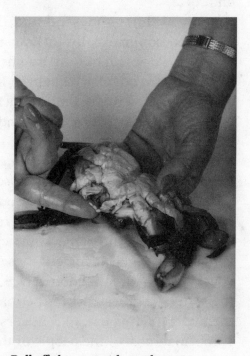

Pull off the eyes and mouth area.

CRAWFISH

The folktale goes that when the Acadians started on the journey to Louisiana, their favorite food, the lobster, decided to come with them. The lobster, like the Acadians, suffered much on the long, hard trip. Many died, many were left scattered along the way. Hunger and hardship changed the Acadian and the lobster, making each strong and sure of his purpose. When they finally reached Louisiana, Acadians became Cajuns, and all that was left of the lobster was the crawfish. These shared experiences made the crawfish and the Cajun inseparable.

There are more than three hundred species of crawfish worldwide. They are found everywhere except Africa, in many size and color variations. The most common variety in Louisiana is the red swamp crawfish. It thrives in the warm, sweet water and can grow ten inches long. Crawfish can walk forward on their legs, but when they are alarmed they propel themselves backward very rapidly with jerks of their tail. In Louisiana the expression "to crawfish" means to back out on a deal.

Between thirty thousand and fifty thousand tons of crawfish are harvested commercially in Louisiana annually. This is estimated to represent 90 percent of all crawfish eaten in the United States. Eighty percent of the crawfish caught in Louisiana are eaten here as well. No one knows how many tons are actually taken from the state's waters because many people catch hundreds of pounds for their own use which are never counted.

Crawfish are easy to catch. During the season, which usually lasts from November to June, one person can catch two hundred pounds a day. The most primitive, childhood way is to fish for them using a piece of Mama's bacon tied to string. Traps get more and more complicated and effective as the demand for crawfish increases. Experiments are being done which involve the use of a tractorlike contraption which shocks the water in a flooded rice field, causing the crawfish to rise in the water. Another part of the machine scoops them up and conveys them to a holding area. Producers are developing new markets, but it seems that most of the people of the United States are not as adventurous as Louisianans when it comes to eating.

Justin tells a story about the gustatory adventurousness of the Louisianans' palate:

> A mama crawfish had a bunch of little bitty bébé crawfish and w'en dey got big enuf to go wid' her she say, "Chirren, brought you'se'f wid me, I'm takin' you out to see the worl' and I don' got much time." So out of the crawfish hole came the mama and the bébé crawfish, and they went out to see the big worl'. They were goin' trew the pasture when all of a sudden the bébé crawfish —*ssshoommmm*—in high-gear reverse, move dose bébés. Mama axed, "What is it chirren? What's wrong?"
>
> "Look at dat, Mama, what that is?"
>
> "Oh don' be scared, chirren," she say. "That's a cow and cows don' like crawfish. Come on, le's go, I got to show you the worl', an' befo' dark."
>
> Well, dey walk about thirty-three more feets an'—*ssshoommmm* —high-gear reverse, dose bébés move. "What's wrong, chirren? What is it?" The bébés look up to see a great big mule.
>
> Mama say, "Don' be silly, chirren, that's a mule and mules don' eat crawfish. Le's go, I got plenty of worl' to show you an' befo' dark."
>
> They walk on some mo' when—*ssshoommmm*—dat mama back-up in double high-gear-reverse. De chirren ax, "What is it, Mama? What's wrong?" She yell, "Run, chirren! Run! Dat's a Cajun an he'll eat anyt'ing."

How to Peel Crawfish

1. Hold the crawfish with its head in one hand, its tail in the other, with claws pointed down. Twist and gently pull to separate the head from the body.
2. Some people throw the head away, but they are missing a treat. I push my forefinger into the head where I get the bright yellow fat. Other people suck the head to get the fat and taste the juices in which the crawfish were boiled. You can then throw the head away.
3. With your thumb and forefinger, press the sides of the top of the tail. The shell will give and should crack. If the crawfish are boiled correctly and you are a seasoned eater, you can pull the whole tail out with your front teeth and eat it right away. If you're peeling the crawfish to preserve, go to steps 4 and 5.

4. Remove the first three segments of the tail. Peel the segments around and off.

5. Pull out the meat. Using your thumb and forefinger, pinch the base of the tail just above the flippers at the last segment, while using your other thumb and forefinger to pull on the exposed meat. The whole tail section should come out.

6. It takes about six pounds of boiled crawfish to get one pound of tail meat. Don't forget to include some fat in the meat for its wonderful flavor.

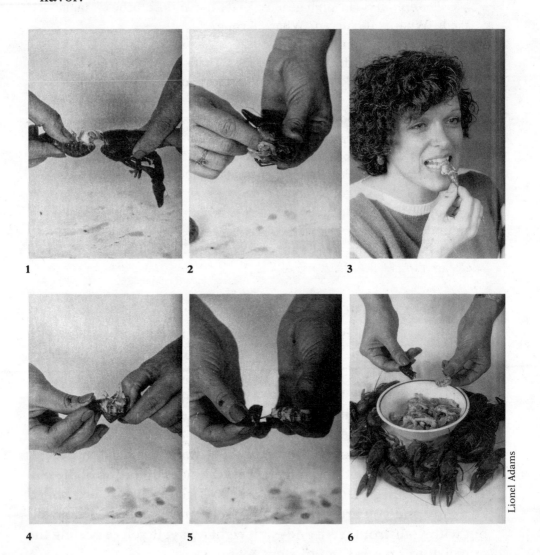

1   2   3

4   5   6

Lionel Adams

Crawfish Étouffée

Every cook has a recipe for crawfish étouffée. I don't make a roux or add anything else because this is basically crawfish and onions smothered down, and that's the way I like it.

4 tablespoons (½ stick) margarine or butter

3 cups chopped onion (or the same volume measure as the crawfish)

1 cup chopped green onions

1 cup chopped fresh parsley

2 teaspoons lemon juice

1 tablespoon soy sauce

2 teaspoons minced garlic

2 pounds crawfish tails, peeled and deveined

Salt to taste

Louisiana hot sauce or ground cayenne pepper to taste

In a large skillet, melt the margarine over medium heat. Then sauté the onions, green onions, and parsley until the onions are clear. Add the lemon juice, soy sauce, and garlic, and cook 10 minutes more. Then add the crawfish, salt, and hot sauce; stir to mix well. Reduce the heat to low, cover, and simmer for 30 to 45 minutes. Serve over cooked rice or pasta.

YIELD: *4 to 6 servings*

Crawfish Boudin

Alligator, shrimp, or fish can be substituted for the crawfish.

¼ cup oil

1 cup chopped onion

½ cup chopped green onions

1 cup chopped fresh parsley

1 cup water

1 teaspoon minced garlic

2 pounds crawfish tails, chopped

4 cups cooked rice

Salt to taste

Ground cayenne pepper to taste

Natural casing (see Note below)

Heat the oil in a large saucepan over medium-high heat, then sauté the onions, green onions, and parsley until the onions are clear. Add the water and garlic and bring to a boil. Add the crawfish, bring back to a boil again, then stir in the rice, salt, and pepper. Cook 5 minutes, then remove from the heat. Let cool, and stuff the mixture into the casing using a sausage stuffer. When ready to serve the boudin, heat it in a skillet with enough water to cover the bottom of the pan. Pierce a few holes in the casing so that it won't pop while heating. Slice and serve hot.

YIELD: *3 pounds; 6 to 8 servings*

NOTE: Natural casing can be purchased at any supermarket that has a meat counter, at a meat shop, or at a sausage supply outlet.

Crawfish and Pasta

¼ cup vegetable oil
1 cup chopped onion
½ cup chopped green onions
¼ cup chopped bell pepper
½ cup chopped fresh parsley
3 cups tomato sauce
1 medium-sized tomato, peeled and chopped
1 tablespoon finely chopped garlic
⅛ teaspoon dried mint

1 cup dry white wine
2 pounds crawfish tails, peeled and deveined
Salt to taste
Louisiana hot sauce or ground cayenne pepper to taste
½ pound cooked pasta
Grated Parmesan cheese to garnish

Heat the oil in a large saucepan over medium-high heat. Sauté the onions, green onions, bell pepper, and parsley until the onions are clear. Add the tomato sauce, tomato, garlic, mint, and wine, and cook, covered, on medium heat for about an hour. Then stir in the crawfish tails, salt, and hot sauce. Reduce the heat to low, cover, and let the sauce simmer while the pasta is cooking. Mix the pasta with the crawfish, sprinkle with cheese, and serve.

YIELD: *6 to 8 servings*

Crawfish Pie

Shrimp can be substituted for crawfish.

¼ cup vegetable oil	1 teaspoon minced garlic
½ cup all-purpose flour	1 pound crawfish tails,
½ cup chopped green onions	peeled and deveined
¼ cup chopped fresh parsley	Salt to taste
½ cup chopped mushrooms	Louisiana hot sauce or
1 cup peeled and chopped	ground cayenne pepper
mirliton (chayote)	to taste
1 cup Fish Stock (see page	One 9-inch pie shell and top,
37) or water	unbaked

Preheat the oven to 350°F. Heat the oil in a large saucepan over medium heat. Then stir in the flour to make a small dark roux (see page 56). Add the green onions, parsley, mushrooms, and mirliton, and cook until the onions and mushrooms are tender, stirring occasionally. Stir in the stock and garlic, and continue cooking and stirring until the mixture begins to thicken. Add the crawfish, salt, and hot sauce, and mix well. Pour the mixture into the pie shell and cover it. Pinch the edges to form a seal, then punch holes in the top to vent. Bake for 1 hour until the crust is golden brown.

YIELD: *6 servings*

Crawfish Stew

This is a favorite winter dish.

½ cup peanut oil	2 teaspoons chopped garlic
1 cup all-purpose flour	Salt to taste
2 cups chopped onion	Louisiana hot sauce or
¼ cup chopped bell pepper	ground cayenne pepper
¼ cup chopped celery	to taste
½ cup chopped fresh parsley	1 cup dry white wine
4 cups stock or water	2 pounds peeled crawfish tails

In a large pot, heat the oil over medium heat, add the flour, and make a thick, dark roux (see page 56). After the roux has darkened, stir in the onions, bell pepper, celery, and parsley; continue cooking and stirring until the onions are clear. Add 2 cups of the stock to the roux and stir until a thick paste has formed. Stir in the garlic, salt, hot sauce, and wine until well blended. Stirring, add the rest of the stock and the crawfish. Reduce the heat to low, cover, and let simmer for 45 minutes. Serve over cooked rice.

YIELD: *4 to 6 servings*

Lazy Crawfish Bisque

Making crawfish bisque usually involves cleaning the heads individually and stuffing hundreds of them by hand, then sautéing them. That's just too much work for me, so I take the lazy way out and make a loaf.

Prepare the Crawfish Stew as explained above. Then:

LOAF:

2 pounds crawfish tails peeled and ground	1 cup finely chopped green onions
1 cup finely chopped onion	1 cup finely chopped fresh parsley

2 teaspoons finely chopped
 garlic
4 large eggs
 Salt to taste

Louisiana hot sauce or
 ground cayenne pepper
 to taste
2 cups plain bread crumbs

Preheat the oven to 350°F. In a large bowl, mix together the crawfish, onions, green onions, parsley, and garlic. In a small bowl, beat the eggs together with the salt and hot sauce, then mix in with the ground tails. Add the bread crumbs and mix well. Form into a loaf on the bottom of a large casserole dish and bake for 20 minutes. Then pour the stew around and over the loaf, cover, and bake for another hour. Serve the stew over cooked rice with a slice of the loaf.

YIELD: *6 to 8 servings*

Crawfish and Zucchini

Shrimp can be used instead of crawfish.

2 tablespoons olive oil
1 cup chopped onion
1 cup chopped fresh parsley
1 cup dry white wine
1 cup water or Fish Stock (see
 page 37)
1 tablespoon minced garlic

6 cups sliced zucchini or other
 summer squash
Salt to taste
Ground cayenne pepper or
 Louisiana hot sauce to taste
2 tablespoons lemon juice
1 pound crawfish tails, peeled
 and deveined

Heat the olive oil in a large saucepan over medium-high heat, and sauté the onions and parsley until the onions are clear. Add the wine, water, and garlic, and continue cooking for 10 minutes. Stir in the zucchini and add the salt, pepper, and lemon juice. Cover and bring to a boil. Stir in the crawfish, bring back to a boil, then reduce the heat to low, cover, and simmer for at least 30 minutes, stirring occasionally.

YIELD: *4 to 6 servings*

FISH

Having the salty waters of the Gulf of Mexico as its southern border, the Sabine River for its western border, and the Mississippi and Pearl rivers for its eastern border, and acre after acre of lakes, rivers, bayous, swamps, and wetlands, it is little wonder that Louisiana is blessed with an abundance of fresh and saltwater fish.

Not only is there a staggering amount of fish in the water, there is an amazing variety of fish that makes up this abundance. Louisiana's fresh and saltwater fish are truly a treasure. Thousands of years ago the Indians quickly learned that there were enough fish on hand to make up for an unsuccessful hunt. Many of the exiled Cajuns were fishermen in Nova Scotia, but they were fascinated with the number of fish and the many aquatic animals in their new land. They devised new methods to catch the new fish. And they are still at it.

As Justin tells it:

> I got a frien' w'at got his boat rigg-up wid' a mirror 6 feets long an 4 feets wide an' it's slant so it flecterizes on da water in Lake Ponchartrain. Ma frien' is out dere 3 week. An' da commercial fisherman see him out dere, an' dey want to ax him about dat mirror but dey don' did dat 'cause dey Cajun too.
>
> Finally one could not stood it some more. He pull up by da side of ma frien' boat, kill da engine an' chunk out da anchor. He ax, "What da hell you doin' wid dat mirror flecterizin' on da water in Lake Ponchartrain?"
>
> "I'm catchin' fish," ma frien' say. An' he point to a bunch of beautimus fish in da bottom of da boat. Da fisherman say, "Man, dose are some fish, I got to fine out how dat work." Ma frien' say, "I can't tole you dat fo' free." "W'at kine of money you talk about?" "One hunnert dollar," say ma frien'. "Here's two fifty dollar bill, I got to know how dat's did. How many have you caught lak' dat?" "You da twelfth one, I garontee."

· ❧ ·

Fish and Potato Cakes

¼ cup oil or shortening
½ cup chopped onion
¼ cup chopped green onions
¼ cup chopped fresh parsley
3 cups boiled, peeled, and mashed potatoes
½ pound fish, cooked and flaked (see Note below)

Salt to taste
Louisiana hot sauce or ground cayenne pepper to taste
1 large egg, beaten
½ teaspoon garlic powder
2 cups seasoned bread crumbs
Oil or shortening

In a small skillet over medium heat, heat the oil, then sauté the onions, green onions, and parsley until the onions are clear. Pour them into a large mixing bowl with the potatoes, fish, salt, and hot sauce, then stir in the egg, garlic powder, and bread crumbs. Form into patties and fry in ¼ inch of oil in a large skillet over medium-high heat, turning once until golden brown on both sides.

YIELD: *10 to 12 three-inch patties*

NOTE: Leftover fish works well for this recipe, but if you don't have leftovers just place the fish in a large saucepan, cover with water, season with salt and pepper, and boil until easily flaked with a fork.

Broiled Fish Fillets

This is diet food for me.

¼ pound (1 stick) margarine or butter
Salt to taste
Louisiana hot sauce or ground cayenne pepper to taste

1 tablespoon lemon juice
½ teaspoon onion powder
1 tablespoon dried parsley
2 pounds fish fillets

In a small saucepan over low heat, melt the margarine, then stir in the salt, hot sauce, lemon juice, onion powder, and parsley. Hold the sauce over a very low heat until ready to be used. Turn on the broiler and preheat the broiler pan. Carefully brush a coat of the lemon butter sauce over the surface of the heated pan. Lay the fish on the pan and place in the broiler, 4 to 6 inches from the heat source. Broil for 10 to 20 minutes, depending on the thickness of the fillets, until done—when easily flaked with a fork. It is important not to overcook fish because it dries out. Remove from the oven and brush the fish with the remaining sauce.

YIELD: *6 to 8 servings*

Fish à la Creole

I have started using farm-raised catfish for many of my fish dishes. It is clean and easy to work with.

2 tablespoons olive oil	1 cup vegetable or tomato
2 cups chopped green onions	juice
½ cup chopped onion	Salt to taste
1 cup chopped fresh parsley	Ground cayenne pepper
½ cup chopped bell pepper	or Louisiana hot sauce
½ cup dry white wine	to taste
1 tablespoon chopped garlic	1 tablespoon Worcestershire
3 cups chopped fresh or	sauce
canned tomatoes	2 pounds fresh fish, cut into
	1-inch pieces

Over medium-high heat in a large skillet, heat the olive oil and sauté the green onions, onions, parsley, and bell pepper until the onions are tender. Add the wine and garlic and continue cooking for 10 minutes more. Stir in the tomatoes, vegetable juice, salt, pepper, and Worcestershire; stir to mix well. Cover, reduce the heat to medium, and continue cooking for another 20 minutes or until the tomatoes fall apart. Add the fish, reduce the heat to low, cover, and simmer until the fish is done, about 20 to 30 minutes. Serve over cooked rice.

YIELD: *6 to 8 servings*

Chris's Catfish Roll-ups

This dish is named for Chris, a wonderful lady for puttin' up with my friend Wayne.

1 quart of oil for deep frying	**DREDGE:**
1 large egg	1 cup corn flour
½ pound lump white crabmeat, picked clean of shells	1 cup all-purpose flour
1 cup finely chopped onion	1 teaspoon onion powder
½ teaspoon peanut oil	Ground cayenne pepper to taste
½ cup plain bread crumbs	Salt to taste
8 catfish fillets	
4 strips bacon	

Fill a deep pot about half full with oil and preheat to 350°F. In a small mixing bowl, beat the egg, then mix in the crabmeat, onions, peanut oil, and bread crumbs. Spread 2 tablespoons of this dressing on each of the catfish fillets, then roll up the fillet, wrap it with a bacon strip, and secure with a toothpick. Mix the corn flour, flour, onion powder, pepper, and salt together in a small mixing bowl and dredge the roll-ups. Fry in oil for 4 to 6 minutes.

YIELD: *4 servings*

• 🌶 •

Baked Salmon Stuffed with Alaska Shrimp

We made this during a trip to Alaska. The shrimp up there have a different flavor, but I made this dish taste good.

One 20-pound salmon, cleaned
    (see Note below)
Salt to taste
Ground cayenne pepper
    to taste
¼ cup peanut oil
1½ cups chopped green onions
½ cup chopped fresh parsley

1 teaspoon dried mint
Louisiana hot sauce
    to taste
Juice of 1 large lemon
Salt to taste
2 pounds peeled and
    deveined shrimp,
    chopped
1 lemon, thinly sliced

Preheat the oven to 350°F. This can also be cooked outside on your barbeque pit. Rinse the salmon, pat it dry, and sprinkle with salt and pepper. In a medium-sized saucepan over medium-high heat, heat the oil and sauté the green onions, parsley, and mint until the onions are tender, about 10 minutes. Stir in the hot sauce, lemon juice, and salt, then add the shrimp, stir, and remove from the heat. Stuff the shrimp mixture into the cavity of the fish. Top with sliced lemon, wrap the salmon in foil, and bake in a flat baking pan 1 to 1½ hours.

YIELD: *enough to feed a party*

NOTE: Other fish can be used, such as catfish, trout, or sea bass.

OYSTERS

Buy only fresh oysters that have no strong fishy or iodine smell. The shells should be tightly closed. Oysters are alive in the shell until they are opened, so keep them on ice or refrigerated constantly. Buy oysters from a good seafood market that will stand behind its goods or from a supermarket that guarantees a fresh product.

If you live near the coast, you can buy oysters right off the boats. Always open the sack to make sure the oysters are the size you want. Then have the oysterman shuck one or two on the spot so you can taste them. People used to say that one should only buy oysters in months that have an "R" in their names. That was partly because most places in the South lacked adequate refrigeration to keep oysters cold and fresh during the long journeys to market. We enjoy oysters year-round, but we have had to become more aware of the water where our oysters are grown because of contamination by pollutants. If you live inland and are able to get fresh oysters infrequently, you can save some large shells, then buy the oysters already shucked and in jars. For a dish such as Oysters Bienville that requires oysters to be baked on their shells, this works well. After they are cooked most people won't be able to tell the difference.

Justin says he always wonders who the very first person to taste a raw oyster was. It must have been a person who was terribly hungry or someone who knew no fear, or both. Whatever made that first person eat oysters, Justin is in his debt. One day he was down in the French Quarter at a place called the Gem, an oyster house. He and some friends devoured eight dozen apiece, then took a walk around the block, and ate some more. In total Justin said he gorged on thirteen dozen oysters that day.

How to Open Oysters

An oyster knife is the best tool for opening oysters. If you don't have one, use a thick-bladed knife that is not too sharp. Rinse off the oyster before opening to keep the shell pieces and sand from getting into your freshly shucked oysters.

I recommend that you use a cotton glove on the hand holding the oyster. Hold the oyster on a stable surface. About halfway between the hinged end and the other end find a place where it is fairly easy to insert your knife. Each oyster is different, and even professional shuckers occasionally find an oyster that is very difficult to open. When you get the knife inserted, twist until the shell pops. This sometimes requires a good bit of force. After you get the knife between the shells, scrape the inside of the upper shell with your knife, where the muscle of the oyster is attached, until the oyster muscle is severed. The top shell can now be lifted off. In the same manner, slide the knife under the oyster and cut the bottom muscle. Clean any bits of shell or dirt away from the oyster resting on the shell. Be sure not to spill any of the tasty juice. Place on a tray of ice, or eat it right away. If you are shucking for uses other than to eat on the shell, dump the juice and oyster in a mixing bowl until you have what the recipe calls for. Be sure to strain the juice before using it.

You can eat raw oysters with a sauce, or just squeeze lemon juice on top of them. They are the best oysters in the world.

Oysters Bienville

This dish is in honor of Jean Baptiste LeMoyne le Sieur de Bienville. He was the explorer, preserver, and often governor of colonial Louisiana.

12 **fresh oysters in the shell** **Rock salt**	¼ **cup finely chopped fresh** **shrimp**
2 **tablespoons (¼ stick)** **margarine or butter**	**Salt to taste**
1 **tablespoon finely chopped** **onion**	**Louisiana hot sauce or** **ground cayenne pepper** **to taste**
1 **tablespoon finely chopped** **fresh parsley**	1 **tablespoon all-purpose flour**
1 **teaspoon minced garlic**	1 **cup Fish Stock (see page 37)** **or milk**
¼ **cup finely chopped** **mushrooms**	

Open the oysters (see page 119). If they are very clean, leave them on the shell. If you must, put the oysters in a separate container so you can make sure that no bits of shell remain on them. Rinse the shells and brush them clean if necessary.

Pour 1 inch of rock salt into the bottom of three 6-inch-square oven-proof dishes (we often use small cast-iron skillets). Place these in the oven while it preheats to 400°F.

Over medium-high heat in a medium-sized saucepan, melt 1 tablespoon of the margarine. Stir in the onions and parsley, and sauté until the onions are clear. Add the garlic and mushrooms, stir, and continue cooking. Add the shrimp, mix well, and season. Turn the heat to low and let cook while preparing the sauce. In a separate small saucepan, melt the remaining tablespoon of margarine over medium heat. Stir in the flour and heat, stirring constantly, until it reaches an ivory color. Slowly whisk in the stock and continue cooking until slightly thickened. Add the sauce to the shrimp mixture and blend well. Remove the heated dishes from the oven and place the oyster shells level on the salt. Place one large oyster or several small ones on top of the shell, then cover with 1 tablespoon of the shrimp sauce and bake for 5 to 10 minutes.

YIELD: *12 oysters on the half shell*

Bar-b-qued Oysters

This makes a wonderful po-boy or is delicious as a main dish with salads and french fries. Shrimp, fish, or scallops can be substituted for the oysters.

1 **quart oil**	1 **teaspoon ground cayenne**
2 **dozen shucked and drained**	**pepper**
oysters	1 **teaspoon onion powder**
½ **teaspoon liquid smoke**	1 **teaspoon garlic powder**
¼ **cup chili powder**	**Salt to taste**
½ **cup all-purpose flour**	1 **teaspoon hickory-smoked**
	salt

Preheat the oil in a large deep fry pot to 350°F. Place the oysters in a small mixing bowl, add the liquid smoke, and let them soak about 10 minutes. Sift together the chili powder, flour, pepper, onion powder, garlic powder, salt, and hickory salt into a small bowl or a small paper bag. Add the oysters and shake to coat well. Deep fry for 3 to 4 minutes or until brown. Drain on paper towels.

YIELD: *2 to 4 servings*

Oysters Étouffée

½ cup olive oil or other
  shortening
4 cups chopped onion
1 cup chopped fresh parsley
1 cup chopped bell pepper
½ cup chopped celery
2 pints shucked oysters, with 1
  cup of the liquor strained
  and reserved

1 teaspoon minced garlic
1 teaspoon Worcestershire
  sauce
2 tablespoons lemon juice
Louisiana hot sauce or
  ground cayenne pepper
  to taste
Salt to taste

Heat the oil in a large skillet over medium heat, and sauté the onions, parsley, bell pepper, and celery until the onions are clear. Add the oyster liquor, garlic, and Worcestershire, and bring to a boil. Reduce the heat to low, add the oysters, lemon juice, hot sauce, and salt, and cook very slowly for 1 hour. Do not allow the mixture to boil after the oysters have been added. Serve over cooked rice.

YIELD: *4 to 6 servings*

Oyster Pie

1 pint small shucked oysters,
  1 cup of the liquor
  strained and reserved
2 tablespoons oil or butter
¼ cup all-purpose flour
1½ cups chopped onion
½ cup chopped fresh parsley
¼ cup chopped celery
1 cup warm milk or cream

1 cup smoked sausage or
  ham, chopped in ½-inch
  pieces
Salt to taste
Louisiana hot sauce or
  ground cayenne pepper
  to taste
1 pie shell and top or
  purchased pie shell

Preheat the oven to 375°F. If the oysters are large, chop them into pieces. In a saucepan over medium heat, warm the oil, then add the flour to make a small roux (see page 56). Stir until the roux has turned a light brown color. Add the onions and stir, add the parsley and celery, and mix well. Cook, stirring occasionally, until the onions are clear. Add the reserved oyster juice gradually, and stir to mix in with the roux to form a thick paste. Then add the milk while stirring. When the mixture begins to thicken, add the sausage and oysters, season, and continue to cook, stirring constantly, until the mixture is thick. Pour into the pie shell, cover with the top crust, and cut 4 small slices in the top. Bake for 45 to 50 minutes.

Y I E L D : *1 pie serves 6*

Oyster Loaf

This is a favorite on a whole loaf of New Orleans bread.

1 quart oil	**1 large loaf of French bread,**
½ cup corn flour	**sliced lengthwise**
½ cup all-purpose flour	**Tartar sauce to taste**
2 teaspoons salt or to taste	**Catsup to taste**
¼ teaspoon garlic powder	**½ head shredded lettuce**
½ teaspoon onion powder	**Lots of sliced dill pickles**
½ teaspoon ground cayenne	**2 large tomatoes, sliced**
pepper	**1 lemon, quartered**
1 pint shucked oysters,	**Louisiana hot sauce to taste**
drained	

Pour the oil into a deep fry pot and heat to 350°F. Mix together the corn flour, flour, salt, garlic powder, onion powder, and pepper in a small flat pan. Dredge the oysters well in the flour mixture and lower them into the oil, being careful not to burn yourself. Fry them in batches until they are golden brown and float. Drain them on paper towels. Make a trough in the bottom of the loaf of bread and toast both halves in the oven. Spread the bread with liberal amounts of tartar sauce and catsup, then arrange the lettuce, pickle slices, and tomato slices on the bottom. Place the fried oysters on top of the pickles, squeeze the lemon quarters over the oysters and apply Louisiana hot sauce, then cover with the top bread. This may be returned to the oven to heat the whole loaf or it may be cut crosswise and served immediately.

YIELD: *one loaf, enough to serve 4 to 6 people*

Shrimp à la Creole

2 tablespoons olive oil	1 tablespoon Worcestershire
2 cups chopped onion	sauce
¼ cup chopped bell pepper	1 cup tomato sauce
1 cup chopped fresh parsley	Salt to taste
½ cup dry white wine	½ teaspoon crushed dried mint
4 cups chopped fresh or	Ground cayenne pepper
canned tomatoes	or Louisiana hot sauce
1 tablespoon minced garlic	to taste
	2 pounds raw peeled shrimp

In a large, high-walled skillet, heat the oil over medium-high heat. Add the onions, bell pepper, and parsley, and sauté until the onions are clear. Stir in the wine, tomatoes, garlic, Worcestershire, tomato sauce, salt, mint, and pepper, then cover and cook over medium heat until the sauce comes to a boil. Reduce the heat to low, cover, and simmer for 1 hour until the tomatoes fall apart. Add the shrimp and continue simmering 30 minutes more, stirring occasionally. Serve over cooked rice or noodles, or use as an omelette filling.

YIELD: *6 to 8 servings*

Shrimp Patties

2 pounds uncooked shrimp,	½ cup minced onion
peeled and deveined	½ teaspoon garlic powder

½ teaspoon ground cayenne   1½ teaspoon salt
pepper   ¼ cup olive oil

Using a meat grinder or food processor, grind the shrimp till they look like ground meat. Wet your hands with water, and mix the ground shrimp, onions, garlic powder, pepper, and salt together in a medium-sized mixing bowl. Heat the oil in a large skillet over medium heat. Form the shrimp mixture into patties, then fry on each side until pinkish and opaque. You should be able to fry at least 3 patties at a time. You can eat this on a bun dressed like a burger or as an entrée.

YIELD: *eight 4-inch patties*

Shrimp Fettuccine

4 cups cooked fettuccine
2 tablespoons olive oil or
    butter
3 tablespoons flour
2 tablespoons minced onion
1 teaspoon minced garlic
2 tablespoons finely chopped
    fresh parsley
1 cup milk or cream

¼ cup grated Parmesan cheese
2 cups shrimp, peeled and
    deveined
Salt to taste
Louisiana hot sauce or
    ground cayenne pepper
    to taste

In a medium-sized frying pan, heat the oil over medium heat, then stir in the flour and make a medium dark roux (see page 56). Then stir in the onions, garlic, and parsley, and cook until the onions are clear. Gradually add the milk and continue cooking over medium heat until thickened. Add the cheese and stir until melted. Then stir in the shrimp, salt, and hot sauce. Cook just until the shrimp are pink and opaque, about 3 or 4 minutes; then stir in the fettuccine and mix well.

YIELD: *4 to 6 servings*

Shrimp Loaf

LOAF:

3 cups cooked rice
2 cups peeled and ground shrimp
½ cup finely chopped onion
¼ cup finely chopped fresh parsley
1 cup mild grated cheese
2 large eggs, beaten
1 cup dry white wine
1 tablespoon Worcestershire sauce
Salt to taste
Louisiana hot sauce or ground cayenne pepper to taste

SAUCE:

1 tablespoon margarine or butter
2 tablespoons flour
2 cups seafood stock or water, or 1 cup of each, mixed
1 cup tomato sauce
1 cup raw shrimp, peeled and deveined
Salt to taste
Louisiana hot sauce or ground cayenne pepper to taste

Preheat the oven to 350°F. In a large mixing bowl, combine all the ingredients for the loaf and mix well. Turn into a greased loaf pan and bake for 45 minutes.

In a small saucepan over medium heat, melt the margarine, then stir in the flour and cook, stirring constantly until it is an ivory color. Gradually stir in the stock and cook until the mixture thickens. Add the tomato sauce, shrimp, salt, and hot sauce, cover, and simmer over low heat until the loaf is done. To serve, turn the loaf upside down onto a platter and pour the sauce on top, then slice.

YIELD: *6 to 8 servings*

Shrimp Scampi

1 pound uncooked shrimp, peeled and deveined

¼ pound (1 stick) margarine or butter

¼ cup finely chopped fresh
   parsley
¼ cup finely chopped onion
1 tablespoon minced garlic
1 tablespoon lemon juice

Salt to taste
Louisiana hot sauce or
   ground cayenne pepper
   to taste

Over medium-high heat in a medium-sized frying pan, melt the margarine. Add the parsley and onions, and sauté until the onions are tender. Add the lemon juice and garlic, stir, and continue to sauté about another 5 minutes. Add the shrimp, salt, and hot sauce, and stir to mix well. Sauté until the shimp are opaque and turn pinkish, about 5 minutes; do not overcook.

YIELD: *2 to 4 servings*

Shrimp Jambalaya

This is the original jambalaya.

¼ cup oil
1 cup finely chopped onion
¼ cup finely chopped green
   onions
¼ cup finely chopped fresh
   parsley
2 tablespoons finely chopped
   bell pepper
One 8-ounce can tomato sauce
2 teaspoons finely chopped
   garlic

1 cup raw rice
2 cups water or stock
2 teaspoons Worcestershire
   sauce
Salt to taste
Louisiana hot sauce or
   ground cayenne pepper
   to taste
1 pound raw shrimp, peeled
   and deveined

In a medium-sized saucepan, heat the oil over medium-high heat. Sauté the onions, green onions, parsley, and bell pepper until the onions are clear. Stir in the tomato sauce and garlic, and continue cooking until the tomato sauce starts to boil. Stir in the rice and mix well, then add the water, Worcestershire, salt, hot sauce, and shrimp.

Continue cooking on medium high, stirring occasionally to prevent the rice from sticking. After all the water has disappeared from the top, turn the heat to low, cover tightly, and let steam undisturbed for at least 45 minutes. Stir to make sure that all the rice is well cooked. If it's not, cover again and let it cook until all the rice is tender, but not mushy.

YIELD: *4 servings*

Cajun-style Over-stuffed Peppers with Shrimp

8	large bell peppers	1½	teaspoons salt
¼	cup olive oil or bacon drippings	1	teaspoon ground cayenne pepper
1	cup finely chopped onion	1½	pounds shrimp, peeled, deveined, and coarsely chopped
½	cup finely chopped green onions		
¼	cup chopped pimento	2½	cups cooked rice
One	8-ounce can tomato sauce	8	bacon strips, cut in half
1	teaspoon minced garlic	1 to 2	cups stock
½	cup dry white wine		

Preheat the oven to 350°F. Slice the tops from the bell peppers, remove the seeds, rinse out, and drain. Heat the oil in a large saucepan and sauté the onions and green onions over medium heat until the onions are clear. Stir in the pimentos, tomato sauce, and garlic, then add the wine, salt, and pepper, and stir. Stir in the shrimp, and remove from the heat. Stir in the rice and make sure everything is mixed together well. Stuff each pepper full with the rice mixture and place them side by side in a shallow pan, one large enough to hold all the peppers. Cross the bacon strips over the top. Fill the pan half full with stock, and bake for 1 hour.

YIELD: *8 servings*

Shrimp Pilau

4 strips bacon, cut into small	**Salt to taste**
pieces	**Louisiana hot sauce or**
½ cup chopped onion	**ground cayenne pepper**
2 teaspoons minced garlic	**to taste**
1 cup raw rice	**1 pound raw shrimp, peeled**
2 cups stock or water	**and deveined**
1 cup minced tomatoes or	
tomato sauce	

In a medium-sized skillet over medium heat, cook the bacon until it is crisp. Remove the bacon and set it aside. To the bacon drippings add the onions, garlic, and rice. Stir and cook until the rice becomes golden brown and the onions are clear, about 15 minutes. Stirring, add the stock, tomatoes, salt, and hot sauce, and bring to a boil. Stir in the shrimp and bacon, reduce the heat to low, cover, and simmer for 30 to 40 minutes or until the rice is tender.

YIELD: *6 to 8 servings*

DEEP FRYING

Deep frying is very popular in Louisiana, and almost any seafood, including many fish species, soft-shelled crabs, shrimp, crawfish tails, soft-shelled crawfish, clams, oysters, scallops, squid, and others, can be successfully deep fried. Some things to remember when you deep fry:

You will need some oil in which to fry. The oil must be heated to at least 350°F to deep fry well, the general rule being to fry seafood between 350° and 375°F. I usually try to preheat the oil to about 15 degrees above the temperature at which I will fry. The oil temperature is then hot enough to fry the breading or batter nice and crispy without burning, while still allowing the inside to get done. I always use an accurate thermometer and try to keep the temperature as constant as possible. Unfortunately many home deep-frying appliances are not equipped with a thermostat sensitive enough to keep a constant temperature. Electric frypans are not well suited to deep frying. Gas heat does a better job because it responds quickly when you raise or lower the heat. Restaurant fryers have circulating filtering systems which do a better job with large amounts of food. The hotter an oil is heated and the longer it is heated, the more it tends to degrade. I use pure peanut oil for most of my deep frying. It has a great flavor, a fairly high smoke point, and it's pure. Corn oil and soy oil are also good if you like their flavors. Many of the commercial oils are a blend of many types of vegetable oil which may not be consistent in quality or may have less heat tolerance.

I do use oil more than once, but it does not last forever. I am careful to strain it and keep the air from it. I also label it and use only fish oil to fry fish again. The darker and thicker an oil gets, the less effective it is. Throw it out if it is the least bit rancid. Everyone has tasted seafood fried in oil that needed to be changed. Don't ruin good and sometimes expensive seafood with old oil.

When frying seafood you usually need some type of breading. I call this a dredge. Many different things are used for breading: all-purpose flour, corn flour, cornmeal, bread crumbs, cracker crumbs, crushed potato chips, or combinations of these. I add all sorts of spices to the breading mix to suit my taste: salt and ground cayenne pepper are standard, but other popular spices include smoked salt, garlic powder, onion powder, chili powder, or any finely ground herb or spice. I don't use black pepper at all, but that doesn't mean you shouldn't use it if you want to.

You'll need a liquid coating to make the dredge stick. I call this a drench. Beaten eggs mixed with milk or water or buttermilk are often used, but I mix my eggs with wine, beer, or stock and add spices to it. A lot of seafood is moist and the coating sticks well without using a drench. But be careful when you deep fry as excess moisture can cause popping and splattering of the grease.

To make a batter simply mix the dredge and the drench ingredients together to get the consistency of pancake batter. Then dip the pieces and put them immediately into the hot oil.

Seafood fried together should be of fairly uniform size. Fry small pieces of seafood in one batch and the large pieces in a different batch. Seafood is done when it is golden and floats easily in the oil. Use enough oil to allow free movement of the pieces when they're frying. Remove the pieces immediately and drain on paper towels or paper bags. Properly fried seafood is golden, light, and crispy on the outside, moist, hot, and tender on the inside. Food cooked in oil that is too hot will burn on the outside and be raw or gummy on the inside. Food cooked in oil that is not hot enough has a gummy, greasy outside and isn't fully cooked, either.

Whole Fried Fish

Use small fish such as catfish, lemonfish, or shark. If you use a fish with scales, you will have to remove the scales. The fish must be gutted and you can remove the head and fins if you prefer, but the tail and fins get wonderfully crunchy and delicious by deep frying. Some preparations call for both a drench and a dredge; some call for neither, and some for just a dredge. Fry until golden brown and crispy on the outside. When you eat whole fish be particularly careful of bones.

Fish Fillets, Fish Fingers, Fish Nuggets

I usually prepare all three of these with a drench and a spicy dredge, then deep fry at 365°F until done.

Fillets are the skinned side portions of the fish with no bones. A whole fillet takes several minutes to cook by deep frying and is often served with a rich sauce spooned over the top.

Fingers are fillets which have been sliced lengthwise about an inch thick. Fingers cook more evenly and faster than fillets. These are often served in restaurants with a tartar sauce.

Nuggets can be cubed fillets or the belly portion that is left after a fish is filleted. Nuggets are popular as finger food (see page 8.)

Soft-shelled Crabs

Soft shells are one of the things that I relish most about living in Louisiana. Because of recent advancements in aquaculture, we are lucky to be able to get these almost year-round, at a reasonable price. As is the case with any crustacean, blue crabs molt several times as they grow during their lives. Before molting a crustacean doesn't eat for several days. Consequently, a soft shell is very clean and 98 percent of the animal can be eaten. These crabs are very fragile, so handle them carefully.

2 quarts oil
1 large or 2 small soft-shells
   per person

DRENCH:
2 small eggs
1 cup milk or white wine
Louisiana hot sauce to taste

DREDGE:
1 cup corn flour
1 cup all-purpose flour
½ cup cracker crumbs
Salt to taste
Ground cayenne pepper
  to taste
Onion powder to taste
Garlic powder to taste

Preheat the oil to 365°F. To clean the crab place it on one hand with the top shell upward. Carefully lift the pointed sides of the top of the shell to expose the tubular lungs (called "dead man") which lie on the main body of meat. Brush them away and replace the upper shell. Repeat this action for the other side. Using shears or your thumb and fingers, cut or tear away the mouth and eyes.

In a small mixing bowl, beat the eggs, milk, and hot sauce together. Sift together the corn flour, flour, and cracker crumbs into another bowl, then season to taste. Carefully drench the crab in the egg mixture. Then place it in the dredge and cover each leg and the entire body completely with the dredge. Lift it out of the dredge and carefully lower it into the hot oil, legs hanging down. Fry several minutes until the crab comes to the surface and it turns a golden brown. Turn over while still in the oil so that the legs point upward. Using pinchers or a slotted spoon, remove it from the oil and drain on paper towels resting on its back. Serve immediately. The legs and swimmerets are crispy, the meat moist and delicious.

Shrimp

Shrimp can be deep fried peeled or unpeeled. If it is peeled the tail is often left on to act as a handle when it's eaten. Large shrimp are often butterflied, or split down the back, filled with a stuffing, coated with a breading or batter, and then deep fried. Use any drench or dredge you like. Fry in oil at 365°F until they float and turn golden brown, about 2 minutes, depending on the size of the shrimp.

Soft-shelled Crawfish

1 quart oil
1 to 2 dozen soft-shelled
   crawfish

DRENCH:
1 large egg
1 cup milk
1 cup all-purpose flour
½ teaspoon ground cayenne
   pepper
1 teaspoon salt

DREDGE:
2 cups all-purpose flour
½ cup seasoned bread crumbs
1 teaspoon salt or to taste
½ teaspoon ground cayenne
   pepper or to taste
½ teaspoon garlic powder

Preheat the oil to 350°F. To prepare the crawfish you will need a pair of kitchen shears or all-purpose scissors. Using the shears, cut through the face diagonally upward, just behind the eyes. Remove the pointed part of the head and gently squeeze. Two small calcium deposits called gastrolith stones should come right out.

In a mixing bowl, beat the egg and milk together, then gradually beat in the flour and seasonings and set aside. In a flat 9-by-9-inch baking pan, mix together the flour, bread crumbs, and seasonings well.

Carefully, one at a time, drench the crawfish in the egg mixture, then coat with the dredge well, being sure to dust each leg and the claws individually. Gently lower the crawfish into the hot oil and fry until golden brown or until the crawfish floats, about 2 minutes. Carefully remove from the oil, drain on paper towels, and serve immediately.

Cajun Popcorn

This is nothing in the world but fried crawfish tails.

1 quart oil
1 pound crawfish tails

DRENCH:
1 large egg
1 cup dry white wine
½ teaspoon garlic powder
½ teaspoon onion powder
Louisiana hot sauce to taste
Salt to taste

DREDGE:
½ cup all-purpose flour
½ cup corn flour
Salt to taste
Ground cayenne pepper
to taste

Preheat the oil to 365°F. In a small mixing bowl, beat together the egg, wine, and seasonings. Into a separate bowl sift the flours, pepper, and salt. Place the crawfish tails in the drench, then coat with the dredge. Fry for about a minute, until they float and turn golden brown. Take out, drain on paper towels, and serve immediately. This dish is often served during a game or as an appetizer before a meal comes.

Oysters

Fried oysters are not my favorite fried seafood, catfish is, but oysters, they are a mighty close second. (See page 121 for great bar-b-que–tasting fried oysters)

1 quart oil
2 dozen large Louisiana
   oysters, shucked and well
   drained

DRENCH:
1 large egg
1 cup buttermilk
   Louisiana hot sauce to taste
   Salt to taste

DREDGE:
1 cup corn flour
1 cup cornmeal
   Salt to taste
   Ground cayenne pepper
     to taste

Preheat the oil to 365°F. Beat together the egg and buttermilk in a small bowl, then add the seasonings. In a separate bowl, mix the flour, meal, salt, and pepper. Pass the oysters through the drench and coat well with the dredge. Fry in batches until they float and turn golden brown, about 2 minutes, depending on the size of the oyster. Take out, drain on paper towels, and serve immediately.

Boiling Seafood

10 small or 5 large onions, cut
   in half
5 lemons, cut in half
1 head garlic, separated into
   cloves, or to taste
1 pound salt or more to taste
   (nearly a brine)

1 cup ground cayenne pepper
   or more to taste
1 package crab boil bouquet
   garni (optional)
25 pounds seafood, such as live
   crawfish, crabs, or fresh
   shrimp

In Louisiana seafood is usually boiled outside in large quantities. A large gas burner and a garden hose with a spray nozzle are essential equipment. First, clean the seafood well by spraying it with clean water. Live seafood can pinch you with its claws, so wear gloves if you will be handling them, though washing live seafood without gloves is a good way to test your reflexes. Often seafood is caught in dirty water, so rinse it several times in clean water to remove mud or plant pieces.

It is a good idea to keep seafood under refrigeration or on ice until it is ready to be cooked. Remove any dead crawfish or crabs. If it is limp and doesn't move, it's dead, but some crawfish play "possum" or play dead. To be sure it's not dead, turn it on its belly and blow. If the legs move it's all right.

You will need a 10-gallon (40-quart) high-walled pot with a lid and a basket. Fill the pot half full with water. Add the onions, lemons, garlic, salt, pepper, and crab boil, cover, and bring to a rolling boil. This mixture of spices needs to be very strong and quite salty. You are going to have to experiment with the amounts to find out what suits your own taste. Let this boil for at least 10 minutes to make sure all the spices are well mixed. Stir occasionally with a large paddle or boat oar.

Add the seafood. Cold seafood will cause the water to stop boiling. Stir around and bring back to a boil. When the water begins to boil again, start timing. Boil 2 to 4 minutes for shrimp, 3 to 5 minutes for crawfish, and 8 to 10 minutes for crabs, a little longer for lobsters. The cooking times vary because the size of the seafood varies. If the shrimp are not uniform, the small ones will cook more quickly than the large ones. Do not overcook.

Turn the burner off and let the seafood soak to pick up the flavor of the seasonings. Test every few minutes, but generally the seafood should soak between 15 and 30 minutes. Crabs should be soaked the longest because their shells are the hardest. If the seafood floats, it can't absorb seasoning as well, so spray cold water on the top and sides of the soaking pot or throw some ice cubes on the top to make it sink.

After you are satisfied with the flavor of the seafood, lift the basket of seafood out of the pot and let it drain a few minutes. Spread several layers of newspaper on a table outside, pour out the seafood, and start eating.

The traditional boil contains all the seasonings and spices mentioned plus corn and potatoes. The corn and potatoes are put in just after the spiced water begins to boil for the first time. Many people eat the onions and garlic after they have been cooked. If smoked sausage or other things are added to the pot, care must be taken that they don't get too spicy. I've even heard of boiling a brisket in the water after all the seafood had been cooked. But don't mix seafood. You can use the spiced water several times in one day, though you may need to add more garlic, salt, onions, pepper, and crab boil. This method of boiling seafood is practiced all over southern Louisiana. There is no better way to spend an afternoon than with a heaping table of freshly boiled seafood, lots of cold beer, and good friends.

Seafood au Gratin

¼ cup olive oil or butter
½ cup all-purpose flour
1 cup chopped onion
½ cup chopped fresh parsley
½ cup chopped green onions
1 cup chopped mushrooms
1 tablespoon minced garlic
2 cups stock or milk or some
  of each
1 tablespoon Worcestershire
  sauce
1 pound crabmeat, picked
  clean of shells

1 pound fish, cut into 1-inch
  pieces
1 pound shrimp, peeled and
  deveined, or 3 pounds
  total of any other seafood
  or fish available
1 cup grated cheddar cheese
1 cup grated mozzarella
  cheese
Salt to taste
Louisiana hot sauce or
  ground cayenne pepper
  to taste
2 tablespoons lemon juice

Preheat the oven to 350°F. In a large saucepan over medium heat, heat the oil, then add the flour and make a light brown roux (see page 56). Add the onions, parsley, and green onions, and sauté until the onions are clear. Stir in the mushrooms and garlic, and cook 10 minutes more. Slowly stir in the stock and Worcestershire. Continue to stir until the mixture begins to thicken, then gradually stir in the seafood, cheeses, salt, and hot sauce. Turn into a large, greased casserole dish, cover, and bake at least 1 hour. Remove the cover, pour the lemon juice over the top, and bake about 20 minutes more, so that the top gets brown and crusty.

YIELD: *8 to 12 servings*

Seafood Casserole

2 large eggplants, peeled and
cut into 1-inch cubes
Water, enough to cover
2 tablespoons olive oil or
bacon drippings
1 cup chopped onion
½ cup chopped fresh parsley
½ cup chopped green onions
2 pounds seafood, any
combination of crab,
shrimp, or cubed fish

1 teaspoon chopped garlic
3 large eggs
1 tablespoon soy sauce
Salt to taste
Louisiana hot sauce or
ground cayenne pepper
to taste
Olive oil, to grease casserole
dish

Preheat the oven to 350°F. Over medium-high heat in a large saucepan,
parboil the eggplants until soft, then drain and set aside. Heat the oil
in the same saucepan over medium heat, then sauté the onions, parsley, and green onions until the onions are clear. Add the seafood and
garlic, cover, and continue cooking for 10 minutes, stirring frequently.
In a large mixing bowl, beat the eggs, then mix in the soy sauce, salt,
and hot sauce. Mix in the seafood with the eggplant and turn into a
large, greased casserole dish and bake for 1 hour.

YIELD *6 to 8 servings*

CHAPTER 8

Meat

In Louisiana one is never far away from farm animals. In the shadow of the Crescent City Connection, the mammoth elevated bridge that spans the Mississippi River in the heart of New Orleans, you will find hog pens. Cattle grazing is carried on within fifteen minutes of the business district. Pork is the meat of choice, and many people still raise and slaughter their own hogs, reminiscent of the days when members of a community butchered a hog and divided the meat in *la boucherie*. The work of slaughtering, curing, smoking, and rendering was divided, too, in this chore-turned-social-event. Cajuns assert that they utilize all of the hog except the squeal. La Boucherie has turned into a festival, along with festivals celebrating cracklings, andouille, and the animal as a whole, the Swine Festival. Many festivals and home parties feature a whole roasted suckling pig, or *cochon de lait,* as a menu centerpiece. Large and small hogs are slow-cooked for hours. The tending of the fire goes to a responsible person who selects a group of helpers and spends the entire night drinking, telling stories, feeding the fire, repositioning the hog, and generally feeling very fortunate to be alive and living in Louisiana.

Besides pork, cattle raising has long been an important occupation. The vast prairies of southwestern Louisiana were used to graze longhorn cattle beginning during the Spanish colonial period. Selective breeding of Brahmin cattle, which tolerate the semitropical climate, with high-meat stock, such as Angus and Hereford, makes Louisiana a major beef-producing state.

The different ethnic backgrounds of many Louisianans gives them an appreciation for organ meats, veal, and lamb. Justin tells about a friend who raised sheep:

> I got to tole you 'bout a frien' wid me who live in Springfield, he got a big schicken farm. He also, too, got hogs, sheeps, an' cattle. An' he got one ol' sheep dat had twin lambs. She didn't want to have not'ing to do wit 'one of dem, but she raise de odder one.
>
> So ma frien's two cute li'l daughters took dat li'l lamb to de house an' fed it on de bottle. Dey also had two lickin' pot houn's dat dey was raisin' an' befo' too long, dat li'l lamb t'ought he was a dog. He would eat wit' dem dogs an' sleep wit' dem. W'en dey chase auromobiles, he would too. He would even go hontin' wit' dem dogs. Well, I got a kick out o' watchin' dat lamb, I really did. Avery time I wen' over dair, I would mos' kill ma' se'f laughin' 'bout dat lamb.
>
> One day I was dair an' I didn't see de lamb an' I ax, "Where dat lamb is, hanh?" He say, "Oh, I had to kill it." "W'atever fo'?" He look at me an' shake his head. "It start killin' sheep."

Twice-smoked Ham

One 10- to 15-pound smoked ham	2 cloves garlic, peeled 1 tablespoon liquid smoke 1 teaspoon crushed dried mint
WATER PAN: 1 cup dry white wine 1 onion, peeled and quartered	¼ cup chopped fresh parsley ½ cup chopped green onions Water

Soak some aromatic wood (pecan, hickory, mesquite, etc.) in water to have it ready to put on the hot coals; you can do that 2 or 3 hours before even lighting the coals. Following the manufacturer's instructions, light the coals and let them heat while you prepare the ham. One 10-pound bag of charcoal briquets is enough to make this recipe. Prepare the water pan by putting in all the ingredients listed and filling it about one quarter full with water. The coals should be getting white around the edges. Place the presoaked smoking wood onto the heated coals. Lower the water pan into place and fill with water to about 1 inch from the top. Place the ham on the rack. Cover and smoke overnight, or put this to smoke in the morning and serve it for dinner. I usually don't even check this after it's on. This is the easiest way to make tasty food for a gathering. After the ham has been removed, lift the water pan away from the heat. This juice with spices can be used as the base for the tastiest gravies, sauces, and soups.

Pork Tenderloin with Stewed Figs

Figs are ripe for only a week or two in midsummer. The fresh stewed ones are the best in this recipe. They grow near the old outhouse.

One 5-pound pork tenderloin	**1 cup chopped mushrooms**
Salt to taste	**2 cups Stewed Fig Sauce (see**
Ground cayenne pepper	**page 66) or 1 cup fig**
to taste	**preserves**
1 cup chopped onion	**½ cup dry white wine**
1 teaspoon minced garlic	

Preheat the oven to 325°F. Sprinkle salt and pepper over the pork loin, then place it in the middle of a flat baking dish. Sprinkle the onions, garlic, and mushrooms around the meat. Spread the stewed figs over the top of the meat until it's completely covered; if you have any left over, put them around the meat. Pour the wine around the meat, cover, and bake until done, about 2 to 3 hours.

Y I E L D : *8 to 10 servings*

Stuffed Pork Chops

1 pound ground pork
1 tablespoon minced garlic
½ cup finely chopped onion
½ teaspoon salt or to taste
1 teaspoon ground cayenne
    pepper or to taste

½ teaspoon finely crushed
    dried mint
Other spices of your liking
1 cup plain bread crumbs
6 pork chops, 1 inch thick,
    with a pocket sliced in the
    middle

Preheat the oven to 350°F. Mix all the ingredients together, except the pork chops, in a bowl. Sprinkle salt and pepper on the outside of each pork chop, then stuff the pocket of each with the meat dressing, and place in a greased baking dish. Bake for 1 to 1½ hours.

Y I E L D : *6 servings*

Strawberry Baked Ham

If you can get homemade strawberry wine, it will make this dish much better. It is also a good idea to sample the wine.

½ cup fresh halved
    strawberries
One 5- to 8-pound smoked ham

1 cup strawberry wine
1 cup water
1 tablespoon creole mustard

Preheat the oven to 350°F. Place the ham in a large roaster and arrange the strawberries on top. Mix the wine, water, and creole mustard together, then pour over the top of the ham, and let it drip down the sides. Bake for 1 hour, basting every 20 minutes. After the ham is baked, slice and serve topped with a Strawberry Sauce (see page 67).

Y I E L D : *This is for a special occasion or holiday.*

• ❧ •

🌶 Pork is the favorite meat in Louisiana and can be prepared many ways.

🌶 Okra à la Creole is a favorite summertime dish.

I get hungry just lookin' at these crabs. Here we have crab salad, marinated claws, and boiled blue crab.

More ways to use peppers.

Opposite: Corn, you can cook it and eat it, or cook it and drink it.

🦢 This is Black Lake—the water is deep and dark. Very few tourists ever see the many beautiful places like this.

🦢 Alligators used to be an endangered species. Now they are controlled by hunting seasons each fall. There are also more and more farms that produce hides and meat.

🦢 *Opposite:* Thank goodness that winter doesn't last long. I miss the green.

I love to eat fresh, raw oysters and you can't get any fresher than these that my good friend and seafood connection, Wayne Levi, is opening right now for me.

Mary and Larry Larrieu bake the best breads. I drive 30 miles to get their breads and pastries.

Baked and Broiled Pork Chops

6 pork chops	1 tablespoon soy sauce
Salt to taste	½ teaspoon garlic powder
Ground cayenne pepper	1 teaspoon onion powder
to taste	1 cup dry white wine

Preheat the oven to 350°F. Salt and pepper the pork chops on both sides. Place the chops in a shallow baking pan and bake in the oven for 10 minutes. While the pork chops are baking, mix together the soy sauce, garlic powder, onion powder, and wine. Turn the oven to broil and continue cooking. After about 5 minutes, pour half of the sauce over the chops and continue broiling another 5 minutes. Turn the chops over, pour the remaining sauce over them, and broil until done.

YIELD: *4 to 6 servings*

Baked Pork Roast

One 8- or 10-pound center cut	1 teaspoon finely crushed
pork loin roast	dried mint
4 large cloves garlic	1 cup water or stock
Salt to taste	1 cup dry white wine
Ground cayenne pepper	½ cup finely chopped green
to taste	onion tops

Preheat the oven to 350°F. Using a sharp knife, pierce 4 deep holes in the pork and stuff with the garlic. Season the roast with the salt and pepper, and sprinkle with the dried mint and pat it into the meat. Place the roast in a roasting pan with a rack. Mix the water and wine together and pour around the roast. Cover and bake until almost done, about 2 hours, basting occasionally. Sprinkle the green onions all over the top, and cook uncovered until brown.

YIELD: *10 to 12 servings*

Pork Jambalaya

A jambalaya is a meal that we like cooking outside as well as inside. When we cook it outside, it's usually done in a forty-quart pot. All the family and friends come over, and we pass a good time. This is a popular dish served at all social gatherings in southern Louisiana.

2 tablespoons oil

1½ pounds pork, cut into 1-inch cubes

1 cup chopped onion

½ cup chopped green onions

2 tablespoons chopped fresh parsley

¼ cup finely chopped bell pepper

½ cup dry white wine

½ teaspoon crushed dried mint

1 teaspoon finely chopped garlic

1½ cups raw rice

Salt to taste

Louisiana hot sauce or ground cayenne pepper to taste

Stock or water

Over medium-high heat in a large saucepan, heat the oil, brown off the pork, then remove from the pot. Add the onions, green onions, parsley, and bell pepper, and cook until the onions are brown. Stirring, add the wine, mint, garlic, rice, meat, salt, hot sauce, and enough water to cover the rice by ½ inch. Continue cooking on medium-high heat, stirring occasionally. Bring the stock to a boil and let boil until it has disappeared from the top, stir again, then lower heat. Cover the pot and simmer for at least 1 hour before lifting the lid. Then check the rice for doneness, stir, cover, and let steam another 15 to 20 minutes.

YIELD: *6 to 8 servings*

Backbones and Turnips

Pork backbone is a country-cut pork chop.

1 cup bacon drippings or oil	1 tablespoon Worcestershire sauce
½ cup all-purpose flour	
1½ cups chopped onion	½ cup dry white wine
½ cup chopped green onions	6 cups peeled and cubed turnips
½ cup chopped bell pepper	
¼ cup chopped fresh parsley	Louisiana hot sauce or ground cayenne pepper to taste
2 pounds pork backbones	
3 cups stock or water	
1 teaspoon chopped garlic	Salt to taste
¼ teaspoon crushed dried mint	

Over medium heat in a large, heavy saucepan, heat ½ cup of the drippings, stir in the flour, and make a dark roux (see page 55). Add the onions, green onions, bell pepper, and parsley, reduce the heat to low, cover, and cook until the onions are clear, stirring occasionally. In a large skillet, heat the remaining drippings and brown the backbones, then remove from the skillet and set aside. Add one cup of the stock to the roux and stir until a thick paste is formed. Add the garlic, mint, Worcestershire, and wine, and stir to mix in well. Add the backbones, turnips, hot sauce, and salt and remaining stock, and stir until the liquid has mixed in with the roux. Bring to a boil, then reduce the heat to low, cover, and simmer for 2 or 3 hours, depending on how long you can wait before you eat this delicious dish.

YIELD: *6 to 8 servings*

Stuffed Ham

This dish is a good meat dish at Easter or anytime you're tired of eating a turkey at Christmas.

One 5- to 6-pound cooked
    bone-in ham, trimmed
    and fat reserved

STUFFING:
2 large eggs
1 cup dry white wine
    Louisiana hot sauce or
    ground cayenne pepper
    to taste
1 tablespoon Worcestershire
    sauce

1 tablespoon prepared
    mustard
10 slices toasted bread, in
    chunks
¼ cup chopped celery
1 cup chopped onion
1 teaspoon minced garlic
1 tablespoon brown sugar
¼ cup chopped fresh parsley
1 teaspoon dried mint

When you buy the ham, ask the butcher to remove the bone and give it to you for use in flavoring vegetables. There will be a large cavity in the middle of the ham which you will be able to stuff.

Preheat the oven to 300°F. Beat the eggs in a large mixing bowl, add the wine, hot sauce, Worcestershire, and mustard, and beat again. Add the bread and mix well, then add the remaining ingredients and mix again. Stuff this into the cavity of the ham. You can lace the end with skewers and string or push a piece of skin over the opening. Bake for 2 hours.

YIELD: *one ham*

Sausage Jambalaya

My guests from out of state like this jambalaya.

2 tablespoons olive oil
1½ cups chopped onion

½ cup chopped green onions
½ cup chopped bell pepper

¼ cup chopped fresh parsley
1 cup tomato sauce
1 teaspoon minced garlic
¼ teaspoon crushed dried
  mint
1 cup dry white wine
1½ cups uncooked long grain
  rice

Salt to taste
Louisiana hot sauce or
  ground cayenne pepper
  to taste
1 pound smoked sausage or
  andouille, sliced thick

In a large, high-walled skillet, heat the oil over medium-high heat and sauté the onions, green onions, bell pepper, and parsley until the onions are clear. Stirring, add the tomato sauce, garlic, mint, and wine, then the rice, salt, and hot sauce, smoked sausage, and enough water to cover the rice by about 1 inch. Cook until most of the juice is gone. Reduce the heat to low, cover, and simmer for 1 hour; don't lift the lid until this has been cooking at least 45 minutes. This makes a red jambalaya.

YIELD: *4 to 6 servings*

Grillades

Grillades are the lean of the sow's belly. When a hog is slaughtered, there will be pieces of meat running through the thick, fatty belly section. In order to make cracklings, or to render lard, these thin strips of lean meat must be carefully removed. Put these thin strips in a greased skillet and brown slowly. Add salt and cayenne pepper to taste. Grillades are often served with grits for any meal.

Maque Chou with Pork

When I made this dish in New York one time, I asked the butcher in the store to give me some jambalaya pork. He didn't know what I was talking about. The meatcutters in southern Louisiana know what I mean, though.

½ cup oil
1 cup chopped onion
½ cup chopped bell pepper
1 cup chopped fresh parsley
3 cups fresh or canned whole
   kernel corn
1 tablespoon finely chopped
   garlic
1 cup dry white wine

1 cup water
Louisiana hot sauce or
   ground cayenne pepper
   to taste
Salt to taste
1 tablespoon soy sauce
2 pounds pork, cut into 1-inch
   cubes

Over medium heat in a large skillet, heat the oil and then sauté the onions, bell pepper, and parsley until the onions are clear. Add the corn and stir, then the garlic, wine, water, and seasonings, and stir again. Reduce the heat to low, cover, and simmer for 30 minutes, then add the pork, recover, and let simmer another hour, stirring occasionally.

YIELD: *6 to 8 servings*

Homemade Pork Sausage

One 5-pound Boston butt or
   meat scraps when you
   butcher hogs
3 cups finely chopped onion
1½ cups finely chopped green
   onions

2 tablespoons minced garlic
Salt to taste
Ground cayenne pepper
   to taste
1 tablespoon dried mint or
   other seasonings to taste

Using a meat grinder, finely grind together the meat and the fat into a large bowl. Mix in the onions, green onions, garlic, salt, pepper, mint, and any other seasonings you would like to use. Using the mixing spoons Mother Nature gave you, your hands, mix all the ingredients together. I usually fry a patty to test for seasonings and because by that time I'm hungry. Then pass the mixture through the meat grinder again to mix very well. You can freeze this in patties with waxed paper in between or stuff into casings. Fry in a skillet when you are ready to serve.

YIELD: *about 5 pounds of sausage*

White Pork Boudin

This is a delicious entrée or appetizer. Boudin is an old Cajun preparation, and every old Cajun has his own recipe. There is also a boudin made from blood called boudin rouge. It is made at the boucherie along with hogshead cheese, grillades, cracklings, and pickled pork.

3 tablespoons olive or peanut oil	1 tablespoon finely chopped garlic
½ cup finely chopped onion	3 cups cooked rice
½ cup finely chopped green onions	5 cups chopped cooked pork (leftovers will work)
½ cup finely chopped fresh parsley	Ground cayenne pepper to taste
1½ cups water	Salt to taste
	Natural casings

Over medium heat in a large saucepan, heat the oil and sauté the onions and green onions until clear. Add the parsley, water, and garlic, and cook another 10 minutes, stirring occasionally. Add the rice and blend well, mix in the chopped pork, and season with the pepper and salt. With a sausage stuffer, stuff the pork mixture into natural pork casings and tie in 4- to 5-inch links. To serve, heat the links in a pan, with a little water, after pricking a few holes in the casing to keep it from bursting.

YIELD: *about 3 pounds*

VARIATION: *Boudin Balls*: Follow the directions for boudin, but do not stuff into a casing. Form the ground boudin into balls about 2 inches in diameter. Deep fry in oil at 350°F for about 2 minutes. Drain and serve immediately.

Ham and Lamb Loaf

2 teaspoons oil or margarine	2 large eggs
1 cup chopped onion	2 tablespoons catsup
2 cups cooked and ground ham	2 teaspoons Worcestershire sauce
2 cups ground lamb	1 tablespoon prepared mustard
1 tablespoon dried parsley	Salt to taste
½ cup plain bread crumbs	Louisiana hot sauce or ground cayenne pepper
½ cup chopped green olives with pimentos	

Preheat the oven to 350°F. Heat the oil in a medium-sized skillet over medium-high heat, and sauté the onions until almost brown. Put the ham and lamb in a large mixing bowl, then mix in the onions, parsley, bread crumbs, and olives. In a small mixing bowl, beat the eggs, then beat in the catsup, Worcestershire, mustard, salt, and hot sauce. Add this mixture to the ham and lamb. Combine well and turn into a well-greased loaf pan and bake for 1 hour. Refrigerate, then slice and serve cold as a luncheon loaf or on a sandwich.

YIELD: *4 to 6 servings*

Rack of Lamb with Fresh Peaches

2 cups stock or water	Ground cayenne pepper to taste
¼ cup all-purpose flour	One 3- to 4-pound rack of lamb with the bone cut through
2 cups peach wine	
1 tablespoon Worcestershire sauce	
1 cup chopped fresh parsley	6 fresh peaches, peeled, pitted, and halved
1 cup chopped green onions	
Salt to taste	

Preheat the oven to 350°F. Over medium heat, pour 1 cup of the stock into a medium-sized saucepan, stir in the flour, and mix well; stirring, cook until thickened. Stir the wine and Worcestershire into the saucepan, then add the parsley and green onions, reduce the heat to low, and simmer for 20 minutes, stirring occasionally. Sprinkle salt and pepper over the rack of lamb and place it in a baking dish with a cover. Pour the thickened flour mixture around the meat and place the peaches on top of the meat. Bake, covered, for 30 minutes, baste, then bake for another 45 minutes or until desired doneness is reached. Slice and serve with the gravy over cooked rice.

YIELD: *6 to 8 servings*

Darn Good Leg of Lamb

One **5-pound leg of lamb**
1 **cup white crème de menthe**
Salt to taste
Ground cayenne pepper to taste
3 **tablespoons crushed dried mint**

¼ **cup olive oil**
2 **tablespoons Worcestershire sauce**
3 **cups dry white wine**
½ **cup Dijon mustard**
2 **cups chopped onion**

Preheat the oven to 350°F. Pat the leg of lamb dry. Massage the crème de menthe into the flesh and place it in a roaster. Sprinkle the top with salt, pepper, and mint. In a small mixing bowl, beat together the olive oil, Worcestershire, wine, and mustard. Pour the sauce into the bottom of the roaster around the meat. Spread the onions over the top, cover, and bake for 2 hours, basting occasionally, until done. Remove the lid and bake another 15 to 30 minutes to brown meat.

YIELD: *4 to 8 servings*

Beef Ribeye Stuffed with Pecans

You will be surprised at how delicious this dish is.

Olive oil
One 10-pound beef ribeye
    or tenderloin
Salt to taste
Ground cayenne pepper
    to taste

2 cups pecan pieces or
    halves
1½ cups dry white wine
1 tablespoon Worcestershire
    sauce
1 cup chopped onion

Preheat the oven to 350°F. Pour enough olive oil into a deep roaster to coat the bottom. Cut a deep pocket on the side of the tenderloin, and season with the salt and pepper, including the inside of the pocket. Stuff the pecans into the pocket and close with skewers. Place the loin in the middle of the roaster, so that the pocket is on the side, not on top. Mix the wine and Worcestershire together and pour around the meat. Sprinkle the onions around the meat, cover, and bake for 2 to 3 hours, depending on how well done you like your beef. Baste every 20 minutes.

YIELD: *10 to 15 servings*

Boiled Beef Ribs

Water
6 to 8 pounds beef ribs
Louisiana hot sauce to taste
1 teaspoon dill seed
1 tablespoon garlic powder
2 tablespoons onion powder

2 tablespoons salt
½ cup dried parsley
1 teaspoon crushed dried mint
1 cup dry white wine
2 tablespoons Worcestershire
    sauce

Pour enough water to cover the ribs in a large pot, and add all the seasonings, wine, and Worcestershire. Cover, bring to a boil over medium-high heat, and let boil for 20 minutes. Add the ribs, and bring the water back to a boil. Reduce the heat to low, cover, and let cook for 1 hour. After the ribs are tender, when the meat starts coming away from the bone, turn off the heat and let the ribs soak in the stock for 1 hour. Serve with Mustard Sauce (see page 58) or horseradish.

After you remove the ribs from the stock, it can be used to cook many of the other recipes that call for beef stock. As a matter of fact, Cabbage Cooked in Stock (see page 183) is an excellent recipe to serve along with your boiled ribs.

YIELD: *6 to 10 servings*

Smoked Beef and Pork Roasts in a Water Smoker

This dish is to be prepared the night before serving, because it can cook while you are sleeping and dreaming of eating it. This is a great special occasion preparation for all your friends and families.

One 10-pound beef roast
One 10-pound pork roast
    Salt to taste
    Ground cayenne pepper
        to taste
10 cloves garlic
10 fresh or pickled cayenne
        peppers
10 green onions

WATER PAN:
1 cup dry white wine
1 onion, peeled and
        quartered
2 cloves garlic
1 tablespoon liquid smoke
1 teaspoon crushed dried
        mint
¼ cup chopped fresh parsley
½ cup chopped green onions
3 tablespoons Worcestershire
        sauce
    Water

Soak some aromatic wood (pecan, hickory, cherry, etc.) in water to have it ready; you can do that 2 or 3 hours before lighting the coals. Following the manufacturer's instructions, light the coals in the smoker, and let them heat while you prepare the rest of the dish. One

10-pound bag of charcoal briquets is usually what I use to smoke this much meat.

With a sharp knife, make five deep punctures in each roast; into each hole, push a clove of garlic, pepper, and a green onion. If the green onion is too long, just cut it off at the surface and throw it into the water pan. Thoroughly salt and pepper the outsides of both roasts. Prepare the water pan by putting in all the ingredients listed and filling it about one quarter full with water. The coals should be ready. Place the presoaked smoking wood on the heated coals. Lower the water pan into place and fill to about ½ inch from the top. Put the middle part of the smoker in place, and position the beef roast on the bottom rack, the pork roast on the upper rack. Cover and smoke overnight, or put this to smoke in the morning and serve it for dinner. I usually don't even check it after it's on. This is the easiest way to make tasty food for a gathering. Save the juice in the water pan to make a gravy.

Oven-baked Rump Roast

One	10-pound beef rump roast	3	tablespoons olive oil
6	small green onions	2	cups dry red wine
6	cloves garlic	1	cup stock or water
6	hot peppers	1	cup coarsely chopped
	Salt to taste		onion
	Ground cayenne pepper to taste		

Preheat the oven to 350°F. With a knife make 6 punctures in the roast and put one green onion, garlic clove, and hot pepper in each hole. Sprinkle salt and pepper over the roast. Pour the oil in a roaster pan and heat it on top of the stove over medium-high heat. Sear the meat on all sides. Pour in the wine and stock and sprinkle the chopped onions around the roast. Cover the roaster, place it in the oven, and bake for 2 hours or until desired doneness is reached. Baste occasionally.

YIELD: *8 to 10 servings, with some left for hash or sandwiches*

Spaghetti and Beef Short Ribs

3 to 4 pounds short ribs
2 cups chopped onion
2 teaspoons salt
½ teaspoon ground cayenne
　pepper
1½ cups dry white wine
1 teaspoon crushed dried
　mint

2 tablespoons soy sauce
2 cups stock
One 8-ounce package spaghetti,
　cooked and drained
　Grated Parmesan or
　Romano cheese

Over medium heat, coat a large Dutch oven with oil, and heat until very hot. Then add the ribs, fat side down, and cook until well browned, about 15 minutes. Add the onions to the pot around the meat, and cook until browned, stirring often. Stirring, add the salt, pepper, wine, mint, soy sauce, and stock. Cover, reduce the heat to low, and simmer for 1½ to 2 hours or until ribs are tender. Heap the spaghetti on a large serving platter. Ring the short ribs around the edges of the spaghetti, and ladle the onions and the meat gravy over the top of the spaghetti. Sprinkle the cheese on top. Serve hot with French bread to soak up the gravy.

YIELD: *4 to 8 servings*

Seven Steaks Étouffée

2 tablespoons bacon drippings
　or olive oil
2 pounds seven or round steak
1 cup chopped onion
1 cup chopped green onions
½ cup chopped bell pepper
½ cup chopped fresh parsley
12 ounces mushroom steak
　sauce or fresh chopped
　mushrooms

1 cup dry white wine
2 teaspoons chopped garlic
¼ cup chopped pimento
1 tablespoon Worcestershire
　sauce
¼ teaspoon bitters
　Salt
　Louisiana hot sauce or
　ground cayenne pepper
　to taste

Heat the drippings in a Dutch oven over medium heat, and brown the meat on both sides, then remove from the pot and set aside. In the drippings sauté the onions, green onions, bell pepper, and parsley until the onions are clear, stirring occasionally. Stirring, add the mushroom steak sauce and wine, then the garlic, and continue cooking another 10 minutes. Add the pimento, Worcestershire, and bitters, then the meat, salt, and hot sauce, and stir again. Cover and let cook on low for 2 to 3 hours. Serve over cooked rice.

Y I E L D : *4 to 6 servings*

Italian Meat Loaf

2 large eggs, beaten
¾ cup seasoned bread crumbs
1½ cups tomato juice
2 tablespoons chopped fresh parsley
½ teaspoon crushed dried mint
½ teaspoon dried oregano
Salt to taste
Louisiana hot sauce or ground cayenne pepper to taste
1 cup grated Parmesan cheese
2 teaspoons minced garlic
2 pounds lean ground beef

¼ pound ham, finely chopped
1 cup grated mozzarella cheese
½ cup finely chopped pickled Italian peppers
½ cup chopped black olives
½ cup chopped green olives
1 cup finely chopped onion
1 teaspoon garlic powder
1 teaspoon salt
½ teaspoon ground cayenne pepper
1 cup dry red wine
2 tablespoons olive oil

Preheat the oven to 350°F. In a large mixing bowl, combine and mix well the eggs, bread crumbs, ½ cup of the tomato juice, parsley, mint, oregano, salt, hot sauce, half of the Parmesan cheese, and the garlic. Then, using your hands, mix in the ground meat, add the chopped ham, and mix again. Turn the meat onto a piece of wax paper. Pat down to about 1 inch thick and into a 9-by-13-inch rectangle. In a separate mixing bowl, combine and mix well the mozzarella, pickled peppers, olives, and onions. Spread this mixture on top of the meat, leaving a 1-inch margin all around. Carefully lift up the paper and roll the meat up like a jelly roll. Then put the meat, seam side down, into a baking dish or pan. Mix the garlic powder, salt, pepper, wine, the remaining tomato juice, and olive oil together, and pour on top of and around the loaf. Place any leftover cheese mixture on the top. Sprinkle with the remaining Parmesan and bake for 1 to 1½ hours. Slice and serve with the tomato gravy over rice or pasta.

YIELD: *8 to 10 servings*

Harry D. Wilson's Hash

Now if you don't have any leftover meat, you can't make this dish, 'cause it won't be Harry D. Wilson's Hash if you don't have leftovers. I GARONTEE!!

½ **cup oil or shortening**	**Leftover meat of any kind,**
1 **cup all-purpose flour**	**cut into 1-inch cubes**
1 **cup chopped onion**	**(amount depends on**
½ **cup chopped green onions**	**what's left)**
¼ **cup chopped fresh parsley**	**Salt to taste**
6 **cups stock or water**	**Louisiana hot sauce or**
2 **teaspoons chopped garlic**	**ground cayenne pepper**
3 **medium-sized raw potatoes,**	**to taste**
peeled and cubed	

Over medium heat in a large, heavy, high-walled skillet, slightly heat the oil, add the flour, and make a dark roux (see page 56). Add the onions, green onions, and parsley, and cook until the onions are clear. Add one cup of the stock and stir until a thick paste is formed. Add the garlic and stir, then add the remaining stock and stir until the water is mixed in with the roux. Add the potatoes, meat, salt, and hot sauce. Cover, reduce the heat to low, and simmer until the potatoes are tender. Serve over cooked rice.

YIELD: *4 to 6 servings*

Natchitoches Meat Pies

This dish is named after the oldest settlement in the Louisiana Purchase, founded in 1714.

CRUST:
- 2 cups all-purpose flour
- 2 teaspoons salt
- 1 teaspoon baking powder
- ½ cup shortening
- 1 large egg, beaten
- 1 cup milk

FILLING:
- ½ pound ground beef
- ½ pound ground pork
- 1 cup chopped green onions
- 2 teaspoons minced garlic
- Ground cayenne pepper to taste
- Salt to taste
- 1 cup cooked butterbeans
- 1 tablespoon all-purpose flour
- 1 quart oil

In a large mixing bowl, sift together the flour, salt, and baking powder. Cut in the shortening until the flour forms tiny balls. Add the egg and mix well, then add the milk and mix well again. Refrigerate for 2 hours. In a large skillet over medium heat, brown the meats. Add the onions and garlic, and cook until the onions are clear. Stir in the salt, pepper, butterbeans, and flour, and heat through. Preheat the oven to 350°F. Turn the pastry onto a floured surface and roll out to about ¼ inch thick. Cut the pastry into 5-inch circles, place one heaping tablespoon of the filling in the lower half of the shell, wet the inside edges with a little water, fold over, and press together to seal. Deep fry until golden brown, about 3 minutes.

YIELD: *about 4 servings*

Justin's Holiday Meat Loaf with Sauce

- 4 pounds lean ground beef
- 1 pound lean ground pork
- 3 large eggs
- 1 teaspoon Worcestershire sauce
- Salt to taste

Louisiana hot sauce or
ground cayenne pepper
to taste
2 cups chopped onion
½ cup chopped bell pepper
1 cup chopped fresh parsley
2 tablespoons chopped garlic
1 teaspoon crushed dried mint
1 cup olives with pimentos

SAUCE:
2 cups tomato sauce
½ cup dry white wine
½ teaspoon liquid smoke
1 tablespoon Worcestershire
sauce

Preheat the oven to 350°F. Mix the beef and pork together in a large mixing bowl. In a small mixing bowl, beat the eggs together with the Worcestershire, salt, and hot sauce. Pour the egg mixture over the meat and mix in well. Add the onion, bell pepper, parsley, garlic, and mint, and mix into the meat well. Add the olives and gently mix in. Form the meat into a loaf and place it in a large roaster. Blend the tomato sauce, wine, Worcestershire, and liquid smoke in a mixing bowl. Pour the sauce over and around the meat loaf and bake for 2 hours, basting every 30 minutes. Slice and serve with the gravy on top.

YIELD: *10 to 14 servings*

Ilse's Rouladen

A wonderful lady named Ilse Ehlers from Germany prepared this for us. We have many German descendants in Louisiana, so it is a popular dish here.

8 pieces round steak, cut ¼
inch thick
Thinly sliced dill pickle
spears
1 cup minced onion
2 strips bacon, cut into 3-inch
pieces
4 strips bacon, cut in half
¼ tablespoon bacon drippings

2 tablespoons all-purpose flour
1 tablespoon prepared
mustard
2 cups stock or water
2 tablespoons Worcestershire
sauce
Salt to taste
Ground cayenne pepper
to taste

In order to slice the meat thinly, you may want to partially freeze it. Or use any other cut of meat and pound it between pieces of wax paper into thin rectangles about 6 by 8 inches. With the short side of one of the pieces of meat toward you, lay one pickle spear and spread 1 heaping tablespoon of onion and a piece of bacon about 1 inch from the end. Carefully roll the steak around the filling, folding the edges toward the center. They will make bundles about 4 inches long and 2 inches in diameter. Then wrap half a slice of bacon around the bundle and secure with toothpicks. Heat the bacon drippings in a Dutch oven, over medium heat, and brown the bundles. Remove them from the pot and set aside. Stir the flour into the hot drippings and make a brown roux (see page 56). Mix in the mustard, stock, Worcestershire, salt, and pepper. Return the bundles to the pot, turn the heat down to low, and cook, covered, for about 2 hours. Remove the toothpicks before serving. The gravy is especially delicious and can be served over rice, or potatoes, or just poured over the meat.

Y I E L D : *4 to 8 servings*

Curt's Fondue

Curt, my father-in-law, makes this fondue in an iron washpot that we sent him. We had to travel up to Montana to make sure he was fixing it right.

About 3 gallons oil or lard

1 pound pork, cut into ½-inch cubes

1 pound beef, cut into ½-inch cubes

1 pound lamb, cut into ½-inch cubes

1 pound chicken, cut into ½-inch cubes

A 36-by-⅜-inch pointed wooden skewer for each person

This is to be done outside at a picnic. Build a campfire and let it burn for several hours until the coals are very hot. Get some help in placing a large cast-iron washpot in the middle of the coals, making sure that it is stable. Add the oil and heat until a piece of white bread browns quickly when thrown in the oil. Each person places his own pieces of meat on the skewers and submerges them in the oil until they are cooked to his taste. The pieces of meat are done in 1 to 3 minutes. Be careful; the campfire is dangerous and the oil is hot.

YIELD: *4 to 6 servings*

Elementary Macaroni

2 pounds ground beef
2 cups chopped onion
1 cup chopped fresh parsley
½ cup chopped bell pepper
1 pound macaroni, cooked and drained
2 cups tomato sauce
½ cup red wine
1 tablespoon Worcestershire sauce
Salt to taste
½ teaspoon crushed dried mint
Louisiana hot sauce or ground cayenne pepper to taste
1 teaspoon garlic powder

Over medium heat in a high-walled skillet, brown the ground beef. Add the onions, parsley, and bell pepper, and cook until the onions are clear. Add the macaroni and blend well. Stirring, add the tomato sauce, wine, Worcestershire, salt, mint, hot sauce, and garlic powder. Reduce the heat to low, cover, and simmer for 30 minutes.

YIELD: *10 servings*

Pan-fried Liver

½ pound bacon strips	1 teaspoon garlic powder
1 cup cracker crumbs	1 to 2 pounds liver, sliced
1 cup all-purpose flour	½ inch thick
Salt to taste	2 large onions, sliced
Ground cayenne pepper	½ cup red wine
to taste	½ cup water

In a large skillet over medium heat, fry the bacon until crispy, then remove from skillet and drain on paper towels. Into a flat-bottomed pan, sift together the cracker crumbs, flour, salt, pepper, and garlic powder. Dredge the liver in the flour mixture and coat well. Turning once, fry the liver in the heated bacon drippings, until done to your taste; I suggest medium. Liver should be pink, not gray, when it is done. Remove the liver from the skillet and arrange on a platter. Increase the heat to medium-high, add the onions and cook quickly, until crunch-tender, stirring constantly. Remove the onions and arrange around the liver, and place the bacon on the top. Add ¼ cup of the flour mixture to the heated bacon drippings, stir, and make a small, slightly browned roux (see page 56). Stirring, add the wine and water. When completely mixed, pour over the liver, bacon, and onions.

YIELD: *6 to 8 servings*

Beef Tongue in Brown Gravy

1 large beef tongue	1 teaspoon garlic powder
Salt to taste	2 teaspoons onion powder
Louisiana hot sauce or	¼ cup oil or shortening
ground cayenne pepper	¾ cup all-purpose flour
to taste	1 cup chopped onion
¼ cup dried parsley	½ cup chopped bell pepper

½ cup chopped fresh parsley

1 tablespoon chopped garlic

½ cup chopped mushrooms

2 tablespoons Worcestershire
   sauce

Place the tongue in a large pot, cover with water, and add the salt, hot sauce, dried parsley, and garlic and onion powders; cover and bring to a boil. Reduce heat to low and simmer for at least 2 hours. Remove the tongue, reserve 3 cups of the stock, and let the tongue cool, then peel off the skin; it should come off easily. Slice the tongue crosswise ½ inch thick, but don't slice all the way through. Place in a small roaster. Preheat the oven to 350°F. Over medium heat in a large skillet, heat the oil, then stir in the flour to make a dark roux (see page 56). Add the onions, bell pepper, and parsley, cover, and cook until the onions are clear. Gradually stir in one cup of the reserved stock until a thick paste is formed. Stirring, add the garlic and the remaining stock. Add the mushrooms and Worcestershire, stir, and let cook for 15 minutes. Remove from the heat, and pour over and around the tongue. Cover the roaster and bake for 1 hour.

YIELD: *6 to 10 servings*

Stuffed and Baked Heart

1 pound ground beef

1 cup chopped green onions

½ cup chopped fresh parsley

1 cup seasoned bread crumbs

2 medium-sized eggs, beaten

½ teaspoon garlic powder

1 whole beef heart
   Salt to taste
   Louisiana hot sauce or
      ground cayenne pepper
      to taste

SAUCE:

1 cup chopped mushrooms

1 cup tomato sauce

1 cup Meat Stock (see page
   38)

2 tablespoons Worcestershire
   sauce

1 cup dry white wine

Preheat the oven to 350°F. In a large mixing bowl, blend the ground meat, onions, parsley, bread crumbs, eggs, and garlic powder. Stuff the meat mixture into the cavity of the heart and place it in a medium-sized roaster. Sprinkle the surface with salt and hot sauce. In another bowl, mix together the mushrooms, tomato sauce, stock, Worcestershire, and wine. Pour the sauce around the heart and bake, covered, for 2 hours. Serve sliced heart with gravy poured over the top. Goes great with rice.

YIELD: *10 to 12 servings*

Sweetbreads

½ cup olive or other oil	½ cup chopped mushrooms
2 pounds sweetbreads, cleaned, any excess fat removed, and cubed	1½ cups cold water
	1 teaspoon chopped garlic
½ cup all-purpose flour	½ cup dry white wine
1 cup chopped onion	Salt to taste
½ cup chopped green onions	Louisiana hot sauce or ground cayenne pepper to taste
¼ cup chopped fresh parsley	

In a large, heavy saucepan, heat the oil, add the sweetbreads, and brown over medium heat. Remove the sweetbreads from the pot and set aside. Add the flour to the oil and make a dark roux (see page 56). Stirring, add the onions, green onions, parsley, and mushrooms; cover and cook until the onions are clear. Add 1 cup of the cold water and stir until a thick paste has formed, then add the garlic and continue cooking another 5 minutes. Stirring, add the rest of the water, the wine, salt, hot sauce, and sweetbreads, and bring to a slow boil. Reduce the heat to low, cover, and simmer for 1 hour. Serve over cooked rice.

YIELD: *4 to 6 servings*

Game

Louisianans are avid hunters. It is said that we will eat anything that doesn't eat us first. But sometimes we eat things that bite us first. Justin says he loves to cook and eat and hunt and fish for something to cook and eat. In a state covered with vast bottomland forest and marshy wetlands where migratory birds make the sky black with their wings, wild animals abound. It was not too many years ago that dinner was made from whatever a man could drag home from the swamp. In a land of such abundance a family didn't go hungry, and some years one could take pride in that fact only.

Justin tells a story about one such proficient hunter:

> Dair was a fallow las' squirrel season wen' out dair de firs' day an' he didn't ree-lize dat peoples had done been in dair an' got mos' of dem squirrel. But de wood is dry, an' he make enuf noise soun' like one o' dem caterpillin' tractors comin' t'rough dair wit' a bush-hog attach to de rearen' o' it. He ain't seen a live squirrel at all. He done shot out some nests in de trees t'inkin' he might fine one sleepin'. But it midday an' dair ain't no squirrel sleepin'.
>
> He jus' 'bout los' his discourage an' he run upon a li'l boy 'bout thirteen or twelve year ol' an' dat li'l boy got squirrel, WHOOEE.

W'at he did, he pull de head up t'rough his belt an' let de tail hang down an' he got squirrel all de way aroun' him. Look like a hula skirt he got so many squirrel.

Dis Cajun say, "W'at you got dair?"

De boy say, "W'at you t'ought I got? I got squirrel. Fo'teen squirrel."

He ax, "Who kill 'em?"

De li'l boy say, "I kill 'em, Mister."

Now he notice dat de li'l boy ain't got no shotgun, no rifle, not even a bow an' arrow. He say, "Son, I ain't one o' dem ol' game warden. If you gat a frien' over sixteen back in dem wood killin' dem squirrel, call him out. I ain't gon' said not'ing. Shucks, I'm jus' proud to see somebody gettin' dem squirrel like dat, I ga-ron-tee."

He say, "Mister, I ain't got no frien' an' I kill dem squirrel mase'f."

He say, "W'at you kill 'em wit'? A rock?"

He say, "Hell no." He reach in his pock-ett an' he pull a steel ball out, one inch in diameter bot' ways. He say, "I kill "em wit' dat steel ball." Ma' frien' say, "Look, I ain't know you t'ree minnits an' you done tole me t'ree lies. You should be 'shamed you'se'f."

He say, "But I'm not lyin', Mister. I kill dem squirrel wit' dis steel ball—SHHHH! Be quiet. Dair's a squirrel on dat lim' r'at up dair."

Well, ma' frien' shut his mout' an' look up dair. Dair's a squirrel up dair—firs' live squirrel he see dat day. Dat li'l boy jus' flick dat lef' han' wit' dat steel ball—WHAM—knock dat squirrel out. He wen' over dair an' pick him up an' BLAP, BLAP, BLAP, beat him ag'inst de tree to make sho' he dead. Den he take off bot' shoes an' begin to feel aroun' for his steel ball in de leaves. Finally he foun' it an' he reach down an' pick it up an' put it back in his pock-ett, den pull dat squirrel t'rough his belt.

Ma' frien' say, "Well, I done see averyt'ing now, but it ain't no use. Nobody gon' bleeve a damn word. Here you are, a li'l bitty ol' lef'-han' boy, chunk up dair an' knock dat squirrel out de firs' time you chunk. Me, I'm lef'-han' an' I could t'row up dair a t'ousan' time an' I wouldn't move a hair. I wouldn't move a fedder on dat squirrel."

Dat li'l boy say, "Mister I ain't lef'-han' me."

Ma' frien' say, "Don' you start dat foolishment wit' me. I jus' saw you t'row up dair lef'-han'. Don' you start dat."

De boy say, "I ain't lef'-han', Mister, I'm r'at-han'."

Ma' frien' say, "How come you did not t'row up dair r'at-han', hanh?"

De li'l boy say, "Papa won't let me."

Ma' frien' say, "How come you' papa won't let you chunk r'at-han'?"

Da boy say, "I tear 'em up too bad."

The best recipe is no good if the game has been improperly handled after the kill. You do not need to marinate game if you like the variations in flavor that the animals' diet of wild berries and plant imparts to its flesh. When game is properly handled it has no objectionable strong taste. Heat, dirt, and moisture encourage the growth of bacteria which can quickly ruin good food.

To prepare your own game for cooking, follow these rules:

1. Immediately after the kill, gut the game to let the heat dissipate and remove the punctured internal organs, which can taint surrounding flesh.
2. If clean water is available, flush the cavity and allow it to drain.
3. If the day is warm, put the carcass on ice. If the day is cool, open the cavity to further speed cooling. Always chill the game as soon as possible.
4. Keep dirt away from the meat. If you must carry or drag the kill, use a bag to cover the carcass. Try to keep any hair away from the flesh.
5. Hang and remove the skin, wash the cavity with clean water, and wipe dry. Remove the sexual organs promptly.

Justin tries to butcher game the same day it is killed, and he usually removes any visible fat and connective tissue before wrapping it securely and freezing it. Some people prefer to hang their game for several weeks, claiming that this ageing period improves flavor and makes the meat more tender. You can do that if you like, but hanging increases the gamey flavor and wastes more of the meat.

Wise game management is the responsibility of every citizen. It makes no difference whether the animal's range is local or, in the case of waterfowl, animals that only use our homes as a resting place. Ducks Unlimited and other conservation groups have done us a great service by preserving animal habitats and thereby preserving our heritage of being able to bring food from the swamps and the field to the table. Our great-grandchildren must be able to enjoy the privileges and joys of hunting for their families.

Venison Sausage

All the small meat scraps from butchering the deer go into this sausage.

50 **percent venison, fat and membranes removed, cut into chunks**
50 **percent pork butts with some fat, cut into chunks**

Ground cayenne pepper to taste
Salt to taste
Pinch finely crushed dried mint or sage
Other spices (optional)

In a meat grinder, grind the venison and pork, mixing the chunks as you go along. Grind the processed meat again to a fine consistency. Season with the pepper, salt, and mint; mix well with your hands. Grind the meat once more, and fry a patty or two for taste; if more seasoning is needed, carefully add it, mixing well with your hands.

This sausage can be made into patties and frozen or stuffed into natural pork casings to make sausage links and smoked or frozen. Casings can be purchased at any meat market.

Venison Finger Steaks

This is a fast and easy recipe.

2 **pounds venison, fat and membranes removed**
1 **cup Worcestershire sauce**

1 **quart peanut oil**
2 **cups all-purpose flour**
Salt to taste

**Louisiana hot sauce or ground
cayenne pepper
to taste**

**Garlic powder to taste
Onion powder to taste**

Cut the meat into 1-by-3-inch strips, making sure to cut across the grain (the meat will be more tender). Soak the strips in the Worcestershire for about 30 minutes. Half fill a deep frying pot with the oil and preheat to 350°F. In a large mixing bowl, mix the flour with the seasonings. Dredge the venison in the spicy flour mixture. Deep fry in the hot oil until the strips float and become golden brown, 2 to 3 minutes.

YIELD: *4 to 8 servings*

Venison Roast with Gravy

3- to 4-pound venison roast
**4 whole fresh or pickled
cayenne peppers**
4 small cloves garlic
**4 fresh green onions
Salt to taste**

**Ground cayenne pepper
to taste**
All-purpose flour
¼ cup olive oil
1 cup dry red wine

Preheat the oven to 350°F. With a sharp knife, puncture four deep holes in the roast, and push into each hole one whole cayenne pepper, one clove of garlic, and one green onion. If the onion extends above the surface of the roast, cut it off even with the meat. Sprinkle salt and pepper over the roast on all sides, making sure to pat the seasonings into the meat; then sprinkle and pat the flour over the entire roast. Heat the oil in a large roasting pan over medium-high heat, on top of the stove, and sear the roast on all sides. Pour the wine around the roast and cover the roaster. Remove from the stove and bake for 1½ to 2 hours. A gravy will form from the meat juices and the wine.

YIELD: *4 to 6 servings*

Stuffed Reindeer with Berries

No, we don't have any reindeer in Louisiana. I got to cook this during my visit to Alaska, and I think that Cajun cooking makes just about anything taste good.

1 large reindeer roast	3 cups fresh berries or jam
Salt to taste	Margarine or butter
Ground cayenne pepper to taste	6 bacon strips

Clean the meat well, making sure to cut off all the fat and membrane. Cut a pocket in the roast with a sharp knife. Salt and pepper the entire roast, inside the pocket also. Mash the berries with the margarine and mix well. Push the berries into the pocket of the roast and strip the top with the bacon. Bake in a large roaster or smoke for several hours. Serve with berries and a wine sauce.

Y I E L D : *10 to 20 servings*

Alligator Sauce Piquant

We like to get together with our friends and family and cook a big black pot of this delicious dish. There are always leftovers for the cook. We always make a big pot of piquant sauce. Nobody would go to this much trouble if the recipe would only feed four people.

5 pounds alligator meat, trimmed of fat and cubed	2 cups chopped fresh tomatoes
1 cup olive oil	8 cups cold water
3 cups all-purpose flour	2 tablespoons finely chopped garlic
5 cups chopped onion	2 tablespoons Worcestershire sauce
2 cups chopped green onions	Juice of one fresh lemon
1 cup chopped bell pepper	Salt to taste
½ cup chopped celery	

Louisiana hot sauce or
   ground cayenne pepper
   to taste

2 cups dry white wine
6 cups tomato sauce

Make a dark roux (see page 56) with the olive oil and flour. When the roux is dark brown, add the onions, green onions, bell pepper, and celery; cover and cook until the onions are clear, stirring occasionally. Then add the tomatoes and continue cooking for 10 minutes; stir often. Add the water and stir to make a thick liquid. Then add the garlic, Worcestershire, lemon juice, salt, hot sauce, wine, and tomato sauce, making sure to mix well. Add the alligator, and enough water to cover the ingredients by 2 inches; stir to mix. Bring to a boil, stirring frequently. After it comes to a boil, turn the heat to low and cover, checking from time to time, and stir to prevent the sauce from sticking. Continue cooking for 3 to 4 hours until the meat is tender. Serve over cooked rice or spaghetti with Parmesan cheese. Freeze the leftovers in serving-size containers.

YIELD: *about 20 servings; this is for a party*

Broiled Alligator Tail with Lemon Butter Sauce

2 pounds alligator tail, trimmed
   of fat and thinly sliced

1 cup Lemon Butter Sauce (see
   page 58)

Lay the alligator slices on a flat broiler pan, and place about 6 inches from the heating element. Broil for 10 to 15 minutes or until done. Remove the pan from the oven and brush the top of the meat with the lemon-butter sauce, making sure to coat the entire surface. Serve immediately.

YIELD: *4 to 6 servings*

Dove Breast Champignon

I like to save the dove hearts and gizzards to include them in this dish.

½ cup all-purpose flour
Salt to taste
Ground cayenne pepper
   to taste
10 dove breasts, well cleaned
½ cup oil
1 cup chopped onion
½ cup chopped fresh parsley
1 cup red wine
1 tablespoon chopped garlic

1 cup chopped mushrooms
1 cup milk
Louisiana hot sauce or
   ground cayenne pepper
   to taste
2 tablespoons strawberry,
   plum, blueberry, or
   muscadine jelly, or fresh
   berries

Season the flour with salt and pepper. In a large, high-walled frying pan, heat the oil over medium heat. Dredge the breasts in the flour and fry each breast for 10 minutes or until golden brown, turning while frying. Remove breasts to a plate when they are done frying. Stir the leftover flour into the frying pan and make a small brown roux (see page 56). This should take about 30 minutes. Once the roux is brown, stir in the onions and parsley, and cook until the onions are tender. Stir in the wine until a paste is formed. Add the garlic and mushrooms; cook for 10 minutes. Stir in the milk and hot sauce to taste. Return the breasts to the frying pan, lower the heat, and cover. Simmer, stirring occasionally, for 1 hour. Remove the lid and stir in the jelly. Serve over rice, mashed potatoes, or pasta.

YIELD: *5 servings*

Rabbit Sauce Piquant

This is for a party and will serve 10 to 20 people. You can freeze what you don't eat for your favorite relations or friends or to eat all by yourself.

½ cup bacon drippings or oil
2 cups all-purpose flour
3 cups chopped onion
½ cup chopped bell pepper
1 cup chopped green onions
¼ cup chopped celery
1 cup chopped fresh parsley
2 tablespoons chopped garlic
2 cups stock or water
6 pounds rabbit, cut into
    2-inch pieces
1 pound mushrooms, sliced

8 cups tomato sauce
2 cups dry white wine
1 cup olives, stuffed with
    pimentos
3 tablespoons Worcestershire
    sauce
Louisiana hot sauce or
    ground cayenne pepper
    to taste
¼ teaspoon crushed dried mint
3 tablespoons salt

With the bacon drippings and flour, in a large pot over medium heat make a roux (see page 56). Add the onions, bell pepper, green onions, and celery, and cook until the onions are clear. Add the parsley and garlic and cook another 10 minutes. Add the stock slowly, stirring all the while, to create a smooth, thick gravy. Add the remaining ingredients and enough water or stock to cover. Bring to a boil, then turn the heat to low, cover, and simmer 4 to 6 hours. Serve over cooked spaghetti or rice.

YIELD: *10 to 15 servings*

Frog Legs and Mushrooms

½ cup (1 stick) of margarine
1 cup chopped bell pepper
3 cups chopped onion
1 cup chopped fresh parsley
1 tablespoon minced garlic
1 pound mushrooms, sliced

8 pairs of frog legs
Salt to taste
Louisiana hot sauce or
    ground cayenne pepper
    to taste
1 cup dry white wine

Over medium heat in a large saucepan, melt the margarine, then add the bell peppers, onions, parsley, and garlic, and sauté about 10 minutes. Stir in the mushrooms, frog legs, salt, hot sauce, and wine, and bring to a boil. Lower the heat and simmer covered for at least 1 hour. Serve over cooked rice.

YIELD: *4 to 6 servings*

Deep-fried Frog Legs

DRENCH:

2 large eggs
1 cup milk
½ teaspoon ground cayenne
   pepper
1 teaspoon salt
½ teaspoon garlic powder
1 cup all-purpose flour

8 pairs of frog legs
1 quart oil

DREDGE:

½ cup corn flour
½ cup cornmeal
2 teaspoons salt or to taste
¼ teaspoon garlic powder
½ teaspoon onion powder
½ teaspoon ground cayenne
   pepper

In a medium-sized mixing bowl, beat together the eggs, milk, and seasonings for the drench. Gradually beat in the flour and set aside. Mix all the dredge ingredients together in a flat pan. Half fill a deep fry pot with the oil and preheat to 360°F. While the oil is heating, prepare the frog legs for frying by dipping each leg in the drench, one at a time, then coating well in the dry ingredients. Put the frog legs, one pair at a time, into the preheated oil, and fry until golden brown, 3 to 4 minutes. Remove from the oil and drain on paper towels. Serve immediately.

YIELD: *4 servings*

CHAPTER 10

Vegetables

Rich alluvial soil and a climate tempered by Gulf winds make Louisiana a perfect place to grow almost any type of vegetable. Until the 1920s, when the swaying hips of Madame Mississippi were corsetted by levees and flood control structures, she used to spread herself regularly over the basins, replenishing the topsoil and increasing the size of her delta. Generations of Louisiana farmers have been nourished by the river's milky sediment. Justin's father was a farmer, his grandson is a farmer. On his papa's sixty-acre farm they grew typical crops, including cabbage, carrots, Irish and sweet potatoes, turnips, peppers, all types of greens, corn, rice, cotton, cane, tomatoes, radishes, kohlrabi, peanuts, beans, strawberries, and many tree fruits. He tells of rising early to cut a huge field of cabbage in the winter dawn's wet chill, then loading a railcar with the dense globes, only to have to send money to cover the freight charges when the market price turned down.

After learning early about fieldwork, Justin decided staying at the house to help Mama was easier. So he began to cook when he was eight years old. Olivet Toadvin Wilson was a fabulous cook, drawing on her French heritage, her inventive mind, and the produce from the farm to improvise tempting meals out of seemingly nothing. Mama's Stuffed

Cucumbers is a dish she created one afternoon when her husband brought a hungry group home. Because he was Commissioner of Agriculture, people were always dropping in at mealtime. She devised signals for the family to let them know the plentitude of the pot. She would sail out of the kitchen, platter in her arms, and announce "F.H.B." That meant Family Hold Back, and don't you dare ask for more. If she said, "Children M.I.K.," that meant More In the Kitchen, go ahead and eat. The company was never aware of her system.

As Justin grew up, he worked as a migrant following the harvest. He says that he is ambiguous, that is, ambidextrous, and so able to pack crates and lugs of produce much faster than most people. When he wasn't packing, he was licensed by the U. S. Department of Agriculture to inspect fruits and vegetables and to certify the grade based on size, conformation, appearance, and insect damage.

Today, more than insects, we have to guard against the chemicals used on our food. Always wash the produce that you don't grow yourself. Better than buying foods, get some containers or grow a small garden. Gardening doesn't take much room or effort, and there is no greater satisfaction than to grow your own food. Eat it right from the plant or use one of Justin's recipes.

In Louisiana vegetables are cooked a long time. Justin refuses to eat what he calls the fad of half-cooked vegetables. He says, let me eat them raw, or else cook them until they are done. And if the food doesn't taste good it won't be eaten anyway, so you'll find vegetables flavored with all types of seasonings and combined with different meats, seafood, and cheeses. When asked what meal won the heart and stomach of his wife, Justin remembered her first meal at his hands and smiled. It was mustard greens, crowder peas, and stewed okra.

· ᔑ ·

Artichoke and Mushroom Casserole

½ cup oil or shortening
1 cup chopped onion
1½ teaspoons minced garlic
1 pound fresh mushrooms, sliced
2 cups quartered artichoke hearts
2 tablespoons lemon juice
½ cup dry white wine

Salt to taste
Louisiana hot sauce or ground cayenne pepper to taste
½ cup grated Parmesan or Romano cheese
½ cup plain or seasoned bread crumbs

Preheat the oven to 350°F. Heat the oil over medium-high heat in a large skillet, then sauté the onions, garlic, and mushrooms until the onions are tender. Add the artichoke hearts, lemon juice, and wine, and mix well. Season with salt and hot sauce, then turn into a greased casserole dish. Mix the cheese and bread crumbs together in a small bowl, then sprinkle on top. Bake for 30 to 40 minutes.

YIELD: *4 to 6 servings*

Red Beans

Red beans and rice is the traditional Monday dish in New Orleans.

1 pound dried small red beans
Water
1 cup dry red wine
3 large onions, chopped
1 tablespoon minced garlic
½ cup chopped fresh parsley
½ cup chopped green onions
½ teaspoon crushed dried mint
¼ cup bacon drippings, ham fat, oil, or shortening

Ham bone and scraps, or salt meat, or pickled pork
8 to 10 cups Ham Stock (see page 38), or Meat Stock (see page 38), or water
Salt to taste
Louisiana hot sauce or ground cayenne pepper to taste

Prepare the beans the night before. Clean and pick through beans to remove foreign objects. Rinse several times in water to make sure beans are absolutely clean. In a large mixing bowl, combine the beans, with enough water to cover by 1 inch, and the wine, onions, garlic, parsley, green onions, and mint. Soak overnight, covered, either refrigerated or unrefrigerated.

The next morning, sauté the ham bone and scraps in the bacon drippings, in an 8-quart pot. Pour the beans, with soaking water and all the seasonings, into the pot, then add enough stock to cover the beans by 2 inches; bring to a boil, then reduce the heat. Cover and simmer for 2 hours, stirring occasionally so the beans won't stick and burn. Season with salt and hot sauce when the beans are tender. To make the beans thicker, mash them with a potato masher or put 1 cup of the cooked beans in a blender and puree them; return them to the pot, and stir in. Serve over cooked rice with chopped onions and hot peppers. The Hot Stuff recipe found on page 249 is also a good topper for these beans. This can be frozen into small portions and served at a later date.

YIELD: *6 to 10 servings*

Rum Baked Beans

This is particularly good if you use several-day-old beans.

1 pound cooked red or white beans (see pages 177 and 179)
6 strips bacon
1 cup firmly packed brown sugar
1 cup catsup
1 tablespoon wine vinegar
½ teaspoon crushed dried mint
½ cup prepared mustard
1 tablespoon mustard seed
½ cup dark rum (optional)
Louisiana hot sauce or ground cayenne pepper to taste

Preheat oven to 300°F. In a large, ovenproof skillet, one with a lid, fry the bacon strips until crispy over a medium heat. Remove the bacon and add the sugar, catsup, vinegar, mint, mustard, mustard seed, and rum to the bacon drippings. Crumble two of the bacon strips into the pan. Add the cooked beans and hot sauce, and stir well. You may want to drain off some of the bean juice. Strip the remainder of the bacon on top of the beans, cover, and bake for at least 3 hours. If the beans are too soupy, uncover, and continue cooking until they are nice and thick.

YIELD: *10 to 12 servings*

White Beans

This recipe can be made with many types of beans or peas. White beans are eaten very often in the country. We usually serve white beans over cooked rice and top them with fresh chopped onions and cayenne pepper.

1 pound dried white beans, picked clean of rocks and rinsed	1 cup chopped fresh parsley Louisiana hot sauce or ground cayenne pepper to taste
1 cup chopped onion	
1 cup chopped bell pepper	2 cups dry white wine
1 tablespoon chopped garlic	7 cups stock or water
2 teaspoons liquid smoke	Salt to taste

In a large pot, combine all the ingredients, except the salt. Cover and bring to a rolling boil. After the water begins to boil, turn the heat to low and cook for about 2 hours; add more water if necessary. Stir occasionally to make sure the beans don't stick to the bottom. When the beans become soft, add the salt. Eat like a soup, sprinkled with chopped onions. This dish can easily be frozen in single serving portions to be eaten later. Take note!! This has *no fat or cholesterol!*

YIELD: *5 to 10 servings*

Fresh Snap Beans with Neckbones

2 cups dry white wine
2 to 3 pounds pork
  neckbones
6 to 8 new potatoes
  Salt to taste
1½ cups chopped onion
1 tablespoon minced garlic
½ cup dried parsley

Louisiana hot sauce or
  ground cayenne pepper
  to taste
1 tablespoon Worcestershire
  sauce
6 cups fresh snapped snap
  beans

In an 8-quart pot over a high heat, combine the wine, neckbones, potatoes, salt, and enough water to cover contents of the pot by 1 inch. Stir in the onions, garlic, parsley, hot sauce, and Worcestershire, then cover and bring to a boil. Add the beans, bring back to a boil, then reduce the heat to low, cover, and simmer until the beans and potatoes are tender, at least 1 hour.

YIELD: *6 to 8 servings*

Garden Beets

Beets from the garden are one of my favorite dishes.

2 pounds fresh whole beets
  (save greens if tender)
  Water
1 teaspoon salt
1 tablespoon oil or shortening

Salt to taste again
Louisiana hot sauce or
  ground cayenne pepper
  to taste

Put whole unpeeled beets in a large pot and cover with water. Add the salt. The young tender leaves may also be boiled and eaten. Cover and bring to a boil, reduce heat to low, and simmer for 30 minutes or until the beets are tender. Drain and let cool, then remove the stems and leaves. The skin should slip off easily when peeled with a knife or rubbed with the fingers. Slice the beets while still warm, then add the oil and season with salt and hot sauce. Toss with the boiled greens, if desired, and serve immediately.

YIELD: *4 to 6 servings*

Sharla's Broccoli and Rice Casserole

1 cup uncooked rice
1 bunch broccoli, rinsed and broken into flowerets (also use the stalks)
1 cup chopped fresh mushrooms or 8 ounces canned mushrooms, drained
1 cup chopped onion
¼ cup chopped fresh parsley
½ cup chopped green onions
1 tablespoon chopped garlic
Salt to taste

Louisiana hot sauce or ground cayenne pepper to taste
2 tablespoons margarine, butter, or shortening
2 tablespoons all-purpose flour
1½ cups shredded cheddar cheese
½ to 1 cup shredded mozzarella cheese (optional)

Cook the rice. Place the broccoli, mushrooms, onions, parsley, green onions, and garlic in a 4-quart saucepan, cover with water, and season with salt and hot sauce. Cover with a lid and bring to a boil. Cook over medium heat until the broccoli is tender, about 25 minutes. Reserve 2 cups of pot liquor before draining and set aside. Drain through a strainer with small holes to catch all the chopped seasonings and broccoli flowerets, and let cool. Preheat the oven to 350°F.

Once cool, peel the outer skin from the broccoli stalks and chop into small pieces. Melt the margarine in the same saucepan over medium heat, and mix in the flour, stirring constantly, until all the flour is blended in with the margarine; don't let the flour brown. Add 1½ cups of pot liquor and cook until thickened, stirring constantly. Stir in half the cheddar cheese until melted, then stir in the cooked rice. Add the broccoli mixture and stir thoroughly. If the mixture is too thick, add some more pot liquor. Turn into a 9-by-9-inch greased casserole dish, and sprinkle the top with the remaining cheddar and the mozzarella cheese. Cover and bake for 20 minutes or until the cheese is melted.

YIELD: *6 to 8 servings*

Brussels Sprouts

At Grand Point, brussels sprouts grow during the winter. They are always included in holiday meals. Select tender, young sprouts for the best flavor.

2 **pounds fresh or frozen brussels sprouts**	1 **cup sour cream**
Water	**Salt to taste**
4 **slices bacon, cut into ½-inch pieces**	**Louisiana hot sauce or ground cayenne pepper to taste**
1 **cup chopped onion**	

If using fresh sprouts, rinse well and cut off any discolored leaves. With a paring knife cut a "plus" sign in the stem end to insure even cooking. Place the sprouts in a large saucepan and cover with water. Bring to a boil and continue boiling for about 10 minutes or until the stem end is tender when pierced with a knife. Drain and set the sprouts aside. In the same pan, fry the bacon pieces. When the bacon is crispy, add the onions and sauté over medium-high heat until tender. Return the sprouts to the pan and stir to reheat. Add the sour cream and remove from the heat. Season with salt and hot sauce, stir carefully, and serve immediately.

YIELD: *6 to 8 servings*

Cabbage Cooked in Stock

8 to 10 cups Meat Stock (see
    page 38) or Ham Stock (see
    page 38)
1 large head of cabbage, rinsed
    and quartered
8 to 10 small new potatoes,
    in skins

4 small whole onions
Salt to taste
Louisiana hot sauce or
    ground cayenne pepper
    to taste

Pour the stock into an 8-quart pot and bring to a boil. Add the cabbage, potatoes, and onions, cover, reduce the heat to low, and simmer until the cabbage and potatoes are tender (when they can easily be pierced with a fork, at least an hour). Remember, the stock is already seasoned, so taste before adding any more seasonings.

YIELD: *8 to 10 servings*

Cabbage Rolls

Large cabbage leaves,
    washed; amount depends
    on size
Water to blanch or parboil
    cabbage leaves
2 tablespoons oil or shortening
1 cup chopped green onions
½ cup chopped fresh parsley
½ tablespoon chopped garlic

½ pound lean ground pork
2 cups cooked rice
Salt to taste
Louisiana hot sauce or
    ground cayenne pepper
    to taste
2 large eggs, beaten
2 cups tomato or vegetable
    juice

Preheat the oven to 325°F. In a large pot, boil enough water to cover the cabbage leaves. Put the cabbage in the boiling water and blanch the leaves until they are soft, about 5 minutes. Heat the oil in a large, high-walled skillet over medium heat, and sauté the onions and parsley. After a little juice has accumulated, add the garlic and continue cooking until the onions are tender. Add the meat to the vegetables and brown. Stir in the cooked rice, salt, and hot sauce. Remove from the heat, pour into a large bowl, and let cool, then add the eggs. Place 2 heaping tablespoons of stuffing in each leaf, roll up, and secure with toothpicks, if needed. Place close together in a baking dish and pour the tomato juice over the cabbage rolls, covering them lightly. Bake for 30 to 45 minutes.

YIELD: *Depends on size of cabbage leaves*

Choux Rouge

1 large head red cabbage, shredded
½ cup bacon drippings
1 large onion, chopped
1 cup dry white wine
¼ cup sugar
¼ cup cider vinegar

1 teaspoon minced garlic
1 apple, peeled, cored, and shredded
Salt to taste
Louisiana hot sauce or ground cayenne pepper to taste

Over medium heat in a large, heavy saucepan, sauté the onions in the bacon drippings until clear. Add the wine, sugar, vinegar, and garlic, stir, and let simmer 5 minutes. Add the shredded cabbage, cover, and simmer another 20 minutes. Add the shredded apple and simmer uncovered, stirring often until the cabbage and apple are tender. Season with salt and hot sauce.

YIELD: *6 servings*

Beryl's Caponata

Beryl lives in New Orleans. All her co-workers and her family and friends agree that she is a fantastic cook and a wonderful lady. We're lucky to know her and to be able to taste the food she cooks often. Caponata is a traditional Italian dish. This can be served as a vegetable dish or put up in glass and served cold as a salad.

3 eggplants, in 1-inch cubes
Water, enough to cover eggplant
Salt, enough to make a strong brine
½ cup olive oil
3 medium-sized onions, sliced thin lengthwise
3 stalks celery, sliced very thin
3 medium-sized bell peppers, in 1-inch pieces
One 8-ounce jar salad olives
One 8-ounce can tomato sauce

16 ounces canned whole tomatoes, chopped, or 2 to 3 large fresh tomatoes, peeled and chopped
1 tablespoon finely chopped garlic
4 fresh basil leaves or 1 teaspoon dried sweet basil
Salt to taste
½ cup white vinegar
¼ cup sugar
Louisiana hot sauce or ground cayenne pepper to taste

Soak the eggplant cubes in the salt and water for 30 minutes. Drain well and pat dry. Heat the olive oil in a 10- or 12-inch frying pan over medium-high heat and fry the cubes until soft, 3 to 4 minutes. Remove them from the fry pan and place in a shallow casserole dish. Over medium high heat, in the pan you fried the eggplant in, add some more olive oil, if needed, and sauté the onions, celery, and bell peppers for 10 minutes, stirring all the while. Add the olives, tomato sauce, chopped tomatoes, garlic, basil, salt, vinegar, and sugar, stirring to mix. Simmer over low heat for an additional 15 minutes. Pour the mixture over the fried eggplant and mix gently.

YIELD: *6 to 8 servings*

Collards and Ham Hocks

Collards are my favorite green. I think people up north are missing a great treat because they don't eat fresh collards. At home I clean the collards, because I want them just so. I wash them carefully in cold water, then remove the middle stem from each leaf, then rinse them again. Some friends of mine grow rows and rows of collards. When they harvest many bunches, they say it saves a lot of time to use their automatic washing machine to rinse and spin the greens dry.

2 pounds smoked ham hocks	2 teaspoons salt
1 cup chopped onion	2 cups dry white wine
1 tablespoon finely chopped garlic	2 pounds collard greens, rinsed and chopped
Louisiana hot sauce or ground cayenne pepper to taste	2 tablespoons soy sauce

Put the ham hocks, onions, garlic, and hot sauce in an 8-quart pot with enough water to cover the ham hocks. Cover and cook over medium-high heat until the water comes to a boil. After it begins to boil, remove the lid and let boil for 5 more minutes. Stir in the salt, wine, and collards, then add the soy sauce and stir again; cover, turn the heat to low, and cook for 1½ to 2 hours, stirring occasionally. If necessary, add more water so that the greens don't stick to the bottom of the pan.

YIELD: *4 to 6 servings*

Creole Corn

4 strips bacon or ham slices	2 medium-sized fresh tomatoes, peeled, seeded, and chopped or one 8-ounce can tomatoes and juice, chopped
2 tablespoons oil or reserved bacon drippings	
¼ cup chopped onion	
¼ cup chopped bell pepper	

2 cups fresh or drained canned
   corn
Salt to taste

Louisiana hot sauce or
   ground cayenne pepper
   to taste

In a large heavy saucepan, fry the bacon until crisp, then remove from the pan. In the bacon drippings, sauté the onions and bell peppers over medium-high heat until the onions are clear. Add the tomatoes and stir, then cover and simmer for 15 minutes. Add the corn, salt, and hot sauce. Crumble the bacon, add to the mixture, mix well, and heat thoroughly. Serve as a side dish.

YIELD: *6 servings*

Mama's Stuffed Cucumbers

This is a variation of a recipe that Mama invented one day when a bunch of people came by to visit and she didn't have anything in the house except a bushel of cucumbers.

Water
4 medium-sized cucumbers,
   cut in half lengthwise
½ cup chopped fresh
   mushrooms
2 tablespoons olive oil
2 tablespoons chopped fresh
   parsley or 1 tablespoon
   dried parsley
1 cup chopped onion
1 teaspoon minced garlic
1 cup chopped uncooked
   shrimp

½ cup seasoned bread crumbs
1 tablespoon Worcestershire
   sauce
Salt to taste
Louisiana hot sauce or
   ground cayenne pepper
   to taste
½ cup dry white wine
½ cup Vegetable Stock (see
   page 39)
Grated Romano cheese

Fill an 8-quart pot half full with water and bring to a boil. Slip in the cucumber halves and continue to boil until tender, about 5 minutes. Drain, reserving 1 cup of the pot liquor, and let the cucumbers cool.

Scrape the cucumber centers into a bowl and chop, then mix in the mushrooms. Preheat the oven to 350°F. In a medium-sized saucepan, heat the oil over medium heat and sauté the onions and parsley 5 minutes, then add the garlic and continue cooking until the onions are tender. Stir in the shrimp, bread crumbs, Worcestershire, salt, and hot sauce, and mix thoroughly. Mix the wine and stock together, then pour into a large baking dish. Stuff cucumber halves with the cooked stuffing and place in the casserole dish. Sprinkle with Romano cheese, cover, and bake for 1 hour.

YIELD: *8 servings*

Fried Eggplant

This can be used as a meat substitute or an appetizer for your next party.

2 medium-sized eggplants, peeled and sliced crosswise ½ inch thick
Water, enough to cover eggplant
1 tablespoon salt
1 quart oil

DRENCH:
2 large eggs
Salt to taste
½ cup dry white wine

DREDGE:
1¼ cups corn flour
½ cup plain bread crumbs
Salt to taste
Ground cayenne pepper to taste
1 teaspoon onion powder
½ teaspoon garlic powder

Place the eggplant in a large bowl, fill with the water, add the salt to make a brine, and soak the eggplant slices for at least 30 minutes. Rinse and pat dry. Fill a deep fry pot half full with oil and preheat to 375°F. Make the drench by beating the eggs, salt, and wine together in a medium-sized mixing bowl. Make the dredge by mixing the corn flour, bread crumbs, salt, pepper, and onion and garlic powders together in a flat pan or large bowl. Drench the sliced eggplant, then coat well in the corn flour mixture. Fry the eggplant in the preheated oil until tender and golden brown, turning the slices over to fry evenly. Drain on paper towels.

YIELD: *30 slices*

Parmesan Eggplant Strata

2 medium-sized eggplants,
    peeled and sliced crosswise
    ¼ inch thick
Water with salt

DRENCH:
2 eggs, beaten
½ cup dry white wine
Salt to taste
Louisiana hot sauce or
    ground cayenne pepper
    to taste

DREDGE:
½ cup all-purpose flour
1 cup plain bread crumbs
½ teaspoon garlic powder
1 teaspoon onion powder
Salt to taste
Ground cayenne pepper
    to taste

1 cup olive oil
3 cups tomato sauce
2 cups grated Parmesan
    cheese

Preheat the oven to 350°F. Sprinkle the eggplant slices with salt on both sides, or soak in brine about half an hour, then rinse and pat dry. In a small bowl, beat the eggs with the wine, salt, and hot sauce. Drench the eggplant slices in egg wash. Then dredge in the mixture of flour, bread crumbs, garlic powder, onion powder, salt, and pepper. Pour about ¼ inch of olive oil into a large flat skillet, and heat over medium-high heat. When the oil reaches 350°F, put several pieces of eggplant in the bottom of the pan and fry. When one side is browned, turn over and brown the other side. Remove and drain on paper towels.

In the bottom of a deep baking dish or a greased casserole, make one layer of fried eggplant. Cover with tomato sauce and sprinkle with the grated cheese. Add another layer of eggplant, tomato sauce, and cheese; continue until all the eggplant is used up. Bake for 30 minutes, until heated thoroughly.

YIELD: *6 to 8 servings*

Stuffed Eggplant

This will feed some gourmets and maybe three or two gourmands.

4 large eggplants, sliced in half lengthwise

½ cup plus 3 tablespoons olive oil

1 cup chopped onion

½ cup chopped fresh parsley

½ pound lean ground pork

½ pound lean ground beef

1 teaspoon minced garlic

1 tablespoon Worcestershire sauce

Salt to taste

Louisiana hot sauce or ground cayenne pepper to taste

1 cup stock or water

2 cups seasoned bread crumbs

Preheat the oven to 350°F. Place the sliced eggplant into a pot of boiling water. Let the eggplant boil until soft when pierced with a fork, then cool and carefully scoop out the pulp; set aside, saving the shells. Heat ½ cup of the olive oil in a 12-inch high-walled skillet over medium heat, and sauté the onions and parsley until the onions are clear. Add the ground meat and brown, then add the eggplant pulp, garlic, Worcestershire, salt, hot sauce, and 1 cup of the bread crumbs. Stir and continue cooking for another 10 minutes, then spoon the mixture into the eggplant shells and place in a baking dish. Pour the stock in the bottom of the dish and bake for 30 minutes; then top with the remaining bread crumbs, drizzle with the remaining olive oil, and bake until golden brown.

YIELD: *8 servings*

Cheezy Grits

Grits are eaten for breakfast, lunch, and dinner.

5 cups water	Salt to taste
1 cup uncooked grits	Louisiana hot sauce or
1 cup grated cheddar cheese	ground cayenne pepper
2 tablespoons olive oil	to taste

Place water in the bottom part of a double boiler, turn the heat to medium-high, and let it come to a boil. Meanwhile, in the top part of the boiler, combine the 5 cups of water, the grits, cheese, olive oil, salt, and hot sauce, and bring to a boil directly over medium-high heat, stirring constantly. Turn the heat to low and continue cooking until the grits begin to thicken, about 20 minutes, stirring occasionally. Then put the pot of grits on top of the boiling water, reduce its heat to low, and simmer for 30 minutes. Serve hot.

YIELD: *4 to 6 servings*

Hoppin' Justin

4 cups cooked field peas (see White Beans recipe, page 179) with juice or other peas or beans	Salt to taste
	Louisiana hot sauce or
	ground cayenne pepper
	to taste
4 cups cooked rice	

Mix the cooked peas and rice together, then pour into a 12-inch high-walled skillet. Cook over medium-low heat until heated through, stirring occasionally. Season with salt and hot sauce. Serve with sliced ham.

YIELD: *6 to 8 servings*

HOMINY

The Indians of Louisiana were the first to enjoy hominy. Hominy is the creamy white inner kernel that remains when a whole kernel of corn is hulled. To make hominy, corn was allowed to mature and then left to dry on the cob. The cobs were then removed and the kernels sun dried several days to make certain they were completely dry.

A large washpot was filled with water. Into the water was put a porous bag which contained at least a quart of hardwood ashes. The dried kernels were added and allowed to soak for a day, after which the pot was placed over a fire and the water allowed to boil for several hours until the kernels became tender. The kernels then were thrown into cold water and washed vigorously until the germ came off, then washed well under cold running water to remove any remaining germ.

Today good hominy is available canned, making this time-consuming preparation unnecessary. Hominy can be eaten simply by boiling in water until the kernels are very tender and soft. Serve them with sugar, cream, or fried with butter and salt. The kernels can also be ground into a fine flour used to make breads and grits. Also, the tender pieces go well in gravies or with meats in tasty sauces.

Fried Mirliton

Mirliton is the French word for a type of summer squash that is native to the Western Hemisphere. It is also called chayote or vegetable pear and is widely available in United States. Mirliton vines are a beautiful light green and sometimes grow hundreds of feet long. In Louisiana mirlitons are eaten raw, in salads, or stuffed then baked, or boiled.

Oil, to deep fry	Ground cayenne pepper
4 fresh mirliton	to taste
Salt to taste	

Fill a deep fry pot half full with peanut oil and heat to 350°F. Wash and peel the mirliton, then cut in half lengthwise, and remove the seed. Slice the mirliton like french fries. Mirlitons contain a lot of water, so set the strips on paper towels to absorb some of the moisture. Carefully lower the strips into the hot oil and fry briefly until they float. Remove from the oil, drain on paper towels, and sprinkle with salt and pepper. Serve immediately.

YIELD: *4 to 6 servings*

Smothered Mirliton

A female mirliton is fleshier and has smoother skin than a male, which is often covered with spines. Many fresh female fruits don't even need to be peeled because they are so tender.

1 tablespoon olive oil	1½ teaspoons finely chopped
1 cup chopped onion	garlic
½ cup finely chopped fresh	Salt to taste
parsley	Louisiana hot sauce
4 mirlitons, peeled, seeds	to taste
removed, and cubed	½ cup dry white wine

Heat the oil in a large saucepan over medium heat, then sauté the onions and parsley until the onions are clear. Stir in the mirliton, garlic, salt, hot sauce, and wine, and continue cooking until it comes to a boil. Reduce the heat to low, cover, and simmer until the mirliton is tender. Stir occasionally.

YIELD: *4 to 6 servings*

• ❧ •

Shrimp-stuffed Mirliton

Water
4 fresh mirlitons, washed, halved, and seeds removed
2 tablespoons margarine
1½ cups finely chopped onion
½ cup finely chopped fresh parsley or ¼ cup dried parsley

1 cup seasoned bread crumbs, reserve ¼ cup
Salt to taste
Louisiana hot sauce or ground cayenne pepper to taste
2 cups chopped fresh shrimp, peeled and deveined

Preheat the oven to 350°F. Half fill an 8-quart pot with water, cover, and bring to a boil, then slip in the mirlitons. Lower the heat to medium, cover, and cook until the mirliton are tender when pierced with a fork, about 15 minutes. Remove from the water and let cool. Taking care not to tear the skins, use a spoon to scoop out the pulp and put it in a large bowl. Arrange the halves on a large baking dish.

In a 4-quart saucepan over medium heat, melt the margarine and sauté the onions and parsley until the onions are clear. Stir in the mirliton pulp, bread crumbs, salt, and hot sauce, and mix well. Turn the heat down to low and let cook for 10 minutes. Add the shrimp, stir, and remove from the heat. Spoon the shrimp mixture into the mirliton shells. Sprinkle the tops with some more bread crumbs and bake for 30 to 45 minutes.

YIELD: *4 to 6 servings*

Okra à la Creole

The longer this cooks the more better it tastes.

2 tablespoons olive oil
1 cup finely chopped onion
1 cup finely chopped fresh parsley

1 cup finely chopped green onions
1 cup finely chopped bell pepper

1 teaspoon crushed dried mint
2 cups peeled, chopped fresh
   tomatoes
1 cup tomato sauce
2 tablespoons minced garlic
2 tablespoons soy sauce
1 cup dry white wine

1 pound smoked sausage,
   sliced ¼ inch thick
10 cups okra, sliced ¼ inch
   thick
Salt to taste
Louisiana hot sauce or
   ground cayenne pepper
   to taste

In a large, high-walled skillet, heat the olive oil over medium heat, and sauté the onions, parsley, green onions, bell peppers, and mint until the onions are clear. Stir in the tomatoes, tomato sauce, garlic, soy sauce, wine, and sausage, cover, and cook over medium heat until it comes to a boil, stirring occasionally. Stir in the okra, salt, and hot sauce, reduce the heat to low, and simmer, covered, stirring occasionally, until the okra is tender, about 45 minutes.

YIELD: *6 to 8 servings*

Boiled Okra

We often use this chilled as an appetizer or salad.

12 to 18 young, tender whole
   okra
Water
Salt to taste
Louisiana hot sauce or
   ground cayenne pepper
   to taste

¼ cup olive oil
2 tablespoons Worcestershire
   sauce
¼ cup white vinegar

Place the okra in a large saucepan, cover with water, and season with salt and hot sauce. Cover and bring to a boil. Reduce the heat to medium and cook until the okra is tender, about 30 minutes. Drain off most of the water, leaving just a little on the bottom. Add the olive oil,

Worcestershire, and vinegar, and season again. Reduce the heat to low and simmer, covered, for 10 minutes, shaking the pot occasionally to get the seasonings all over the okra.

YIELD: *4 to 6 servings or enough for one hungry Cajun!*

Okra and Shrimp Maurice

Maurice is a Mississippi Cajun, and a damned fine cook. He says to eat this like a cochon. *That's like a pig.*

¼ cup oil	1 teaspoon salt
1½ pounds okra, stems cut off and sliced thin	¾ teaspoon ground thyme Louisiana hot sauce or ground cayenne pepper to taste
1 large onion, chopped	
2 large tomatoes, peeled and pureed	
4 large cloves garlic, crushed and pureed (talk about needing twin beds!)	1 pound raw shrimp, peeled and deveined

Heat the oil in a large, high-walled skillet over low heat. Simmer the okra, onions, tomatoes, and garlic together 1½ to 2 hours or until the okra cooks apart and the other vegetables come together. Stir often to avoid burning. Add the salt, thyme, hot sauce, and shrimp, and cook until the shrimp turn pink, only a few minutes.

YIELD: *6 to 8 servings*

Stuffed Onions

Try this recipe with any type of ground meat or seafood or cheese substituted for the bread crumbs. This is a favorite at our house.

4 to 6 medium-sized onions,
   peeled
Water
2 teaspoons salt
¼ cup shortening or oil
¼ cup finely chopped fresh
   parsley

1 tablespoon minced garlic
1 cup seasoned bread crumbs
Salt to taste
Louisiana hot sauce or
   ground cayenne pepper
   to taste
2 eggs, well beaten

Preheat the oven to 325°F. Fill a large pot half full with water, add the salt, and bring to a boil. Using a knife or a melon baller, remove the center of each onion to make a cavity. Drop the onions into the boiling salted water, reduce the heat to low, and simmer until the outer layers of the onion are tender, about 10 minutes. Remove the onions from the water, let drain, and cool. Chop up the center parts of the onions and sauté in the heated oil in a large skillet, with the parsley, over medium heat. When a little juice has accumulated, add the garlic and cook until the onions are clear, stirring occasionally. Remove from the heat, add the bread crumbs, and season with the salt and hot sauce. Add the beaten eggs to the sautéed vegetables and mix well. Fill the onions gently with the stuffing, mounding it on the top. Bake for 20 to 30 minutes, then turn on the broiler and brown the tops.

YIELD: *4 to 6 servings*

Stuffed Bell Peppers

6 large bell peppers
1 tablespoon olive oil
½ pound lean ground beef
   (see Note)
½ cup chopped green onions
½ cup chopped fresh parsley
1 cup chopped onion
2 teaspoons chopped garlic
1 cup chopped tomatoes

2 cups cooked Seasoned Rice
   (see page 71)
Salt to taste
Louisiana hot sauce or
   ground cayenne pepper
   to taste
One 8-ounce can tomato sauce
½ cup dry white wine
½ cup water

Clean the bell peppers by slicing through the top, close to the stem. Take out the seeds and wash inside and out, then allow to drain. Preheat the oven to 350°F. Over medium-high heat in a medium-sized skillet, heat the oil and brown the meat, stirring occasionally. Add the green onions, parsley, onions, garlic, and tomatoes; stir and continue cooking until the onions are clear. Add the cooked rice, salt, and hot sauce; mix well. Remove from the heat, stuff into the peppers, and place in a baking dish. Mix the tomato sauce, wine, and water together, and pour around the stuffed peppers, not on top. Bake for 1 hour.

Y I E L D : *6 stuffed peppers*

N O T E : Try using different meats or seafoods. Don't be afraid to experiment with this or any other recipe.

Fried Bell Pepper Rings or Green Tomatoes

This recipe can be used to fry shrimp, onion rings, or whatever else you are frying that takes a batter.

DRENCH:

- 2 cups buttermilk
- 1 teaspoon salt
- 1 teaspoon cayenne pepper
- ½ teaspoon onion powder
- ½ teaspoon garlic powder
- 1 teaspoon Worcestershire sauce
- 1 cup flour

DREDGE:

- 2 to 3 cups all-purpose flour
  Salt to taste
  Ground cayenne pepper to taste
- 4 large bell peppers, sliced in rings
- 2 quarts oil

Pour the oil in a large deep pot and heat to 350°F. To make the drench, pour the milk into a medium-sized mixing bowl. Beat in the salt, pepper, onion and garlic powders, and Worcestershire. Gradually stir in the flour, making sure to blend well. It should look like pancake batter. To make the dredge, sift the flour, salt, and pepper into a flat pan. Soak the pepper rings in the drench, then pass them through the seasoned flour, coating well. Deep fry in the hot oil until golden brown, about 3 minutes. Remove from the oil and drain on paper towels. Serve immediately.

YIELD: *4 to 6 servings*

VARIATION: *Fried Green Tomatoes:* Use 3 large green tomatoes, sliced ¼ inch thick, and add 1 teaspoon of sugar and a pinch of crushed dried mint to the dredge. Otherwise follow the instructions above exactly. The tomato slices will take about 3 minutes to fry.

Andouille and Potatoes

3 tablespoons bacon drippings
or olive oil
1 cup chopped onion
½ cup chopped bell pepper
1 cup finely chopped parsley
1 cup dry white wine
1 tablespoon finely chopped
garlic
1 tablespoon soy sauce

1 to 2 pounds andouille or
other heavily smoked
sausage
Louisiana hot sauce or
ground cayenne pepper
to taste
Salt to taste
6 medium-sized potatoes,
thinly sliced

Heat the bacon drippings in a large, heavy saucepan over medium-high heat, and sauté the onions, bell pepper, and parsley, stirring occasionally until the onions are clear. Add the wine, garlic, soy sauce, and andouille, and mix well. Add the salt and hot sauce and stir. Add the potatoes, stir, cover, reduce the heat to low, and simmer, stirring occasionally until the potatoes are tender, about 30 minutes.

YIELD: *6 to 8 servings*

Stuffed Potatoes

4 large baking potatoes	Louisiana hot sauce or
½ cup oil	ground cayenne pepper
4 strips bacon	to taste
1 cup chopped green onions	And any other fish, meat,
½ cup chopped fresh parsley	vegetable sauce, nuts,
1 cup sour cream	cheese, shrimp, pork, or
1 cup grated cheddar cheese	piquant sauce you might
Salt to taste	want to add

Preheat the oven to 375°F. Rub the potatoes with the oil and bake for 1½ hours or until they are soft when squeezed. Allow to cool. Cut the potatoes in half lengthwise and scoop out the pulp, leaving the skin and about ½ inch of the pulp intact. Place the pulp in a large mixing bowl and set aside. In a skillet, fry the bacon until crisp, and crumble into the bowl with the pulp. Sauté the onions and parsley over medium heat in the bacon drippings until the onions are clear; turn into the potato pulp and mix well. Add the sour cream, cheese, salt, hot sauce, and anything you think would taste good, and mix well. Stuff the potato mixture back into the skins and bake until heated through and tops are brown, 20 minutes or less.

YIELD: *8 halves*

Justin's Succotash or Something

3 tablespoons bacon drippings or oil	2 cups dry white wine
1 cup chopped onion	Two 10-ounce cans baby green lima beans
1 cup chopped bell pepper	4 cups fresh corn kernels, boiled and cut from cob
One 16-ounce can whole tomatoes, diced	½ cup dried parsley

2 tablespoons Worcestershire
   sauce
¼ teaspoon crushed dried mint
¾ teaspoon garlic powder
1 cup chopped boiled ham

1 cup fresh mushrooms, sliced
Salt to taste
Louisiana hot sauce or
   ground cayenne pepper
   to taste

Over medium-high heat in an 8-quart pot, heat the drippings and sauté the onions and bell pepper until the onions are clear. Add the diced tomatoes, wine, beans, corn, parsley, Worcestershire, mint, and garlic powder; stir to mix. Cover and bring to a boil, stirring occasionally. Once it boils, add the ham, mushrooms, salt, and hot sauce, and stir to mix well. Cover, reduce the heat to low, and simmer 1 hour.

YIELD: *6 to 8 servings*

Baked Squash

¼ pound (1 stick) margarine
½ cup chopped bell pepper
½ cup chopped fresh parsley
½ cup chopped onion
½ cup chopped green onions
1 pound tender summer
   squash, sliced ¼ inch
   thick

1 cup pecan pieces
Salt to taste
Louisiana hot sauce or
   ground cayenne pepper
   to taste
1 cup grated mild cheddar
   cheese
½ cup seasoned bread crumbs

Preheat the oven to 325°F. In a large saucepan, melt the margarine over medium heat and sauté the bell pepper, parsley, onions, and green onions until the onions are clear. Stir in the squash and pecans and mix well. Season with the salt and hot sauce, then pour into a greased 9-by-9-inch baking dish. Sprinkle with the cheese and bread crumbs and bake for 45 minutes.

YIELD: *6 to 8 servings*

Baked Sweet Potato

1 medium-sized sweet potato　　**Oil or bacon drippings**
per person

Preheat the oven to 350°F. Wash the sweet potatoes and dry them. Rub oil onto each potato and place on a baking sheet. Now, I could tell you in hours or minutes how long to cook sweet potatoes, but the best way to tell when they're done is by touch. Squeeze the sweet potato with your fingers, being sure to protect your hands from the heat; if it is soft to the touch, then it is ready. Serve hot with margarine on top. To eat as a dessert, drizzle cane syrup on top. They taste good cold, too.

Y I E L D : *1 serving per person*

Sweet Potato Sweet

This is a vegetable dish, but it tastes like a dessert. I garontee!!

3 pounds cooked or canned　　**2 teaspoons ground cinnamon**
sweet potatoes or yams,　　½ **cup packed brown sugar**
cut into ¼-inch slices, well　　**1 cup pecans**
drained　　**1 cup moist grated coconut**
1 cup honey　　**Large marshmallows**

Preheat oven to 325°F. If the sweet potatoes are fresh, boil them in a large saucepan, with enough water to cover, until they are soft to the touch. The potatoes are much easier to peel after they have been boiled. Remove the potatoes from the water and let cool. Then peel and slice, and place in a greased 9-by-9-inch casserole dish or baking pan.

　In a medium-sized mixing bowl, combine the honey, cinnamon, and brown sugar, and mix well. Stir in the pecans and coconut and mix well again, then pour over the potatoes and cover the top with the marshmallows. Bake until the marshmallows are melted and golden brown, about 45 minutes.

YIELD: *10 to 12 servings*

VARIATION: Substitute cooked cranberry sauce for the coconut. That is a southern holiday dish that suits northerners, too.

Fried Sweet Potatoes

5 sweet potatoes, washed, peeled, and sliced like french fries
　Peanut oil, for deep frying

　Salt to taste
　Ground cayenne pepper to taste

Half fill a deep fry pot with the oil and heat to 350°F. If the potatoes are wet, blot them with paper towels before frying. Use a large cooking spoon to lower the potatoes into the hot oil. Fry until tender, about 4 minutes. Remove, drain on paper towels, and sprinkle with salt and pepper, or some people like to sprinkle with powdered sugar and ground cinnamon.

YIELD: *about 6 servings*

Baked Tomatoes

6 large fresh, ripe tomatoes
1 tablespoon oil or shortening
½ cup chopped onion
¼ cup chopped fresh parsley
1 cup white lump crabmeat
1 cup grated mild cheese
1 cup seasoned bread crumbs
　Juice of one lemon

　Salt to taste
　Louisiana hot sauce or ground cayenne pepper to taste
2 cups tomato juice
2 tablespoons Worcestershire sauce

Preheat the oven to 350°F. Slice off about 1 inch of the stem end of the tomato, and, using a spoon, carefully scoop out the center of the tomato and try not to split it. Save the pulp. In a small skillet, heat the oil over medium heat, and sauté the onion and parsley until the onions are clear. Remove from the heat and add the crabmeat, cheese, bread crumbs, tomato pulp, and lemon juice. Season with salt and hot sauce. Fill the tomato shells gently with the stuffing. Mix the tomato juice and Worcestershire together and pour into a baking pan. Arrange the stuffed tomatoes in the pan and bake for 30 to 40 minutes until tender but not mushy.

YIELD: *6 servings*

Potatoes/Tomatoes

½ cup oil or shortening
1 cup chopped onion
½ cup chopped parsley
5 medium tomatoes, peeled and diced, or one 16-ounce can whole tomatoes, chopped

10 small red potatoes, sliced ¼ inch thick
2 cups Meat Stock (see page 38) or water
Salt to taste
Louisiana hot sauce or ground cayenne pepper to taste

In a large pot with a lid, heat the oil over medium heat, and sauté the onions and parsley until the onions are clear. Add the tomatoes and potatoes, then pour in the stock, and season with the salt and hot sauce. Cover, reduce the heat to low, and simmer until potatoes are tender, about 30 minutes. If too juicy, cook uncovered for a while.

YIELD: *6 to 8 servings*

· 🐚 ·

Stewed Tomatoes

4 tablespoons (½ stick)
  margarine or shortening
½ cup chopped onion
¼ cup finely chopped celery
¼ cup chopped fresh parsley
1 pound fresh tomatoes,
  peeled, seeded, and cubed,
  or one 16-ounce can whole
  tomatoes, cubed with juices

¼ cup dry white wine
2 slices stale bread or toast,
  crumbled or cubed
Salt to taste
Louisiana hot sauce or
  ground cayenne pepper
  to taste

In a large saucepan over medium-high heat, melt the margarine and sauté the onions, celery, and parsley until the onions are tender. Add the tomatoes and wine, reduce the heat to low, and simmer for 5 minutes. Add the bread and mix well. Season with salt and hot sauce, then simmer 15 more minutes to remove any extra juice.

YIELD: *4 to 6 servings*

Buttered Turnips or Kohlrabi

2 pounds fresh turnips or
  kohlrabi, peeled and cut
  into ½-inch cubes
Water
Margarine or butter

1 tablespoon fresh lemon juice
  (optional)
Salt to taste
Louisiana hot sauce or
  ground cayenne pepper
  to taste

Put the turnips in a large saucepan, and add enough water to cover; bring to a boil, then reduce the heat to low, and simmer for 30 minutes or until tender. Drain, pour the turnips into a serving dish, and top with margarine, lemon juice, salt, and hot sauce. Stir to mix well.

YIELD: *6 servings*

Turnips au Gratin

Olive oil

6 to 8 large turnips, peeled and sliced thin

1 cup grated Swiss cheese

6 to 8 large onions, sliced thin

1 cup grated mild cheddar cheese

1 cup grated Parmesan cheese

1 cup chopped fresh parsley

4 large eggs, beaten

2 cups dry white wine

Salt to taste

1 teaspoon garlic powder

Louisiana hot sauce or ground cayenne pepper to taste

1 cup grated Romano cheese

Preheat the oven to 350°F. Grease a large casserole dish with the olive oil. Starting with the turnips, put a single layer on the bottom of the dish, then a layer of Swiss cheese, a layer of onions, a layer of cheddar and Parmesan cheese, and then sprinkle with the parsley. Make as many layers as you can, but save some onion for the top. Beat the eggs with the wine, then one at a time mix in the salt, garlic powder, and hot sauce. Pour the egg mixture over the vegetables and cheeses, then top with the Romano cheese. Bake 1 to 1½ hours or until turnips are tender.

Y I E L D : *8 to 10 servings*

This is the makin's for Red Beans and Rice, a traditional New Orleans dish for lunch on Mondays.

I'm so glad to have guard dogs for my smoker cooker.

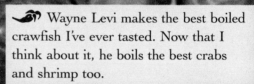 Wayne Levi makes the best boiled crawfish I've ever tasted. Now that I think about it, he boils the best crabs and shrimp too.

This is the Old State Capital of Louisiana, where I, as a child of ten, worked as a page during the legislative session. Some of the other pages and I used to catch the goldfish in the pond, then cook and eat them.

These fine young fellows are going to make me a fine crab dinner.

My favorite time of the year—when the garden gives me a salad every night. Of course, I help it along. Here I'm making Surplus Salad.

This 20-gallon washpot full of Leftover Turkey and Andouille Gumbo will feed us today and tomorrow and I will give some away to our friends and maybe if there's some left we'll freeze a little for later on in the winter.

CHAPTER 11

Breads

The variety of bread consumed in Louisiana is not surprising, given the diversity of the population. From the cornbreads of northern Louisiana to the wonderful light French bread in New Orleans neighborhoods, to the many fried breads, fritters, and griddle cakes of south Louisiana, the right bread is important. In the 1920s, his mentor, Judge Schneider of Tallulah, used to send a fourteen-year-old Justin forty miles over gravel roads in his Packard limousine to fetch him a special bread from that den of iniquity, Natchez Under the Hill. Today Justin travels twenty miles to buy his bread from a little Bavarian bakery, where they import special flour from Europe.

In the areas of Italian settlement, each yard had its own cupola-shaped brick oven. These families spent a whole day mixing the dough according to old Italian and Sicilian recipes, firing the oven, then finally baking dozens of loaves in olive-oil cans. We have included plans (see next page) and a recipe for baking bread like the Monteleone family does in Tangipahoa Parish.

When Justin was growing up, it was rare to get white bread, as cornbread and biscuits were the norm. Only when someone rode the train home from the city were they treated to New Orleans baker's bread. This supreme bread was also baked in wood-fired brick ovens.

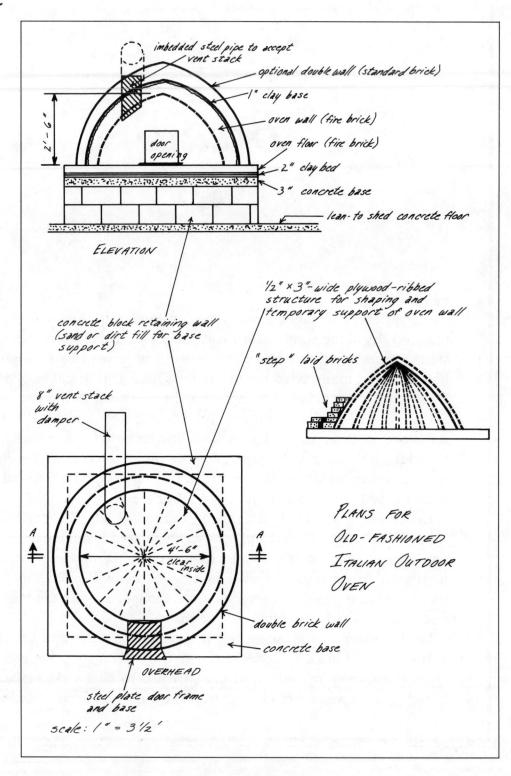

imbedded steel pipe to accept vent stack

optional double wall (standard brick)

1" clay base

oven wall (fire brick)

oven floor (fire brick)

2" clay bed

3" concrete base

lean-to shed concrete floor

2'-6"

door opening

ELEVATION

concrete block retaining wall (sand or dirt fill for base support)

½" × 3"-wide plywood-ribbed structure for shaping and temporary support of oven wall

"step" laid bricks

8" vent stack with damper

A   A

4'-6" clear inside

PLANS FOR
OLD-FASHIONED
ITALIAN OUTDOOR
OVEN

double brick wall

concrete base

OVERHEAD

steel plate door frame and base

scale: 1" = 3½'

Though many have tried, they can't seem to duplicate the qualities of New Orleans bread. Some hold that it is the humid climate of the city that makes this bread distinctive, some say it is the skill of the bakers. This bread is very light, with uniform air spaces, tender, even porous in character—it seems to melt on the tongue. The crust is very thin and crisp. Piles of crumbs on the tablecloth after a meal at a fine New Orleans restaurant are not a sign of careless eating, they are an indication that the bread was perfect.

Breads in Louisiana make use of our abundant produce. Ground corn and hominy, originating with the Indians, are still used to make both baked and fried breads. One can still visit an operating grist mill to have grain custom ground. Cooked rice and rice flour are used more in southwest Louisiana. And leftover breads are used in French toast or that favorite breakfast or late-night snack, cold buttermilk poured over crumbled cornbread. Justin tells a story about educating cornbread:

I got a frien' an' he got one boy chirren dat finish high school, an' he smaht enuf where he can go to college. An' somebody tole dis frien' wit' me about dat good school in Bat-ohn Rouge, L.S.U. So he morgage averyt'in w'at he got to sen' his boy to school.

But he don got some money to brought hisse'f home avery week even dough iss jus' t'irty mile. An' also too he want his boy to learn real good in school how to be somet'in. His son wrote him a postcard an' tole him he's gonna brought hisse'f home fo' Christmas an w'at day to expec' him. Man, dat Cajun got in his pirogue boat an up an' down de bayou he tole all his frien' "My boy gonna brought hisse'f home, we gonna have a sauce piquant an a jambalaya, averthin' you want we gonna have-brought you'se'f."

W'en his son got home dair must have been ninety-nine peoples dair to meet him. Now his proud papa say, "Son, we so proud fo' you to see us, an' we proud wit' you at L.S.U. learn to did somet'in wit' youse'f. Would you please tole us w'at you learn up dair?"

He say, "Papa, you jus' don't go an' say w'at you learn up dair."

He say, "Boy, w'at you took up dair. W'at kine of schoolin' you took?"

"Papa, I took algebra."

"Hokay, son, say somet'in' in algebra r'at now."

"Oh Papa, I can't did dat."

He say, "Look, boy, I done spen' my las' money w't I got to get you some educate, an here you come tole me you can't said somet'in' in algebra. You better said somet'in or you won't be able to go back to school no time. I'm gonna beat you head from you."

De son say, "Hokay Papa. Pi R square."

Blap! His papa hit him an say, "Now if dat ain't a damn fool. Averybody know pie are roun'—cornbread are square."

Cornbread

This is a crunchy, thin, not sweet cornbread. It's just right for eating with greens at night and for breakfast the next morning, crumbled up in a bowl with cold buttermilk poured over it. My cornbread are round.

2 tablespoons shortening, heated (I use bacon drippings)	2 teaspoons salt
	1 tablespoon baking powder
	1 teaspoon baking soda
2 cups cornmeal	3 medium-sized eggs
1 cup all-purpose flour	1½ cups buttermilk

Preheat the oven to 400°F. I cook this in two cast-iron frying pans, one large and one small. I put the shortening in the pans while the oven is heating so the oil will be hot and ready to add to the cornmeal.

Into a large mixing bowl, sift together the dry ingredients. In a small mixing bowl, beat the eggs and buttermilk together, then mix this with the dry ingredients and stir well. Take the pans with oil, which have been heating in the oven, and pour the oil into the batter and stir immediately. Pour the batter back into the greased frying pans and bake for 50 minutes or until golden brown. Turn the cornbread over and put it back in the oven for another 5 minutes. This is called "sweating" the cornbread.

YIELD: *one 9-by-13-inch thin cornbread or one 9-inch and one 6-inch round cornbread*

VARIATION: Add 1 cup grated cheese, or 1 cup whole corn, or ¼ cup chopped cayenne pepper, or 1 cup minced cracklings, or ½ cup chopped onion. Just mix what you add in with the other ingredients before adding the hot oil.

Corny Hush Puppies

1 quart oil for deep frying
1 cup all-purpose flour
1 teaspoon salt
1 teaspoon baking soda
2 teaspoons baking powder
½ teaspoon garlic powder
½ teaspoon ground cayenne pepper

2 cups yellow cornmeal, more or less
½ cup chopped green onions
1 cup fresh sweet corn or 1 cup canned whole sweet corn, well drained
2 large eggs
½ cup buttermilk
2 tablespoons hot oil

Fill a 3-quart saucepan half full with oil and heat to 350°F. In a large mixing bowl, sift together the flour, salt, baking soda, baking powder, garlic powder, and pepper, then stir in the cornmeal and green onions. Add the corn. In a separate bowl, combine the eggs and milk, then pour into the cornmeal mixture; stir to blend. Add the hot oil and stir. This stiff batter should be thick enough to stay on a spoon without dripping off the sides. You may need to stir in more cornmeal if it's too runny or milk if it's too dry. Very carefully drop the batter by teaspoons into the oil, and cook until golden brown, about 2 minutes on each side. The puppies usually turn over by themselves to cook the other side, but you might have to help them out a little. Drain on paper towels and serve immediately.

YIELD: *about 3 dozen*

Cornmeal Justin Cakes

1 cup cornmeal	2 medium-sized eggs, beaten
½ cup all-purpose flour	2 cups buttermilk
1 teaspoon salt	2 tablespoons melted
½ teaspoon baking soda	shortening or hot bacon
½ teaspoon ground cayenne	drippings or oil
pepper	¼ cup oil for frying

Into a small mixing bowl, sift together the cornmeal, flour, salt, baking soda, and pepper. In a large mixing bowl, combine the eggs and buttermilk, then gradually add in the dry ingredients until well mixed. Pour the 2 tablespoons melted shortening into the cornmeal mixture and stir; it should have the consistency of a thick batter. In a 10-inch skillet, pour in ¼ cup of oil, and heat until the batter sizzles when a drop is placed in the oil. Pour ¼ cup of the batter at a time into the skillet, cook like a pancake until golden brown, then flip and fry the other side.

YIELD: *6 to 8 cakes*

Buttermilk Biscuits

Serve with jam, or butter, or anything you prefer. I like to eat mine with gravy on top or use them to sop.

2 cups all-purpose flour	1 teaspoon baking powder
½ teaspoon baking soda	⅓ cup oil or shortening
1 teaspoon salt	½ to ¾ cup buttermilk

Preheat the oven to 450°F. In a large mixing bowl, sift together the flour, baking soda, salt, and baking powder. Mix in the oil or cut in the shortening, then add the milk and mix well. The dough should be easy to handle and hold together. Turn out onto a floured surface, flour your hands, and gently knead the dough to form a smooth ball. Flatten with your hands and roll the dough out to about a ½-inch thickness. Cut with a biscuit cutter and place the biscuits on a greased cookie sheet. Roll the leftover dough back into a ball, roll out, and cut again. Bake for 15 minutes or until golden brown.

YIELD: *10 to 20 biscuits, depending on the size of the cutter*

Sweet Milk Biscuits

2 cups all-purpose flour
1 tablespoon baking powder
½ teaspoon salt

⅓ cup oil or shortening
½ cup milk

Preheat the oven to 450°F. Sift together the flour, baking powder, and salt into a large mixing bowl. Mix in the oil or cut in the shortening. Add the milk and mix well. The dough should be easy to handle. Turn out onto a floured surface, flour your hands, and gently knead dough to form a smooth ball. Flatten the dough with your hands and roll out to a ½-inch thickness. Cut with a biscuit cutter and place on a greased cookie sheet. Roll the leftover dough back into a ball, roll out, and cut. Bake for 15 minutes or until golden brown.

YIELD: *10 to 20 biscuits*

Rice Bran Muffins

2 cups all-purpose flour
1 cup rice bran
⅓ cup cane syrup or molasses
1 teaspoon baking soda
2 large eggs, well beaten

⅓ cup peanut oil
1 cup buttermilk
1 cup fresh blueberries
   (optional) (see Note)

Preheat the oven to 350°F and grease a muffin tin. Sift the flour and rice bran together into a large mixing bowl and set aside. Pour the syrup into a small mixing bowl and stir in the baking soda; stir until the syrup lightens. Pour the beaten eggs into the syrup and stir. Add the oil and buttermilk, mix well, then stir the mixture into the flour and rice bran, mixing well. Carefully fold in the blueberries, then spoon into the greased muffin tins till half full. Bake for 30 minutes.

YIELD: *12 to 18 muffins*

NOTE: Instead of blueberries, you can also use pecans, raisins, chopped fruit, or anything you might like to try.

Apple Pancakes

1 cup all-purpose flour
1 teaspoon baking powder
½ teaspoon baking soda
½ teaspoon salt
1 large egg, beaten
1 cup buttermilk
1 tablespoon oil or melted shortening
1 cup Apples in Wine and Cinnamon Sauce (see page 67)
Extra oil to coat the pan

Into a medium-sized mixing bowl, sift together the flour, baking powder, baking soda, and salt. In a small mixing bowl, combine the egg and buttermilk and mix well. Add the oil and mix again. Stir the mixture into the dry ingredients and mix well. Fold in the apples. Heat the oil over medium heat in a medium-sized skillet or griddle, then pour out ¼ cup of the batter at a time onto the surface. Cook until brown on one side, then flip and brown the other. Serve alone or with cane syrup, maple syrup, or honey.

YIELD: *6 to 8 pancakes*

• 🙋 •

Crepes

This is a basic crepe recipe and can be filled with anything from apples to zucchini.

3 medium-sized eggs	1 cup all-purpose flour
1 cup milk	¼ teaspoon salt
1 tablespoon melted shortening or oil	Extra oil or melted shortening to grease pan

In a large mixing bowl, beat together the eggs, milk, and oil. Sift the flour and salt together into the bowl and beat until smooth. Cover the bowl and refrigerate for at least 1 hour. Heat a small amount of oil in a crepe pan or small frying pan over medium-high heat, then ladle about 2 tablespoons of batter into the hot pan. Grasp the pan handle and rotate at an angle so that the batter forms a thin coating on the bottom about 6 to 7 inches round. Return to the heat and let cook for about 1 minute. The underside should be light brown and easy to lift and turn over. Heat the other side about 30 seconds, then flip out of the pan. Each crepe can be filled, then rolled and served with a sauce. If you plan to freeze the crepes, place a sheet of waxed paper between each crepe.

YIELD: *Twenty-five 6-inch crepes*

VARIATION: If you use the crepes to make a dessert, add ¼ cup sugar to the mixture.

Calas

Cala is a Spanish word meaning a small piece or plug, and that's just how these look. Years ago street vendors in New Orleans fried these up fresh for the children. Serve them hot with cane syrup or fruit, rolled in sugar for breakfast, or as a delicious snack.

1½ cups all-purpose flour	½ teaspoon ground cinnamon
⅓ cup sugar	1½ cups cooked soft rice
Dash salt	1 medium-sized egg, beaten
1 teaspoon baking soda	1 quart oil for deep frying

Half fill a large, deep saucepan with the oil and preheat it to 375°F. In a medium-sized mixing bowl, sift together the flour, sugar, salt, baking soda, and cinnamon. Stir in the rice and then the egg. You may have to add a bit more flour to make this a stiff batter. Carefully drop by spoonsful into the hot oil and fry until golden brown, about 3 minutes.

Y I E L D : *about 30 calas*

Beignets *(Oreilles de Cochon)*

Beignets are fried bread that is served in restaurants in the French Quarter. Out in the country they are called oreilles de cochon, *or pigs' ears. I call them the hole from the doughnut.*

2 cups all-purpose flour	3 tablespoons sugar
1 teaspoon salt	1 cup milk
1 tablespoon baking powder	¼ teaspoon vanilla extract
1 teaspoon ground cinnamon	1 quart oil for deep frying
1 medium-sized egg	Confectioners' sugar

Half fill a large, deep saucepan with oil and preheat it to 375°F. Sift together the flour, salt, baking powder, and cinnamon into a large mixing bowl. In a separate bowl, beat the egg well, then beat in the sugar, milk, and vanilla. Pour the egg mixture into the flour and mix slightly until moistened. Turn onto a floured surface and knead lightly. Roll the dough out to a ¼-inch thickness. Slice into diamond shapes, about 3 inches long. Fry in oil, turning once, until they are golden brown and puffed up. Remove, drain on paper towels, and sprinkle with confectioners' sugar. Serve immediately with with café au lait.

Y I E L D : *about 20 pieces*

Dumplings

You can add minced pieces of parsley, onion, or garlic for more flavor.

2 cups all-purpose flour	½ cup shortening
1 teaspoon salt	½ cup milk
1 teaspoon baking powder	1 large egg, beaten

Sift the dry ingredients together into a large mixing bowl. Cut in the shortening until well mixed. Add the milk to the beaten egg, then pour into the flour. Mix well. Drop by tablespoonsful into a simmering stock or soup, and cook, uncovered, over medium heat about 15 minutes. Dumplings should hold together, yet be tender and fluffy on the inside.

YIELD: *10 to 12 dumplings*

Pain Perdu

Pain perdu is French for lost bread, which means it is too old or stale for eating. Stale bread works best for this dish because it soaks up the egg batter and holds its shape better.

1 large egg	1 teaspoon vanilla extract
½ cup milk	⅛ teaspoon ground cinnamon
2 teaspoons cane syrup or honey or sugar	4 to 6 slices old bread
	2 tablespoons oil

In a flat-bottomed, rectangular dish, beat the egg, beat in the milk, syrup, vanilla, and cinnamon. Heat the oil in a griddle or large, flat, heavy frying pan over medium-high heat. Dip the bread in the egg mixture, let soak a few moments, then turn over and soak the other side another few moments. Put on the hot griddle, brown one side, then turn over and brown the other side. Serve immediately, topped with cane syrup, honey, jam, or fruit butter, or sprinkled with confectioners' sugar.

YIELD: *2 servings*

Doris's Mountain Lion Bread

Doris and Junior Monteleone bake their bread in an old-fashioned brick oven that Junior built himself by remembering the ovens used during his childhood. They bake enough bread for their family, and have great fun doing it. This makes a great gift, but don't forget to keep at least one loaf for yourself.

5 pounds bread or all-purpose flour	1½ cups vegetable shortening
5 level teaspoons salt	5 cups lukewarm water
5 level teaspoons sugar	⅙ pound (2½ ounces) fresh yeast

Preheat the oven to 350°F. In a very large mixing bowl, sift together the flour, salt, and sugar, then cut in the shortening. Dissolve the yeast in the lukewarm water, then mix in the flour and work together until well mixed. Cover with a cloth and let rise in a warm, draft-free spot until doubled in size. Punch down and knead the dough. Return to the bowl, cover, and let rise again until doubled in size. Grease 5 bread pans, then cut the dough into 5 equal parts. Knead the dough into loaf shapes and place in the pans. Cover and let rise in the pans until the dough is coming out of the pans. Bake for 50 minutes.

YIELD: *5 large loaves*

C H A P T E R   1 2

Desserts

When Justin wrote his first cookbook nearly thirty years ago, it didn't even include a section for dessert. To paraphrase Justin himself, there were three reasons why the book contained no desserts: first, he said he didn't like dessert too much; second, he cited his girth and indicated that soon he would approximate the volume of a dwelling if he didn't quit eating; and third, he maintained that after feasting on a real Cajun meal, eating a dessert was a physical impossibility.

Now as Justin gets older some changes have occurred: he gets more of a sweet tooth, he buys bigger clothes, and he simply waits several hours after eating a meal to enjoy a dessert, often with coffee and a brandy. So this book includes some decidedly Louisiana sweets. These desserts use native products: pecans, widely grown all over the state; the juicy fruits, strawberries, peaches, and oranges, as likely to come from the backyard as from the huge commercial field; rice and sweet potatoes, which are so versatile they can play the role of starch, vegetable, or dessert course; and, finally, the sweetness that binds everything together, honey, syrup, and sugar. In Louisiana one can cut cane in the field at sunrise, then enjoy it as ribbon cane syrup at sunset.

Speaking of syrup, Justin tells a story about a rogue sweet tooth:

I got a frien' in Sout' Louisiana saveral year ago w'en we didn't get paid much. He made a dollar a day I t'ink, an dat was 75 cent mo' den I was makin'. He got a teet' dat hurt him so bad, he don' know w'at he gon' did and he don' got enuf money to go to dem dentis'. He work for six week an' dem damn teet' hurt him all de time. Jus' 'bout drove him plum' crazy. W'en he got enuf money to go to de dentis' he say, "Doc, pull dis damn t'ing an' r'at now." De doctaire say, "I don' know." He say, "Don' talk 'bout it. Pull it. I can't stood it summore." Well de doc-taire get a pair of dem pliers, an he get in dair an' Owweeee, he pull dat jaw teet' out w'at had hurt dat Cajun for six long week.

He ax, "Doc, would you min' lettin' me took dat teet' home wit' me?" De Doc say, "No, I don' mind. You can have dat teet'." He wrap it up an' give it to him. Dat Cajun get home an' he get a platter, a great big platter. He put dat teet' in de middle of dat platter an' he got a whole half gallon o' syrup, dat ol' sugar cane syrup, an ' he pour it on dat teet'. Den he tell dat teet', Go on an' hurt, damn you. Hurt all you wan' to.

Bread Pudding

Bread Pudding is one of the most popular desserts served in Louisiana. It is a great way to use dry or stale bread.

1 loaf stale French bread or toast
1 quart milk
2 cups sugar
4 large eggs, beaten
1 tablespoon vanilla extract
1 cup peeled and diced apples
1 cup raisins
Oil or shortening to grease pan

Preheat the oven to 350°F. Break the bread into chunks into a large bowl. In another large mixing bowl, beat the milk and sugar into the eggs. Mix in the vanilla, apples, and raisins, then pour over the bread, and mix everything together. Let it set until the milk is absorbed into the bread, mixing once or twice. Turn into a greased 9-by-9-inch casserole or baking pan. Bake for 30 to 40 minutes. Serve warm with Rum Sauce (see recipe below) or vanilla ice cream on top.

YIELD: *10 to 12 servings*

Rum Sauce

2 large eggs
¼ cup rum
1 cup confectioners' sugar

1 cup cream, whipped to
soft peaks

In a small saucepan, beat the eggs, adding the rum, and place over low heat. Gradually add the sugar, stir, remove from the heat, fold in the whipped cream. Pour over warm bread pudding.

YIELD: *about 2 cups*

Brown Rice Pudding

They say that brown rice is good for you, but I really like the way it tastes, too.

4 cups cooked brown rice
½ cup honey
1 cup dry white wine
½ teaspoon vanilla extract

¼ teaspoon ground cinnamon
1 cup raisins
4 large eggs, beaten
Meringue (see page 222)

Preheat the oven to 325°F. Combine the honey, wine, vanilla, and cinnamon in a medium-sized saucepan. Heat slowly over medium heat until the honey has dissolved, then add the raisins. Continue cooking until mixture begins to boil, then remove from the heat. Combine the eggs and rice in a large mixing bowl, then pour in the honey mixture and mix well. Turn into a greased 9-by-9-inch deep casserole dish and bake for 45 minutes to 1 hour. Top with the meringue and bake until golden brown.

YIELD: *6 servings*

Meringue

6 large egg whites, at room temperature
½ teaspoon vanilla extract

¼ teaspoon cream of tartar
6 tablespoons granulated or confectioners' sugar

All your utensils need to be clean and free of oil. In a small, deep mixing bowl, beat the egg whites on high until frothy with some large air pockets. Add the vanilla, cream of tartar, and sugar, and continue beating on high until stiff peaks form. Spread the meringue on top of your pie, bringing the meringue to the edges of the pie crust.

YIELD: *tops one 9-inch pie*

Tarte à la Bouille

This is an old Cajun dessert still made and sold on special days by the women of the villages.

CRUST:

1 cup flour
½ teaspoon baking powder
⅛ teaspoon salt
4 tablespoons (½ stick) margarine, butter, or shortening

1 large egg, well beaten
½ cup sugar
¼ cup milk (more or less)

FILLING:

3 cups milk

1½ cups sugar

1 teaspoon vanilla extract

3 large eggs, well beaten

2 tablespoons margarine

Make the crust several hours ahead of time or the night before. Sift the flour, baking powder, and salt together into a large mixing bowl. Cut in the margarine with a pastry cutter. In a small bowl, beat the sugar into the egg. Pour the egg mixture into the flour and mix well. Gradually add the milk until the dough can easily be handled and forms a ball. Refrigerate for several hours or overnight. Roll out the dough ⅛ inch thick and larger than a 9-inch pie plate. Place the dough over the pie plate. Don't trim the edges of the pie dough, as they are folded over the filling later.

Preheat oven to 350°F. In a medium-sized saucepan, mix the milk and sugar together. Bring the milk to a boil over medium heat, stirring occasionally. Once the milk begins to boil, you will need to stir frequently. Continue cooking over medium heat until thickened, about 10 minutes. In a small mixing bowl, beat the vanilla together with the eggs and set aside. Then stir the margarine into the heated milk and continue cooking until melted. Stir a little of the hot milk into the egg mixture, then pour the egg mixture into the milk and stir. Remove from the heat and let cool a few minutes, then pour into the unbaked pie shell. Fold the edges of the crust over the top so that it rests on top of the filling. Bake for 30 to 40 minutes or until the crust is golden brown.

YIELD: *one 9-inch deep-dish pie*

VARIATION: For a different taste, 1 cup shredded coconut can be added to the filling, or you can press pecans into the bottom of the crust.

· 🐦 ·

Fruit Cream Pie

¼ cup all-purpose flour
1 cup sugar
1 teaspoon salt
1 cup milk, scalded
3 large egg yolks, beaten, whites reserved for the meringue

2 tablespoons margarine or butter
2 cups fruit puree (melon, peach, strawberry, etc.)
1 baked 9-inch pie shell
Meringue (see page 222)

Preheat the oven to 350°F. Sift the flour, sugar, and salt together into the top of a double boiler over medium heat. Slowly stir in the scalded milk, then cook until thickened, about 15 minutes. Stir half a cup of the hot mixture into the egg yolks, then pour the yolks into the double boiler and continue cooking, stirring, until thick. Add the margarine and fruit puree, stir, and cook until it gets very thick. Remove from the heat, pour into the baked pie shell, top with the meringue, and bake until the meringue is golden brown, about 15 minutes. Serve well chilled.

YIELD: *one 9-inch deep-dish pie*

Sweet Potato Pie

This is pure goodness and often served at holiday feasts.

1½ cups mashed boiled sweet potatoes
½ cup honey
1 teaspoon ground cinnamon
½ teaspoon salt
3 large eggs

½ cup sugar
1 teaspoon vanilla extract
1 cup pecan pieces or whole pecans (optional)
One 9-inch unbaked pie shell

Preheat the oven to 350°F. Mix the sweet potatoes, honey, cinnamon, and salt together in a large mixing bowl. In a separate bowl, beat the eggs, then gradually beat in the sugar and vanilla. Pour the eggs into the potato mixture and mix well. Add the pecans, if desired, and pour into the pie shell. Bake for 1 hour or until a knife inserted in the middle comes out clean.

YIELD: *one 9-inch deep-dish pie*

Pecan Pie

A traditional Southern favorite.

3 large eggs	1 cup molasses
1 cup sugar	1 teaspoon vanilla extract
1 tablespoon melted margarine	½ teaspoon salt
3 tablespoons all-purpose flour	2 cups pecan halves
	Two 9-inch unbaked pie shells

Preheat the oven to 350°F. In a large mixing bowl, beat the eggs, then gradually beat in the sugar, margarine, and flour. Beat in the molasses, vanilla, and salt, then stir in the pecans. Pour the filling into the two unbaked pie shells and bake for 1 hour or until firm in the middle.

YIELD: *two 9-inch pies*

King Cake

According to tradition, the Mardi Gras season starts on Kings' Night, or the Feast of the Epiphany, and runs until Ash Wednesday. King cakes are baked and served throughout the carnival season. Secretly baked in the dough of the cake is a small object, possibly a bean, a coin, a porcelain figurine, or, commonly today, a hard plastic doll. The person receiving the piece of cake with the object becomes the "king" for the day and is responsible for buying or baking the next cake and throwing the party where it will be eaten. In New Orleans King cakes come in several sizes and are now being air-shipped all over the world. The pastries are glazed, then topped with sugar granules in the carnival colors of purple, green, and gold.

½ cup butter or margarine	4 to 5 cups all-purpose flour
½ cup milk	Some "prize" to bake in the
½ cup sugar	cake: a large bean, a large
½ teaspoon salt	button, or a plastic baby
⅓ cup warm water	doll
2 packages dry yeast (½ ounce)	
3 large eggs, beaten	**GLAZE:**
1 teaspoon grated lemon rind	1½ cups confectioners' sugar
1 teaspoon ground nutmeg or cinnamon	1 tablespoon lemon juice
	1 tablespoon water

Preheat the oven to 375°F. Over medium heat in a large saucepan, heat the butter, milk, sugar, and salt until the butter melts and the mixture steams. Do not let it scorch. Remove from the heat. Pour the warm water into a large bowl, then dissolve the yeast in it. Add the warm milk mixture, the eggs, lemon rind, nutmeg, and 2 cups of flour. Mix well until free of lumps. Stir in 2 more cups of flour. Then add more flour as needed to make a dough that holds together and is easy to handle. Dust a surface with flour, turn out the dough and knead it for 5 minutes until it gets springy. Grease another large bowl, place the dough in it and cover with a cloth. Set the bowl in a warm draft-free place and let it rise until it doubles in volume, about 2 hours. Punch it down and knead it again for about 5 minutes. Divide the dough into 3 equal parts and roll each piece into a rope about 30 inches long. Grease a large baking sheet and carefully braid the ropes close together, curving the braid around to form an oval. Wet the ends and press them together. Push the "prize" underneath and hide it. Cover the sheet again with a towel and let the braid rise for about an hour. Then bake for about 20 minutes until golden brown. Let the cake cool. In a small mixing bowl, blend the ingredients for the glaze well. Drizzle or paint on the top of the cake and sprinkle it with alternating colors of granulated sugar.

YIELD: *one large cake*

Cheesecake

CRUST:
- 1 cup self-rising flour
- ½ cup firmly packed brown sugar
- 4 tablespoons (½ cup) melted butter or margarine
- 1 cup ground pecans

FILLING:
- 2 pounds cream cheese, softened or at room temperature
- One 16-ounce container prepared whipped topping
- 2 tablespoons sugar
- 1½ tablespoons vanilla extract or other flavoring extract

Preheat oven to 450°F. In a large mixing bowl, combine all the crust ingredients and press into the bottom and sides of a deep 9-inch baking pan. Bake for 10 to 15 minutes until golden brown. Let cool.

The filling is easily prepared with an electric mixer. On medium speed in a large bowl, beat the softened cream cheese until it is free of lumps. Gradually alternate beating in the whipped topping and sugar until mixed with the cream cheese. Add the vanilla extract and beat until mixed. Turn the filling into the crust, and refrigerate at least 2 hours.

YIELD: *one 9-inch cheesecake*

VARIATIONS: I like to experiment with this recipe. Any kind of fruit can be used in the filling, or you can top a plain cheesecake with pieces of fresh fruit. Try adding chocolate bits or mint bits with the extract. You can also use other kinds of nuts for the crust, walnuts or almonds, for example.

Fig Cake

Almost every yard in Louisiana has its own fig tree.

3 large eggs	1 teaspoon baking powder
¼ cup sugar	1 cup chopped pecans
½ teaspoon salt	2 cups fresh ripe figs, peeled
½ cup oil	and chopped fine or
1½ cups all-purpose flour	mashed, or fig jam
½ teaspoon baking soda	

Preheat the oven to 350°F. Grease and flour a 9-by-9-inch baking pan. Beat the eggs in a large mixing bowl, then beat in the sugar and salt. Add the oil and beat again. In a separate bowl, sift together the flour, baking soda, and baking powder. Mix the flour into the eggs, and stir in the nuts and figs. Pour into the baking pan and bake for 30 to 35 minutes or until a knife inserted in the middle comes out clean.

YIELD: *10 to 12 servings*

Cream Cheese Frosting

8 ounces cream cheese, softened	½ teaspoon vanilla or rum extract
2 cups confectioners' sugar	½ cup chopped pecans (optional)
¼ pound (1 stick) margarine or butter, at room temperature	

Beat the cream cheese in a small mixing bowl until smooth. Gradually add the sugar while you continue beating. Then mix the margarine in well and add the vanilla. If you are using pecans, you can mix them in with the vanilla or just sprinkle on top and serve. This is good served on butter cookies, brownies, or Fig Cake (see above).

YIELD: *about 2 cups*

Pineapple Down-side-up Cake

I once won a baking contest with a recipe for this cake!

¼ pound (1 stick) margarine or
    butter
½ cup firmly packed brown
    sugar
6 to 9 pineapple rings (reserve
    ½ cup of the juice)
½ cup chopped pecans

2 large eggs, beaten
½ cup sugar
1 teaspoon vanilla extract
1 cup flour
½ teaspoon baking powder
  Dash salt

Preheat the oven to 350°F. Melt the margarine in a deep 9- or 10-inch ovenproof skillet or baking dish. Stir in the sugar and arrange the pineapple slices in the sugar. Then sprinkle the pecans over and around the pineapple. In a large mixing bowl, combine the eggs and add sugar, then stir in the reserved pineapple juice and the vanilla. Sift the flour, baking powder, and salt into the bowl, and mix well. Pour the batter over the pineapple slices and bake 45 to 50 minutes. Cool slightly, then invert a platter over the pan and, while holding it, turn it down-side-up. The cake will fall onto the platter. Remove the baking dish. Serve warm or cold.

YIELD: *one 9- or 10-inch cake*

Strawberry Shortcake with Soda Crackers

This works well with strawberries that are ripe and soft.

1 pint strawberries, washed
    and stemmed
1 cup sugar or to taste

1 teaspoon ground cinnamon
One 4-ounce pack soda crackers
Whipped cream (optional)

Put the berries in a medium-sized mixing bowl. Mix the sugar and cinnamon together in a small mixing bowl, then pour over the berries, mix well, and mash the berries with a masher or the back of a spoon. Let them sit for at least 30 minutes and stir again. Place the crackers on the bottom and around the sides of an 8-inch dish. Pour the berries into the dish and refrigerate for 3 to 4 hours or overnight. Serve just like it is or topped with whipped cream.

YIELD: *4 to 6 servings*

Peach Cobbler

A favorite summer dessert served with vanilla ice cream.

FILLING:
- ¼ pound (1 stick) margarine or butter
- 1½ cups sugar
- 2 tablespoons flour
- Pinch of salt
- 8 ripe peaches, peeled and thinly sliced
- ½ cup water or brandy

CRUST:
- 4 tablespoons (½ stick) margarine or butter
- ½ cup sugar
- 1 cup flour
- 1 teaspoon baking powder
- ½ teaspoon salt
- ½ cup milk or fruit juice

Preheat the oven to 350°F. To prepare the filling, melt the margarine in a medium-sized saucepan over medium heat. Stir in the sugar, flour, and salt; mix well. Then add the peaches and the water. Stir and heat thoroughly, about 5 minutes. Pour into a greased, deep 9-by-9-inch casserole dish and set aside. To prepare the crust, in a medium-sized mixing bowl cream the margarine with the sugar, then add the flour, baking powder, salt, and milk; mix well. Pour the batter over the peaches and bake for about 1 hour or until golden brown.

YIELD: *6 to 9 servings*

Peach Sherbet

Almost any type of fruit puree or flavoring agent may be used in this recipe. Try strawberry, canteloupe, or fig.

<table>
<tr><td>2 cups peach puree</td><td>½ teaspoon vanilla extract</td></tr>
<tr><td>3 large eggs, well beaten</td><td>3 cups milk (lowfat milk can</td></tr>
<tr><td>¾ cup sugar</td><td>be used)</td></tr>
<tr><td>¼ teaspoon salt</td><td></td></tr>
</table>

Combine all the ingredients in an ice-cream freezer can. Place the can in the ice-cream freezer, add the ice and salt around the freezer can, and follow the manufacturer's directions for operating the machine.

YIELD: *1 quart*

Pralines

<table>
<tr><td>1½ cups sugar</td><td>1 tablespoon margarine or</td></tr>
<tr><td>1½ cups firmly packed brown sugar</td><td>butter</td></tr>
<tr><td>1½ cups evaporated milk</td><td>1 teaspoon vanilla extract or other flavoring extract</td></tr>
<tr><td>Dash of salt</td><td>2 cups chopped pecans</td></tr>
</table>

In a medium-sized saucepan over medium-high heat, mix the sugar, brown sugar, and milk together. Cook until the firm ball stage (240°F on a candy thermometer), stirring occasionally. Add the salt and the margarine and stir until melted. Set the pot aside and let cool until the bottom of the pot is cool enough to hold in your hand. Add the vanilla, beat until creamy, then stir in the pecans and spoon the mixture onto wax paper by the teaspoonful and let harden.

YIELD: *about 3 dozen pralines*

Pecan Cocoons

½ pound (2 sticks) margarine
  or butter
½ cup confectioners' sugar
1 teaspoon vanilla extract
2 cups all-purpose flour

¼ teaspoon salt
1 cup finely chopped pecans
  Confectioners' sugar to roll
  cocoons in

Preheat the oven to 325°F. In a large mixing bowl, cream the margarine with the sugar, then stir in the vanilla and mix in the flour, salt, and pecans. The dough should be easy to handle and shape. Form into small cocoon shapes the size of your finger. Place on a cookie sheet and bake for about 15 minutes; don't allow them to get brown. Remove from the oven and, while they are still warm, roll in confectioners' sugar to coat completely.

Y I E L D : *about 40 small cookies*

• ❧ •

Beverages

A *votre santé,* to your health, the toast that has been heard for centuries in Louisiana: to the health of your family, to an abundant harvest, to many fish in your net, to grandchildren in your late years, to a good story told by a friend to make you laugh. In Louisiana food and drink cannot be separated; they belong together.

Louisianans have enjoyed spirits from the beginning of their history. The LeMoyne brothers, being Frenchmen, were probably the first to enjoy food and drink together. New Orleans has always had the reputation for wonderful combinations and inventions of drink. Because it was a port city with a constantly changing and varied population, new spirits were demanded by and supplied to the inhabitants. The Creoles prepared and enjoyed cordials, ratafias, ponches, and liqueurs.

The cocktail was invented in New Orleans. In the 1790s, Antoine Peychaud, a refugee concoctor, served up a mixture of bitters and cognac in a small egg cup, or *coquetier.* The thick-tongued Americans mispronounced this mixture as *cocktail,* and a whole tradition of mixing spirits was born, each new cocktail reflecting a growing, sophisticated city courted by the next colonial power or group of refugees.

The largest group of refugees, the Cajuns, stayed well clear of New Orleans but spread throughout the south of Louisiana. The Cajun cus-

toms of fortified coffee and well-lubricated *fais-do-do* and family cele-
brations meant that imbibing was not reserved to a single sex or class.
Cajuns married solid and liquid refreshment at every life event, from
a birth to a wake. The Italian and Slavic immigrants brought skilled
winemaking to the strawberry- and orange-producing regions, and a
more catholic appreciation of the benefits of spirits.

As southern Louisiana was settled by Mediterranean peoples, northern Louisiana was accommodating groups of Americans and Anglo-
Saxon pioneers. They brought entirely different ideas about "likker"
with them. The Americans drank "whatever anybody else has." Justin's
papa used to say that when he was in northern Louisiana if he passed
around his jug he was lucky to get his cork back. Some of the finest
moonshine and corn likker is made in north Louisiana. Justin tells a
story about it:

> One day I was in Johnny Guitreau's barroom saloon cocktail
> lounge restaurant general store with some of my friend'. A fallow
> walked in holding a jug on his han' and strode up to dis frien' with
> me. He said, "Hey my frien' won't you take a drink from my jug?"
> Ma frien', hearing from his speech that he was not from the area,
> told him, "No thank you very much." The other fellow said, "Come,
> have a drink from my jug." "No, thank you very much," said my
> frien'. The stranger pulled his gun from his waist, cocked it, and
> pointed it at my frien'. "How about having a drink from my jug?"
> he axed. With such an incentive my frien' quickly obliged him with
> a swig and then remarked at the smoothness of the liquor. The
> stranger brightened considerably, then announced, "Good, now
> hold this gun on me and make me taste it."

These few recipes are just a sampling of drinking fashion in Louisiana. Many people make their own wine. A neighbor makes wonderful
wine from apples, carrots, blackberries, strawberries, raisins, musca-
dines, grapes, peaches, sassafras roots, pineapples, and anything else
that grows well or is cheap and abundant. For centuries men and
women have combined herbs with spirits to soothe and cure some
ill-defined malady. Bartenders and mixologists in the cities are proud
of their heritage and vie to discover new and better formulas for their

customers. Nonalcoholic drinks are gaining in popularity because it is the fellowship that is most important in life—not getting drunk.

The ports of New Orleans and Baton Rouge import millions of tons of coffee beans each year, and much of that cargo is processed and enjoyed morning, noon, and night from the demitasse, or half cups, right here in Louisiana.

The important wish is still the one that says "to your health": may you enjoy this drink and this fellowship, and may your life be a good one.

Orangeade

This is not a strongly flavored beverage; rather, it is light. The varieties of citrus that grow in Plaquemines Parish deep in southern Louisiana on the rich black soil that has been laid down by the Mississippi River are a connoisseur's delight. The yielding delicacy of its pulp, overflowing with juice, has a flavor no other orange can match.

3 oranges or satsumas	1 lemon
½ cup sugar	8 cups water

Wash one of the oranges well in warm soapy water, then dry it. Cut it crosswise into ¼-inch thick slices. Put the slices in the bottom of a large pitcher, then pour the sugar over them and let them sit for at least 30 minutes. Squeeze the juice from the other two oranges and the lemon and pour into the pitcher. Add the water and stir to mix well. Chill or serve over ice.

YIELD: *4 servings*

VARIATION: You can substitute 6 lemons for the oranges and make lemonade.

Eggnog

Eggnog is a traditional holiday drink in Louisiana, too. Calories . . .
whoooo booooy!!

6 large eggs, separated and at
　room temperature
1 pint very cold whipping
　cream

6 tablespoons sugar
6 to 8 ounces brandy or
　bourbon
Ground nutmeg (optional)

In a large mixing bowl, beat the egg whites until they form soft peaks.
In another large mixing bowl, beat the cream until stiff peaks form,
then fold in the beaten egg whites and store in the refrigerator. Using
two large mixing bowls that fit inside each other, put ice in the bottom
bowl and place the other bowl on top. Pour in the egg yolks and beat.
While beating, gradually add the sugar until the yolks have turned
quite light. Add the brandy and continue beating. Gently fold the
cream with the whites into the yolks, mix well, and keep chilled. When
ready to serve, you can sprinkle nutmeg on top.

YIELD: *6 to 8 servings*

Sazerac Cocktail

The Sazerac is named after a bar in the French Quarter. Herbsaint is
a substitute for absinthe, an addictive drink made from the herb worm-
wood. Pernod can be used instead of herbsaint.

1 lump sugar
　Dash Peychaud bitters
1 tablespoon herbsaint

Ice
2 jiggers brandy or bourbon
Lemon peel

Put the sugar, bitters, and the herbsaint into a rocks glass and mash
with a muddler or a long-handled spoon. Some mixers spin the glass

rapidly in the air to coat the inside. Just before serving, put two solid ice cubes in the glass, add the brandy, and stir. Rub the lemon peel around the rim of the glass, then twist the lemon and drop into the glass.

YIELD: *1 serving*

Mint Julep

When I was a boy and staying with Judge Schneider in Tallulah, he used to serve juleps to his houseguests after they rose in the morning. They often had several before breakfast.

Traditionally prepared in silver goblets, mint juleps now are often prepared in tall iced-tea glasses. We prepare these a dozen at a time, and place them in the refrigerator to allow the mint to flavor the drink.

Fresh mint leaves	1 to 2 jiggers bourbon
1 teaspoon sugar	Water
Ice	Lemon peel (optional)

In a tall, heavy glass, muddle a few mint leaves with the sugar. To muddle, use a muddler or a long-handled teaspoon to crush and bruise the mint leaves against the grains of sugar. If you're preparing many drinks, refrigerate them now. Just before serving, fill the glass with ice, add the bourbon to taste, and fill the rest of the glass with water. Pass the lemon peel around the glass rim, then put it in the glass. Stir and serve with a sprig of fresh mint leaves.

YIELD: *1 serving*

• 🐟 •

Party Punch

This is good served at your next office party or family get-together.

8 cups strong tea	1 bottle gin, vodka, or rum
4 cups cola	(optional)
4 cups cranberry juice	Pieces of fresh fruit or
2 cups sugar	canned fruit cocktail
8 cups water	(optional)
4 cups ginger ale	

This can be mixed together right in your large punch bowl. Mix the tea, cola, and cranberry juice together well, then dissolve the sugar into the mixture. Now add the water and ginger ale and mix well. This can be refrigerated until ready to serve. Just before the party starts, stir in as much booze as you like and the fruit cocktail. Drop big chunks of ice into the bowl of punch.

YIELD: *30 to 40 servings*

Home Brew

Mama and I used to make Home Brew during Prohibition. When I was working in Alexandria in 1931, a whole batch of home brew that had been stored underneath my bed blew up. I thought a war had started.

5 tablespoons fresh yeast	3 pounds Blue Ribbon malt,
1 cup warm water	light hop flavor
5 pounds sugar	Water

In a small mixing bowl, dissolve the yeast in the warm water with 1 tablespoon of sugar. In a 10-gallon container, mix the sugar and malt together, then stir in the dissolved yeast. Mix in enough water to come to 6 inches below the top of the container to allow for expansion during the foaming action. Place the crock in an out-of-the-way place, and let it sit for 4 days to 1 week at room temperature. Test the brew after 4 days by putting a little in a glass and stirring. If it forms a heavy foam, let it sit a few more days. Then keep testing until the brew quits foaming and it doesn't bubble. Pour into bottles, then cap tightly and store at room temperature until the brew is clear. When ready to serve, chill, but be careful not to disturb the sediment on the bottom of the bottle.

YIELD: *as many bottles as you can fill*

Milk Punch

Children of all ages drink milk punch in Louisiana.

1 tablespoon sugar	**Ice**
1 to 2 jiggers brandy or rum	**1 cup milk**

In a small cup, dissolve the sugar in the brandy. Fill a tall glass with ice. Pour the brandy and then the milk over the ice, stir, and serve.

YIELD: *1 serving*

COFFEE

There is nothing quite like waking up to a bayou sunrise and the intoxicating smell of a pot of freshly dripped coffee. Café noir and café au lait are traditions in Louisiana, and one would have trouble convincing a Louisianan that there is a better cup of coffee to be found anywhere else. In some families, like Justin's, making coffee was a morning ritual. It was so important that Justin's PapaBoy made it himself. Coffee making is not to be taken lightly or done halfheartedly, and everyone drinks coffee, even small children. Justin remembers well the shadowy figure of PapaBoy waking him as a little-bitty boy with the rich, pungent aroma and welcoming warmth of café au lait. PapaBoy said that he had more one-way cups than anybody; they never did find their way back to the kitchen. Justin usually rises first at his house, makes coffee, and carries it to his wife who is still asleep.

Our coffee is a rich and dark roasted blend of many types of beans. Visitors tell me that they have never tasted coffee as strong as we make it. Many people drink coffee when they first get up, have a midmorning cup, a cup after a large lunch, a midafternoon cup, and a cup with their brandy or cognac after dinner. A guest to a home is always offered a cup of coffee. Many people drink coffee all day long, nursing one or two cups through an afternoon. Gentle sips from a demitasse are comforting in home or office surroundings.

Some southern Louisianans believe that good strong coffee helps them live longer. Old Cajun physicians believed in the efficacy of coffee as a preventor of infectious disease. A doctor would pass through a room holding a dish of burning coffee beans to deodorize the house. Many successful people testify to its ability to stimulate the brain—they claim it makes them more alert and smarter. And another thing, if you drink coffee standing up you will never be rich, hear?

To make coffee as in olden times, one must first roast the beans. Roasting was usually done only once a week and care was taken not to roast too much, because if the parched beans are not used promptly they tend to lose their flavor. After the beans are parched and allowed to cool, the coffee is ground. Grinding the beans was one of Justin's jobs as a child. And they only ground what they needed for that day. Coffee in southern Louisiana is dripped, not boiled. This allows for every bit of the flavor to be extracted.

Café Noir

To make good coffee, you must:

1. *Use a clean coffee pot*
2. *Use freshly roasted and freshly ground coffee*

3. Start with cold water
4. Never boil the coffee, only the water
5. Serve promptly after brewing.

For each cup of water, use 1 tablespoon of freshly ground dark-roast coffee or coffee with chicory. Place the ground coffee in a drip pot or biggin. Bring the water to a strong boil. Slightly moisten the grounds with boiling water, then continue pouring the boiling water through the grains. When all the water has dripped through, remove the grounds. Stir the coffee and serve at once. The pot may be kept warm in a pan of water on the stove.

Café au Lait

1 part Café Noir (see page 240)   Sugar (optional)
1 part milk, scalded

The coffee and the milk should be close to the same temperature. Simultaneously pour the heated milk and hot coffee into individual cups, or into another pot, to mix well. Add sugar, if desired, and serve immediately.

Pousse Café

Many Cajuns took their pousse café with them to the field. The coffee was dripped fresh in the morning and poured into a pint bottle. The brandy or bourbon was added to fill the bottle. Into the back pants pocket went the bottle. It stayed warm from the body all day and enabled many farmers or fishermen to labor long hours with only an occasional pousse break.

Café Noir (see page 240)   1 teaspoon brandy, cognac,
                                bourbon, or benedictine

Mix the freshly dripped Café Noir with the liquor of choice. Serve in a demitasse or pour into a bottle as the Cajuns do. Sugar or honey may also be added.

Café Brûlot

Café Brûlot is the perfect ending to a special meal.

6 **cups Café Noir (see page 240)**
6 **lumps sugar or 6 teaspoons**
6 **whole cloves**
Six **ounces (4 jiggers) brandy or cognac, warmed**

2 **sticks cinnamon**
The peel of 1 small lemon (wash it first)
The peel of ½ orange or satsuma (wash it first)

This after-dinner preparation is usually made in a silver bowl about 10 inches in diameter. Pour boiling water into the bowl and let it heat; then pour the water out and dry the bowl. Into the warm bowl put the sugar, cloves, brandy, cinnamon, and lemon and orange peels; stir lightly. Lower the lights in the room. Very carefully touch a flame to the mixture. The brandy will flame readily if the bowl and the brandy have been warmed. Let it burn only 15 to 20 seconds, stirring the mixture with a ladle. Pour the coffee down the side of the bowl, stirring all the while. Ladle into demitasse cups and enjoy immediately.

YIELD: *6 to 10 servings*

• 🐚 •

Preserves

We are lucky in Louisiana because the mild climate allows us two or three crops each year. There is always some fresh delight maturing in the soil or on the tree. We can walk into the garden to pluck a sun-warmed tomato from the vine, add some salt, and bite into a taste of heaven. Years ago life was planned around planting and harvest. The ripening of fruits and vegetables dictated life events. Today, efficient transportation systems make us accept as fresh produce woody tomatoes, hard peaches, and unsweet corn.

Many Louisianans get great satisfaction and excellent results from their practices of putting food by. They have learned to preserve the abundance of the season against the months when absolutely fresh fruits and vegetables are not available.

Justin's Mama and PapaBoy were dedicated preservers. They put up much of the food from the farm, canning field peas, crowders, beets, tomatoes, figs, strawberries, and many jams, jellies, and pickles. Then when she cooked that food, Mama could coax out the flavor of the sun and the stirring breeze that went into those same jars, flavors that seem to have disappeared in our mass-produced processed foods.

The boucherie, or hog-killing, provided fresh meat and many cuts which needed to be salted or smoked in order to preserve them. Sun drying has been practiced for more than a century on red peppers. The fishermen around Barataria Bay sun dry thousands of pounds of "sea bobs" or small shrimp for use as snacks and in gumbos. More seafood is frozen and shipped to world markets. Many different vegetables are pickled commercially and in home kitchens. Sugar and sweet syrups, combined with wild and domesticated berries and fruits, yield jellies, jams, marmalades, and preserved pieces of fruit for pies and other desserts.

Canning is big business in Louisiana, with several canneries operating in the southern part of the state. Almost everything that is processed in a plant can be preserved in the home. Cleanliness is the most important consideration. If the food that you put up is the least bit discolored or bubbly, throw it away.

These are just a small sampling of some foods that we preserve. If you would like to learn more about food preservation, get a book from a manufacturer of equipment or from the library.

Mayhaw Jelly

Mayhaws are like cranberries, but they grow wild on a small tree. The early spring finds the swampy lowlands of home white with mayhaw blossoms. After a few days, the petals fall and look like snow around the bases of the trees. It's my pleasure to let neighbors pick the berries, then furnish me with their wonderful homemade jelly. The finished color of this jelly is almost an opalescent light pink.

4 pounds fresh mayhaws, cleaned	1 box pectin
Water	5 cups sugar, or the same amount as the juice

Pour the mayhaws in a large, heavy pot and cover with water. Over medium-high heat, bring to a boil, then cover and continue to boil about 15 minutes, until the skins pop. Remove from the heat and allow to cool. Use a potato masher to mash the berries into a pulp. While the fruit is still warm, strain through a damp jelly bag or a cheesecloth or an all-cotton pillowcase (make sure the pillowcase is an old one, because the berries will stain it). Discard the pulp or feed it to the hogs.

In a large saucepan, mix the juice with the pectin and bring to a rolling boil over medium heat; stir frequently. Add the sugar and continue stirring. When the juice comes back to a strong boil and cannot be stirred down (220° F), cook for 1 minute longer, then remove from the heat and skim off any bubbles or scum that has formed. Immediately ladle into sterilized jars and seal with sterilized new lids, following the manufacturer's directions. Cool and label. Store in a cool, dark, and dry place.

YIELD: *about 6 pints*

Tangipahoa Strawberry Jam

Tangipahoa is an Indian word that means cob without much corn. Tangipahoa Parish, where Justin was born, was the strawberry capital of the world in the 1930s. The berries from southeast Louisiana are sweeter and finer than any others. The problem with strawberries is that everything that is done to them is done bending over. Justin first worked loading the railcars filled with berries in 1923.

5 cups ripe strawberries,	**5 cups sugar**
washed, stemmed, and	**1 box granulated pectin**
drained	

In a medium-sized saucepan over medium-low heat, combine the berries and sugar. Using a potato masher, break up the berries. Add the pectin and stir while slowly bringing the mixture to a boil, one that cannot be stirred down. Boil for three minutes, stirring constantly so that it won't scorch. Carefully spoon into sterilized jelly glasses and seal with sterilized new tops and rings, according to the manufacturer's instructions. Serve on breads or ice cream.

YIELD: *about 4 pints*

FILÉ

American Indians gave us filé powder. In Louisiana, filé is sprinkled on gumbo and soups after they are cooked and just before they are served. Filé has a delicate flavor and also thickens the liquid to which it is added.

Filé is made from the leaves of the sassafras tree, which grows wild throughout Louisiana. At the end of summer, about the middle of September, we gather the leaves. Sometimes small branches are cut off, and sometimes just the leaves are picked from the trees. Then the leaves are cleaned and left to dry in the sun.

After the leaves are thoroughly dried (they'll crush easily in the hand when ready), we take off the stems and remove the big spines. Then we either pound them in a heavy canvas sack with a mallet or a big paddle or put them in a food processor or blender and grind them into a fine powder. We sometimes then put the powder through a fine strainer to get out any larger pieces. Store the filé in airtight containers. We make new filé every year in September.

LOUISIANA PEPPERS

We can thank Christopher Columbus for the feisty intensity of Louisiana cooking. Though peppers are native to the Western Hemisphere, explorers carried the plant back to Spain, Europe, and eventually throughout the world. This plant is not at all related to black pepper, which is the dried fruit of a shrub native to India. Peppers are members of the genus *Capsicum* and called variously chilis, agi, pimienta, or by any of hundreds of separate variety names: bell, habanero, jalapeño, anaheim, ancho, tabasco, cayenne.

Peppers are widely grown in the United States, both commercially and for family consumption. Even city dwellers grow peppers in small containers. In Louisiana the main variety, the cayenne, will produce all year if protected from the occasional killing frost. Cayenne pepper is the favorite seasoning of the Cajuns and Creoles, and is used to flavor regional dishes. It gives seafood specialties a special zest.

Cayenne is used primarily for flavor, but through the centuries it has been used in a number of other ways. Medicinally, it has been used to treat sore throats, malaria, colic, and digestive ailments. "Tabasco" pepper sauce is the thumb-sucking preventive of choice. Pepper tea mist and ground pepper powder are used to keep animal and insect pests away from valued plants.

Cayenne pepper is named for the region of the Cayenne River in French Guiana. The pods grow anywhere from 4 to 12 inches in length, and the color matures from a deep, shiny green to orange-red to deep red. Selective breeding is producing a shorter, thicker pod with more pulp for commercial uses. Many Louisianans grow cayenne for themselves, plus enough to give to neighbors and friends.

The pods are harvested by hand and then used fresh, dried, or ground and processed into various sauces and powders which add flavor to foods. Many people from outside Louisiana have the mistaken impression that Cajun and Creole foods are terribly hot with piquant pepper. Though southern Louisianans especially use more pepper than is generally used farther north, the dishes prepared by any skilled cook depend on cayenne merely to enhance the flavor of the ingredients, not to mask the food's true flavor or to make the taster uncomfortable.

Justin tells a story about some newcomers to southern Louisiana:

There was one preacher down in Sout' Louisiana, whenever a new fambly brought isse'f into de community, he always go call on dem. An' he been live dair all his life, an' he love dat Louisiana hot sauce, green an' red pepper an' all dem pepper sauce. An' he notice dese peoples w'at he goin' to visit brought deyse'fs from way up Nort' where dey don't got to use hot sauce so he brought his own hot stuff wit' him when dey set de meal out fo' him. He put some on his food an' dis young fallow wit' his papa an' mama he say, "We better go along wit' him," an' he put some jus' like de preacher dues on his food an' dey eat, but it was too strong.

An' dat young fallow can't stood it, he say, "Preacher, I wanna ax you somet'ing." De preacher say, "Well, go ahead, son."

De young fallow say, "You preach hellfire an' brimstone an' damnation an' all dat, hanh?" De preacher say, "I t'ought dass ma' duty to do dat to show peoples whuss gonna happen to dem."

An' de boy say, "Well I've heard dat all ma' life, but you're de firs' preacher I ever saw dat took his samples along wit' him, I ga-ron-tee!"

Ground Cayenne Pepper

Please protect your eyes, nose, and hands when handling or harvesting hot peppers.

Harvest red, ripe, cayenne peppers. As the peppers get more mature, their potency increases. Allow the pods to dry either by stringing them on a strong thread and hanging them in a dry, dark place or by sun drying them on sheets for a few days. After the pods are dry, leathery, and shriveled, remove the stems. You may allow them to dry further if you live in a damp climate. Put them in a food processor or a blender and grind them into a powder. You may want to do this outside so any wayward pepper dust gets blown away. Store the ground pepper in an airtight container. This seasoning is the cornerstone of Louisiana cooking.

Justin's Louisiana Hot Sauce

There are dozens of hot sauces in Louisiana. All of them enhance rather than destroy the flavor of foods. I hope that you will experiment with hot sauces to come up with your own brand name.

3 cups stemmed and finely
   chopped cayenne peppers
   (see Note below)
1 cup white vinegar

½ cup water
1 tablespoon finely chopped
   garlic
1 tablespoon salt

In a medium-sized saucepan, combine all the ingredients. Over medium-low heat, simmer, covered, until the peppers are very soft, stirring occasionally. Then remove from the heat and mash with a potato masher. Press the mixture through a sieve so that all that remains in the sieve are the seeds and skins; discard. If the mixture is too thick to pour, more salt and vinegar may be added. Pour into sterilized jars and put on the sterilized new lids according to the manufacturer's directions. This can be stored in your pantry for about 6 months. We always use it up before then.

YIELD: *4 cups*

NOTE: When handling hot peppers, please protect your hands with rubber gloves, and *don't* touch your eyes.

Hot Stuff

This is great served over beans, gumbos, stews, or just about anything you want.

2 cups finely chopped onion
2 cups stemmed, seeded, and
   chopped fresh hot peppers
   (see Note below)

1 teaspoon salt per quart jar
   or ½ teaspoon salt per
   pint jar
¾ cup white vinegar
¼ cup water

Mix the onions and peppers together in a large mixing bowl, then spoon into sterilized canning jars and add the salt. In a small saucepan, mix the vinegar and water together and heat. Don't bring to a boil. Stir the liquid with your finger; when it gets too hot to keep your finger in, it's ready. Pour it into the jars, making sure to cover the peppers and onions. Seal with sterilized new lids, following the manufacturer's directions. Let sit for three to four days before using. This will keep for at least a year. I usually don't refrigerate pickled preserves.

YIELD: *2 pints*

NOTE: When handling hot peppers, please use rubber gloves to protect your hands, and *don't* touch your eyes.

Creole Catsup

This was made in many homes, and many older cooks have their own recipes that they still make for their own families.

20 hot pepper pods, stemmed and chopped (see Note below)	1 cup water
	3 medium-sized onions, chopped
3 large tomatoes, peeled and chopped	1 tablespoon minced garlic
	Salt to taste
2 cups red wine vinegar	

In a medium-sized saucepan, combine all the ingredients. Cover and simmer over medium heat until the onions are very soft, stirring occasionally. Remove from the heat and mash with a potato masher. Force the mixture through a sieve until only the seeds and the skins are left; discard. This may now be diluted with vinegar if it is too thick or too strong. Pour into sterilized bottles and seal with sterilized new lids, according to the manufacturer's directions.

Y I E L D : *about 1 quart*

N O T E : When handling hot peppers, please protect your hands with rubber gloves, and *don't* touch your eyes.

Hot Pepper Jelly

Try this on meats, vegetables, or sandwiches. Mama made this all her life, and it continues to be very popular today.

1 bell pepper, ground or finely chopped	6 cups sugar
1½ cups cider vinegar	6 ounces liquid pectin
½ cup stemmed, seeded, and finely chopped hot peppers (I use cayenne peppers—see Note below)	4 drops green food coloring (optional)

Place the bell pepper in a blender with the vinegar, and pulse until the pepper is chopped into about ⅛-inch pieces; mix in the chopped hot peppers. Place this liquid in a medium-sized saucepan with the sugar, and cook over medium-high heat, stirring frequently. Bring to a rolling boil, then continue to boil and stir constantly for 10 minutes. Remove from the heat and stir in the pectin and food coloring. Pour into sterilized jars and seal with sterilized new lids, following the manufacturer's directions. Cool and label.

Y I E L D : *6 cups*

N O T E : When handling hot peppers, use rubber gloves to protect your hands, and *don't* touch your eyes.

· ☙ ·

Bell Pepper Relish

This relish is pretty and tastes great with meats and as a base for a sauce served with hors d'oeuvres.

12 ripe red bell peppers, stemmed, seeded, and finely chopped	2 cups white vinegar
	1 tablespoon salt
1 hot pepper, stemmed, seeded, and finely chopped (optional—see Note below)	1 tablespoon minced garlic
	2 cups sugar

An easy way to chop the peppers is in a blender with the vinegar and salt. Pulse them together until the peppers are finely chopped. Then pour into a medium-sized saucepan and stir in the garlic and sugar. Over medium-high heat, bring to a boil, stirring frequently. Reduce the heat and simmer, stirring frequently, until the peppers are as thick as a spread. Spoon into sterilized jars and seal with sterilized new lids, according to the manufacturer's directions.

YIELD: *about 4 cups*

NOTE: When handling hot peppers, please protect your hands with rubber gloves, and *don't* touch your eyes.

Pickled Okra

Tiny, tender okra fresh from the garden is the best to preserve in this way. When the okra ripens in the summer and you get tired of eating it fried, stewed, and boiled, this is the next best way to enjoy it.

20 fresh small okra
1 teaspoon salt per quart jar
or ½ teaspoon salt per
pint jar

4 hot peppers, whole or
chopped (see Note below)
1 clove garlic, cut in 8 pieces
3 parts white vinegar
1 part water

Put the okra into two sterilized quart jars, add the salt, hot peppers, and 3 or 4 pieces of garlic, depending on how much you like garlic. In a medium-sized saucepan, mix the vinegar and water together, then heat slowly. Don't bring to a boil. Stir the liquid with your finger; when it gets too hot to keep your finger in, it's ready. Pour into the jars, making sure to cover the okra completely, and seal with sterilized new lids, following the manufacturer's directions. Let set for one to two weeks before using.

YIELD: *2 quarts*

NOTE: When handling hot peppers, please use rubber gloves to protect your hands, and *don't* touch your eyes.

Dot's Garlic in Oil

Dot is my neighbor and comes from a long line of excellent cooks. This can be used as seasoning when cooking or for a salad dressing. We grow a lot of garlic in Louisiana. Large, mild elephant garlic is popular.

12 to 15 large cloves garlic,
peeled
2 green hot peppers, washed
and dried (see Note below)

2 red cayenne peppers,
washed and dried (see
Note below)
Olive oil, enough to cover
garlic

Alternating between the garlic and red and green peppers, fill a pint jar. Pour in olive oil to cover and screw on the lid tightly. This has a shelf life of 4 to 6 months.

YIELD: *1 pint jar*

NOTE: When handling hot peppers, use rubber gloves to protect your hands, and *don't* touch your eyes.

Mint Jelly

1 cup packed fresh mint
   leaves and stems, rinsed
   and drained
½ cup cider vinegar
1 cup water

3½ cups sugar
3 ounces liquid pectin
2 drops green food coloring
   (optional)

Place the mint in a medium-sized saucepan. Using a muddler or heavy glass tumbler, bruise the leaves, then add the cider vinegar, water, and sugar. Over medium-high heat, stirring frequently, bring to a rolling boil. Stir in the pectin and food coloring, and bring back to a boil, stirring often. Remove from the heat and skim off any bubbles or scum that may have formed. Pour or strain into sterilized jars and seal with sterilized new lids, following the manufacturer's directions. Cool, label, and store in a cool place.

YIELD: *about 2 cups*

• ☙ •

Glossary of Terms

A votre santé: A French toast, "To your good health."

Al dente: Italian for "to the teeth." Pasta cooked al dente is soft on the outside and firm on the inside.

Andouille: A type of sausage used in cooking. Originally made using pieces of intestine or chitterlings stuffed into a large casing with pork or ham, onions, garlic, and cayenne, then smoked.

Bacon drippings: The fat that is rendered after bacon has been fried until crispy.

Barataria Bay: A large body of water located south of New Orleans, where much commercial fishing is done.

Beignet: French for "fritter," a doughnut-type batter usually deep fried in oil and sprinkled with confectioners' sugar. A New Orleans favorite often served with café au lait.

Bisque: A type of soup usually made with a cream base. In southern Louisiana, often made with a dark roux and crawfish, shrimp, or fish, and highly seasoned.

Boucherie: French for "butchery." *La boucherie* evolved into a communal event where all participants shared the slaughtering and meat-preserving chores, then divided the fresh meat, lard, and other smoked and salted products.

Boudin blanc: A unique Cajun sausage made of pork, rice, onions, and other seasonings, stuffed into a casing.

Boudin rouge: Blood sausage made from the blood of a freshly killed animal, fat pieces, garlic, and cayenne.

Café: French for "coffee."

Café au lait: French for coffee with milk.

Café brûlot: French for a coffee that is flamed.

Café noir: French for black coffee.

Cajun: A descendant of the original Acadian refugees or anyone absorbed into the Cajun culture by marriage or choice. Cajuns settled mostly in southern Louisiana.

Casing: The large or small intestines of an animal which are stuffed to make sausage. Casing can be purchased at a butcher store or supermarket meat counter. Synthetic casings are also available.

Cayenne pepper: The very pungent fruit of a variety of capsicum. Fresh or pickled, ground or whole, this seasoning is used in cooking many foods.

Cochon de lait: French for a suckling pig. A *cochon de lait* is often slow-roasted over a bed of hot coals. It is usually cooked for a special occasion or holiday meal.

Coquetier: French for an egg cup.

Cordial: A strong, sweetened, aromatic, alcoholic liquor. A liqueur.

Corn flour: Corn finely ground to the consistency of flour. Cornmeal is ground more coarsely.

Crab boil: A bouquet garni, or porous bag, filled with the seasonings used to boil and flavor shrimp, crabs, or crawfish.

Crawfish: A freshwater crustacean related to and smaller than a lobster. Also called crayfish.

Creole: A term generally applied to a native-born descendant of Mediterreanean ancestry.

Creole mustard: A seasoned, coarsely ground prepared mustard.

Crowley: A city in southwestern Louisiana, home of the Rice Festival held every October.

Demitasse: French for "half cup." A small coffee cup.

En brochette: French for "on a skewer."

Étouffée: French for smothered. A dish made with onions, seasonings, and meat, fish, or vegetables smothered and slowly cooked.

Fais-do-do: A Cajun dance.

Falernum: A lemony almond sweet syrup, created in the Caribbean Islands. Used to flavor drinks.

Filé: A seasoning used in Louisiana to thicken gumbos. Made from the dried leaves of the sassafras tree.

Grillades: The lean strips of meat from the belly part of the hog.

Gumbo: A soup made with a dark roux and water, also with seafood and meat. Eaten with rice and sprinkled with filé. It's also Bantu for the okra plant or pod.

Herbsaint: A substitute for absinthe.

Hogshead cheese: An aspic made from the head, feet, and sometimes other meat of the hog. Also called souse.

Jambalaya: A very popular dish made in Louisiana. It consists of rice, meat, or seafood, with onions, garlic, and other seasonings, cooked in one pot.

Jigger: A small measure of liquor, usually holding 1½ ounces.

Lard: The rendered fat of hogs. The best lard is made from the belly fat.

Maque chou: Young tender corn, cut off the cob, fried in a small amount of fat, then simmered. Meat or seafood can be added for variety.

Mardi Gras: "Fat Tuesday," the day before Ash Wednesday. The Mardi Gras season begins in January and is celebrated with parades and parties.

Mayhaw: A type of berry grown on trees in the wild. Used for jam, jellies, and wine.

Mirliton: A squash, also known as a vegetable pear or chayote.

Muddler: A stick for stirring drinks.

Muscadine: A grape grown in the wild or harvested at home. Used to make jams, jellies, and wines.

Natchitoches: The site of the oldest permanent white settlement in the Louisiana Purchase. Natchitoches was founded in 1714.

Okra: A vegetable often boiled or stewed, and also used in gumbo.

Pilau: A dish of sautéed rice steamed in bouillon with meat, poultry, or shellfish and seasonings.

Pistolets: Small individual French breads about the size of a fist.

Po-boy (poor-boy): A New Orleans tradition. Made with a loaf of fresh French bread, sliced in half lengthwise. Filled with meat or seafood with lettuce, tomatoes, onions, and many other ingredients. A submarine.

Pope's nose: The fleshy protuberance at the posterior of a dressed fowl. Also called a parson's nose.

Pousse café: French for "coffee pusher." A shot of liquor served with or in coffee, or a drink with several liqueurs arranged in layers.

Praline: A candy made with brown sugar, milk, and pecans.

Ramekin: A small dish in which food can be baked and served.

Ratafia: A liqueur flavored with fruit kernels or fruit.

Roux: Flour browned in fat; used to thicken gravies, gumbos, and sauces.

Sassafras: The leaves of the sassafras tree are dried to make filé. Medicinal tea and flavoring oils are also made from its roots.

Satsuma: A type of mandarin grown in extreme southern Louisiana.

Sauce piquant: A highly seasoned gravy with meat or seafood. Often made with tomatoes and served over rice or pasta.

Tangipahoa: Indian word meaning "cob without much corn." The name of a parish in southeastern Louisiana and a river and community in that parish.

Tarte à la bouille: Milk custard pie.

Tasso: Smoked pork, highly seasoned and then smoked again. Used to flavor vegetables, seafood, pasta, or gumbo.

Resources

For more information on Louisiana

Baton Rouge Convention and
　Visitors Bureau
P. O. Drawer 4149
Baton Rouge, LA 70821
(504) 383-1825

Louisiana Department of Agriculture
　and Forestry
P. O. Box 94302
Baton Rouge, LA 70804-9302
(504) 922-1234

Louisiana Department of Culture,
　Recreation, and Tourism
P. O. Box 94361
Baton Rouge, LA 70804-9361
(504) 342-8115

Louisiana Department of Wildlife
　and Fisheries
P. O. Box 98000
Baton Rouge, LA 70898-9000
(504) 765-2803

Louisiana Fairs and Festivals
　Association
Route 3, Box 174
DeRidder, LA 70634

Louisiana Farm Bureau
　Federation, Inc.
P. O. Box 95004
Baton Rouge, LA 70895-9004
(504) 922-6200

Louisiana Restaurant Association
2800 Veterans Boulevard, Suite 160
Metairie, LA 70002
(504) 831-7788

New Orleans Tourist and Convention
　Commission
1520 Sugar Bowl Drive
New Orleans, LA 70112
(504) 566-5011

Kliebert Turtle and Alligator Tours, Inc.
1264 West Yellow Water Road
Hammond, LA 70401
(504) 345-3617

To order Vidalia onions

Bland Farms
P. O. Box 506
Glennville, GA 30427

To order the Cookin' Cajun Smoker Cooker

Bosmans Industries
P. O. Box 3726
Shreveport, LA 71103
(318) 925-6933

To order Magnalite cookware

General Housewares Corp.
P. O. Box 4066
Terre Haute, IN 47804
(800) 457-2665, ext. 273

To order electric kitchen equipment

K-Tec
74 Northwest State Road
American Fork, UT 84003
(800) 288-6455

To order specialty barbecue equipment

Pitt's and Spitt's
14221 Eastex Freeway
Houston, TX 77032
(800) 521-2947 or (713) 987-3474

To order sweet onions

Ransom Onions
Route 4, Box 138
Monroe, LA 71205

For more information on rice

The Rice Council
P. O. Box 740123
Houston, TX 77274
(800) 888-7423 or (713) 270-6699

To order specialty liquor products

Sazerac Company, Inc.
Jefferson Highway
New Orleans, LA 70121
(504) 831-9450

To order kitchen appliances

Sears, Roebuck and Company
Sears Tower
Department 698/731A
Chicago, IL 60684

To order ice-cream freezers

Waring Products
P. O. Box 349
New Hartford, CT 06057
(203) 379-8573

To order kitchen cabinets

Wood-metal Industries, Inc.
1 Second Street
Kreamer, PA 17833
(717) 374-2711

Selected Bibliography

Andrews, Jean. *Peppers: The Domesticated Capsicums.* Austin, TX: University of Texas Press, 1984.

Chambers, Henry E. *Mississippi Valley Beginnings: An Outline of the Early History of the Earlier West.* New York: The Knickerbocker Press, 1922.

Conrad, Glenn R. *The Cajuns: Essays on Their History and Culture.* Lafayette, LA: The Center for Louisiana Studies, University of Southwestern Louisiana, 1983.

Daigle, Rev. Msgr. Jules O. *A Dictionary of the Cajun Language.* Ann Arbor, MI: Edwards Brothers, Inc., 1984.

Davis, Frank. *The Frank Davis Seafood Notebook.* Gretna, LA: Pelican Publishing Company, 1983.

Del Desto, Steven L., and Jon L. Gibson. *The Culture of Acadiana: Tradition and Change in South Louisiana.* Lafayette, LA: The University of Southwestern Louisiana, 1975.

Diler, J. Hanno. *The Settlement of the German Coast of Louisiana and the Creoles of German Descent.* Philadelphia: American Germanica Press, 1909.

Fontenot, Mary Alice, and Julie Landry. *The Louisiana Experience.* Baton Rouge, LA: Claitors Publishing Division, 1983.

Hillman, Howard, and Lisa Loring. *Kitchen Science.* Mount Vernon, NY: Consumers Union, 1988.

Land, Mary. *Louisiana Cookery.* Baton Rouge, LA: Claitors Publishing Division, 1970.

Lockwood, C. C. *Discovering Louisiana.* Baton Rouge, LA: Louisiana State University Press, 1986.

Marchand, Sidney A. *Acadian Exiles in the Golden Coast of Louisiana.* Donaldsonville, LA: Sidney A. Marchand, 1943.

Post, Lauren C. *Cajun Sketches: From the Prairies of Southwest Louisiana.* Baton Rouge, LA: Louisiana State University Press, 1962.

Robotti, Frances D., and Peter J. Robotti. *French Cooking in the New World.* Garden City, NY: Doubleday and Company, Inc., 1967.

Rushton, William Faulkner. *The Cajuns: From Acadia to Louisiana.* New York: Farrar, Straus and Giroux, 1979.

Sunset. *Fresh Produce.* Menlo Park, CA: Lane Publishing Company, 1987.

Taylor, Joe Gray. *Louisiana: A History.* New York: W. W. Norton and Company, 1984.

The Magnolia Mound Plantation Kitchen Book: Being a Compendium of Foodways and Customs of Early Louisiana 1795–1841. Baton Rouge, LA: Magnolia Mound Plantation House, 1986.

The Service League of Natchitoches, Inc. *Cane River Cuisine.* Natchitoches, LA, 1974.

The Times-Picayune. *The Original Picayune Creole Cook Book.* New Orleans: The Times-Picayune Publishing Company, 1942.

Visser, Margaret. *Much Depends on Dinner.* New York: Grove Press, 1987 (hardcover); Collier Books (paperback).

Index